D1722446

The Bible and Asia

The Bible and Asia

*From the Pre-Christian Era
to the Postcolonial Age*

R. S. Sugirtharajah

Harvard University Press
Cambridge, Massachusetts
London, England
2013

Library of Congress Cataloging-in-Publication Data
Sugirtharajah, R. S. (Rasiah S.)
The Bible and Asia : from the pre-Christian era to the postcolonial age /
R.S. Sugirtharajah.
    pages   cm
Includes bibliographical references and index.
ISBN 978-0-674-04907-9 (alk. paper)
    1. Bible—Criticism, interpretation, etc.—Asia.   I. Title.
BS511.3.S84   2013
220.095—dc23   2013009720

Contents

The Bible and Asia

Introduction

This volume is about the Bible and Asia. So the inevitable question is: What is Asia? Or, which Asia? Defining Asia has not always been easy. In Asian languages or in the dominant ancient Asian cartographical categories, there was no single term, "Asia," that covered the whole region, as the designation "Europe" did that continent. There were expressions such as the "Sea of China" or the "Sea of Hind," which had an analogous meaning in Arabic and in some of the Indian languages.[1] This reluctance and absence of naming was partly due to the fact that the multiple religious, linguistic, and ethnic groups that inhabited the continent did not conceive of themselves as a collective unit. Whereas Christianity and dynastic alliances provided a structure for a common identity for Europe, there was no such framework helping to sustain a similar pan-Asian identity. In contrast with the European essentialist view, Asians saw themselves as diverse and plural civilizations.

Asia and the East are vague constructions. The term "Asia" occurs for the first time in 1584 in one of the maps of the Italian Jesuit Matteo Ricci. Ricci's naming was not the routine orientalist exercise of structuring and categorizing the "other" but reflected the "official

Chinese interpretation of the concept."[2] He was simply reproducing the Chinese characters for *yaxiya*, which meant "inferior"—indicating Asia as a marginal place and China in the middle encircled by "various barbarians, such as the European folangji, Japanese wako pirates, or Mongolian enemies, in the north."[3] This deprecatory term indicated that these people who lived on the borders belonged to Asia and did not refer to the Chinese themselves. The Chinese characters for *yaxiya* were so consistent that Pekka Korhonen, who has studied the usage of the term, concluded that it might well have been "the result of a logical and intentional act of naming."[4] It may be an uncomplimentary term, but it was the term Asians "themselves chose four centuries ago."[5]

Before the modern "discovery" of Asia and the East, these terms were used so interchangeably and broadly that Egypt figured in the maps of Asia. Often India was seen as the symbol of, and indistinguishable from, Asia and was used as a comprehensive term to cover the continent. As late as the sixteenth century, Maximilian of Transylvania wrote that "the natives of all unknown countries are commonly called Indians."[6] The celebrated case in point is that of the Iberian conquistadores naming Native Americans as Indians. Ironically, when the Portuguese reached the Japanese island of Tanegashima, the Portuguese were themselves greeted as Indians.[7] This imprecise usage continued even as recently as the eighteenth century, when the East was defined as "all regions beyond the Arabian Sea and the Kingdom of Persia."[8]

The concept of Asia, not as a geographical unit but as a cultural unit, emerged only at the height of modern colonialism, when Indian reformers (such as Swami Vivekananda, Keshub Chunder Sen, and P. C. Mozumdar), Sinhala nationalists (such as Anagarika Dharmapala), and the Japanese Kinza Rigue M. Hirai were trying to invoke a common Asian spirituality as a critique of Western materialism at the Chicago Parliament of Religions (1893). Subsequently, Rabindranath Tagore used Asian values to criticize Indian and Japanese nationalism. In a sense, the current usage of "Asia" as a continental unity is a combination of two factors—the Western habit of naming the "other" and the Asian strategy of invoking Asian values to withstand Western materialism.

In current political discourse, the continent is seen as plural. There are at least four Asias—West Asia (the Arab world), Central Asia (republics of the former Soviet Union), East Asia (extending to the western Pacific nations), and South Asia (sub-Himalayan countries, sometimes referred to as "the subcontinent"). This volume is primarily about West, East, and South Asia.

The story and the events that lie behind the testaments of the Bible encompass only a tiny proportion of the history and religion of a very small part of West Asia. The history of the arrival of these books, and their reception in East and South Asia, is a long one and goes back at least to the third century of the first millennium. In reality, however, the Bible's substantial presence has been felt more recently, with the advent of modern colonialism.

It was the Church of the East, popularly but condescendingly known as the Nestorian Church, that first introduced the Bible to India, Java, and China. There are three remarkable features about this precolonial reception of the Bible in Asia. First, the Bible did not arrive with the conquering army of a superior civilization in order to subjugate a weak and barbarous people but came with those on the fringes of society to parts of the world where civilization was thriving. The early harbingers of the good news were a motley crowd of missionaries, merchants, persecuted Christians, and travelers with hardly any political power or ambition to conquer. Second, the Bible remained remote and untranslated, especially in India, for more than a thousand years. In the Malabar churches, the Bible was seen as an object of veneration but little read. The congregations learned about the message of the Bible through the liturgy. Third, unlike the aggressive and intrusive instrument that the colonialists' Bible became, the biblical message was of a gentler and less triumphalist form of Christianity. Other early Christian literature closely associated with India—the Gospel of Thomas and the Acts of Thomas—likewise offer a different message. The Gospel of Thomas, in George Gispert-Sauch's view, reads like the Upanishads, and the Acts of Thomas presents Jesus not announcing his message tinged with the heavy artillery of Semitic images and vocabulary but replicating what the Buddha did a few centuries before—expounding the virtues of detachment and an ascetic form of life. In China, when the Bible encountered indigenous texts, biblical precepts were melded with the beliefs of the Buddha and Lao Tzu. The scrolls, known as the Jesus Sutras, portray Jesus as a wise sage who redeemed humanity, not from sin, which was one of the chief tenets of evangelical Christianity in Asia, but from the wheel of reincarnation.[9]

All this changed when the Bible in its present form reached Asia and other continents. With the emergence of modern colonialism, the Bible was introduced as an artifact of modernity in the form of the King James Bible, the "national Bible" of the English people. In this incarnation, the Bible became a very European book, lost all its oriental traits, and became less Asiatic. This Asian estrangement was further compounded by two additional factors: the Bible's role as a legitimizing document for European invasion and the Protestant conviction of the indispensability of the Bible for the salvation of the native souls. The centenary report of the British and Foreign Bible Society proudly claimed that the Bible carried the "secret of the surest happiness for individuals and the surest prosperity for nations. . . . [The Society] has gone into every corner of the earth distributing the scriptures in the languages which the inhabitants can understand."[10] Asians, who were comfortable with and hospitable to each others' sacred texts, found an intruder in their textual landscape. The result was that they could not accord the Bible the same status as they did their own religious books. The imported "white man's book" was seen as a strange instrument, an entrapment to lure them away from their own traditions.

An Asian reading of the Bible has, consequently, not always been a smooth one. It is a contrived reading and not as natural as a Hindu reading of the Bhagavad Gita, a Buddhist reading of the Dhammapada, or a Chinese reading of the Analects. The Asian reading of the Bible, as George Soares-Prabhu remarks, is a "forced and somewhat artificial exercise."[11] Most of the time, the Bible has to be read against the indigenous religious texts. This volume explores Asian Christians' complex and complicated relationship with the Bible, which has been at times stimulating, at times seditious, and at times synthetic.

Chapters, Summations

Chapter 1 narrates an often-overlooked hermeneutical aspect—the presence of Asia and India in the Christian Bible. Traditionally, it has been assumed that the Israelites were influenced only by the cultures around the Mediterranean and that early Christian writings drew heavily from Roman culture. This chapter challenges this view and provides examples of how not only Indian goods (ivory), birds (peacocks), animals (monkeys), and fruits (pomegranate) but also religious ideas, theological concepts, and moral stories traveled from the

East. The chapter assembles the evidence that has been all along known to orientalists and Indologists but has been given a wide berth by biblical scholars. The chapter registers that, along with Indian merchandise, a number of Indian moral stories have found their way into the books of the Old Testament. One is the famous judgment of Solomon. The chapter also explores the possibility of a poetical genre typical of Tamil literature, in which a girl pines for her lover, providing the literary impetus for the Song of Songs. The major concern of the chapter is the vexed question of Buddhist and Indian ideas in the New Testament. It asks whether it is reasonable to attribute some of the biblical phrases and concepts that have no possible Hebraic or Hellenistic roots to Buddhist or Indian origins. The chapter does not idealize or romanticize the Indian presence and input. Its aim is to demonstrate that first-century Palestine was not an isolated territory and to place the Bible in a wider, universal religious history.

Chapter 2 deals with the European search for a possible replacement for the Old Testament and the potential influence of Vedic thinking on biblical religion. At a time when missionaries and some orientalists were trying to introduce Christianity as the remedy for native degeneracy, there were other orientalists who were trying to find imaginary Vedic texts not only to strengthen Christianity but also to demonstrate that it was these Eastern texts from which the biblical religion drew its strength. Two such men were John Z. Holwell and Louis Jacolliot, both colonial officers, the former for the British and the latter for the French. Their hermeneutical enterprise was diametrically opposed to the concerns of liberal Protestants of that time. It was not the souls of the "heathens" but, rather, the spiritual degeneration of those Westerners that occupied these interpreters. While oriental and biblical scholars were scrutinizing Christianity's relationship to Near Eastern culture with regard to both the testaments, these two colonial administrators were more concerned with the East and its impact on the biblical thought world and were seeking to provide an alternative to Judaic and Hellenistic traditions.

Chapter 3 challenges the popular perception of Asian biblical interpretation as a mindlessly tedious and imitative affair without any spicy heretical disputes or animated disagreements. It brings to the fore the intervention of three Asians—Raja Rammohun Roy, Hong Xiuquan, and J. C. Kumarappa—who confronted the missionaries' version of Christianity and colonial power by using the same weapon provided by the missionaries—the Bible. All were favorably predisposed toward missionaries. All three had different hermeneutical opponents and agendas but certain common features. They thought they were better and more effective at interpreting the Bible than the missionaries themselves; they all had self-belief in the moral decency of their indigenous cultures; and, above all, they were convinced that the Bible that came with the missionaries needed a vigilant redaction and revision. In their hands, the Bible gained a new dimension. What their hermeneutics shows is that the ultimate power is not in the Bible but in the ability to create a new cultural, political, and moral world that would appeal to their own people.

Chapter 4 focuses on the hermeneutical enterprise of Angarika Dharmapala, a Sinhala nationalist who was tirelessly involved in reviving Buddhism in colonial Sri Lanka. Dharmapala was one of those natives who was not enamored of the grandeur of the British but was very proud of the civilizational repute of Sri Lanka. Dharmapala's hermeneutics could be easily dismissed as the mindless mimicry of the colonized or the unreflective posturing of an uppity native. Rather, as outlined in the chapter, his hermeneutics was a specific and calculated attempt to defeat colonialism and its enabling partner, the Christian mission. The chapter focuses on three aspects. First, it analyzes for the first time the often overlooked vast number of biblical references interspersed in Dharmapala's writings. He used the very book—the Bible—over which Christian missionaries thought they had control. He drew on the cherished book of the Christian preachers to attack them at their own game but on his own terms. Second, it shows how his exercise in decolonization repeated many colonial tendencies; and third, it demonstrates the terrible irony in Dharmapala's discursive work. While he was anticolonial and resisted the British presence and imperialist Christianity, he was equally colonial in defining a national identity that excluded the indigenous Tamils and Muslims. This chapter, in effect, undermines Dharmapala's hallowed status as a spokesperson of Sinhala nationalism. His case is a reminder that Asians, too, can produce and perpetrate illiberal, prejudiced, and communalist discourse while claiming to be progressive and speaking on behalf of the people.

In Western hermeneutics, the apostle Paul is seen as a European hero who not only paved the way for European Christianity but also liberated Judaism from its archaic and narrowly ethnocentric attitudes and opened it up for all comers. Chapter 5 looks at how Paul and his writings have been embraced, mimicked, transformed, and rejected by orientalists, missionaries, and Asian Christians. In Asian biblical hermeneutics, Paul's place is an ambiguous one. His image varies from being a collaborator who supported the empire to a companion in solidarity or a fellow samurai upholding chivalric values, as portrayed by some Japanese Christians. While some of the missionaries tried to present Paul as a nonpolitical but loyal imperial hero, some Asian Christians who felt suffocated by the Western form of dogmatic and institutionalized Christianity enthusiastically embraced Paul's message of direct experience of God, as a way of subverting the faith introduced by the missionaries. This chapter demonstrates how Paul takes on a new vitality outside mainstream Western thinking, and that an Asian reading goes beyond the traditional Pauline teaching of law giving way to grace and faith replacing work. It also analyzes the complex and uneasy relationship Asian women have with Paul. The chapter has two extra features. First, it rereads Paul's Athenian speech—supposed to be a model for interfaith dialogue—and exposes its colonizing tendencies. Second, it revisits the ever irresolvable question of whether Paul was an ally of the empire, or drafted in but still resisting its power, or totally opposed to the colonizing impulses of the empire.

Asian biblical hermeneutics is itself a very marginal discipline, but within this minority discipline, new voices have recently emerged that have been left aside by pan-Asian theology. Chapter 6 narrates the story of these forgotten and overlooked voices. There was a time when Asian theologians were articulating a theology for the whole of Asia and in the process ignoring the concerns of their own doubly oppressed—the women, Indian Dalits, Japanese Burakumins, and tribals (that is, tribal peoples) who inhabit the continent. The chapter explores how the "imported" text became an important vehicle for asserting the agency of these marginalized Christians and how, situating themselves in the biblical narratives, they appropriated biblical symbols and personalities to make sense of their lives, offer resistance, and articulate their minority status. This chapter introduces two new entrants to Asian biblical interpretation. One is the emergence of diasporic hermeneutics undertaken by Asians who live outside the continent. It looks at how Asian Americans with their racial and ethnic identities have been reading and writing about the Bible, how these interpreters negotiate individual and community formation and survival, and how their articulations have been influenced not only by the history, politics, and culture they left behind but also by the history, politics, and culture of the host community. The interesting feature of diasporic hermeneutics is how these scholars are constantly forced to formulate and reconstitute both their identity and their attitude to Christian, Hindu, Confucian, and Taoist texts. The other new entrant is postcolonial biblical interpretation. Here we analyze how Asian biblical scholars have employed this critical tool. The chapter ends with a consideration of benefits and risks associated with such a strongly identitarian minority hermeneutics.

The wide-ranging impact of the Bible on Western culture, especially on its literature, is well documented. However, the Bible's influence on Asian literature is not as profound and penetrative as that of the Bible on the Western imagination. Rather, it is minimal, largely because Asian storytellers draw heavily on indigenous resources such as the Mahabharata and a vast number of Chinese, Korean, and other indigenous folktales for imagery and ideas. Chapter 7 deals with the minimal use of the Bible by Asian novelists and storytellers. What is noticeable is that these novels are not profusely littered with biblical citations, and more alarmingly to the traditionalists, biblical narratives and biblical personalities are often read against the received perception. The Bible has a different function in these novels—often used to critique the institutionalized church and Western colonialism, at times used to provide scriptural warrants to perpetuate a very stern form of Christian fundamentalism, and occasionally characters in these novels are drawn to it as a magical object endowed with divine properties. The Asian novels discussed here give the impression that the Bible is an unattractive book, and as one of the characters in a novel featured here said, it had to be rejected.

The volume ends with a conclusion that charts some of the future tasks that await Asian biblical interpreters.

On Method, Language, and Versions

In this volume, I use insights from postcolonial criticism, but the reader will notice that I hardly indulge in heavy theorizing. Theorizing looks like a specialized business, accessible only to those with arcane epistemological tools. My intention is to work with specific hermeneutical examples and subject them to critical practices that are assembled around the label "postcolonialism," rather than apply an already worked-out and complex theory that is liable to impose artificial structures and obfuscate the material under consideration.

Those readers raised with language sensitivity will find the sexist and racial language in the text awkward and uncomfortable. All these offensive passages occur in quotations that come from earlier centuries where such sensitivities were scarcely exercised or even recognized. I have cited them without sanitizing them, to show how our attitude toward gender and race issues has evolved over the years. Biblical quotations come from different versions depending on by whom and in which century they were used.

As I finished this volume, I came across commentaries on Matthew (1898) and John (1906) written by Ponnanbalam Ramanathan (1851–1930) during the colonial days in Sri Lanka. Ramanathan was solicitor general of Ceylon and was actively involved in politics. His commentaries were important for three reasons: first, they were probably the first commentaries in Asia to follow the modern line-by-line analysis of the text; second, they were written by a Hindu who knew Greek, Hebrew, and Latin and who, more pertinently, made use of his knowledge of biblical languages to challenge the translation of the King James Version where it did not agree with his Saiva philosophy; and finally, unlike orientalists, missionaries, and Indian converts who used the Sanskritic Vedas and Upanishads in interpreting the biblical message, Ramanathan's commentaries use the Tamil Saiva Sidhanta to illuminate the text and in the process almost make the Gospel writers look like Saiva Jnanis (saints) following Saiva Sidhanta doctrines; they make use of and challenge some of the leading exponents of Western biblical scholarship of the time; and, crucially to our purpose, so far no one has done any extensive work on them. Ramanathan, like Rammohun Roy, had the class confidence, academic sophistication, and caste arrogance to tell Westerners that Easterners were better interpreters of the West's cherished book—the Bible. It was too late to include them in this volume, but I intend to return to them at a later date.

Finally, I end with two observations. Although the volume has a rather grand title, I will be the first to admit that it does not cover the entire continent or the vast time frame that the title suggests. It is impossible to explore every hermeneutical issue or to study every work of every Asian biblical interpreter. A volume that prides itself on a postcolonial approach and omits hidden voices and suppressed histories will be seen as guilty of a cardinal sin, but the task is too much for one person. What I have done is to draw attention to a selection of stunning examples of Asian exegetical sedition, idiosyncrasy, vitality, and imagination.

At the height of colonialism, Stanley Cook claimed that the West got far more out of the Bible than ever the East had done. What this Regius Professor of Hebrew at the University of Cambridge observed, nearly nine decades ago, still holds true. In the field of biblical studies, the West still dominates. The words of Ashis Nandy, spoken in a different disciplinary context, are equally true for biblical studies: "The West is now everywhere, within the West and outside; in structures and in minds."[12] This volume may not shatter the West's pervasive presence, but I will be more than pleased if it makes even a small dent in it.

1 Merchandise, Moralities, and Poetics of Aryans, Dravidians, and Israelites

Readers of any standard work on the Bible will get the impression that there is a tacit agreement among biblical scholars that both testaments were influenced by Near Eastern and Hellenistic cultures. Before Napoleon's campaign in the Mediterranean (1798–1801), scholarly investigation of biblical religion and culture was largely confined to the sources supplied by Greco-Latin classical writings. Subsequent to the opening of the Orient, however, and the discovery and decipherment of Sumerian, Hittite, and Ugaritic inscriptions, the history of Israel was placed within what biblical scholars designedly configured as a Near Eastern context. Such a placement radically challenged biblical history, its chronology, and its theological precepts. It has always been taken for granted that the New Testament was produced under Roman colonial rule. Roman administration not only provided economic and political stability but also supplied philosophy, language, and customs that shaped the New Testament writings and the early church. In other words, it has become a scholarly convention to assume that those adjoining countries that often invaded Israel and the occupying power—the Roman empire—offered cultural provisions and sustenance to both testaments. This chapter aims to broaden the cultural catchment area of the Bible by including Asia as a potential contributor to the life and thought of the biblical people and their culture.

The chapter, then, will do three things in particular. It will draw attention to the presence of India and Asia and how these were represented in various biblical books; provide examples of the exchange of both commercial commodities and cultural products, such as myths, stories, and religious concepts, that took place between India and the biblical world; and explore the possibility of Eastern religious thought, especially the alleged influence of Buddhism, on the New Testament. It will conclude with a consideration of some of the hermeneutical implications surrounding the potential influence of Eastern religions on the emerging Christianity.

Asia in the Bible

I begin by listing instances where Asia and India have been mentioned, first in the Hebrew scriptures, then through the intertestamental writings, the New Testament, and other books that are left out of the canon.

One of the earliest biblical writings to mention India is the Book of Esther. It has two references. The first appears in the opening verse of the book: "This happened in the days of Ahasuerus, the same Ahasuerus who ruled over one hundred twenty-seven provinces from India to Ethiopia" (1:1 New Revised Standard Version [hereafter NRSV]). The other occurs as part of an edict: "The king's secretaries were summoned at that time, in the third month, which is the month of Sivan, on the twenty-third day; and an edict was written, according to all that Mordecai commanded, to the Jews and to the satraps and the governors and the officials of the provinces from India to Ethiopia, one hundred twenty-seven provinces, to every province in its own script and to every people in its own language, and also to the Jews in their script and their language" (8:9 NRSV). The purpose of mentioning India as the eastern border of the Ethiopian empire in Esther, according to Randal Bailey, is to indicate the power of the southern empires. Because the book of Esther was written during the Greek rule of Southern Syria, Bailey's contention is that it could be an anti-Greek polemic that called attention to the superiority of southern nations over the north. Ethiopia and India are not just geographical markers but the benchmark against which Israel is evaluated.[1]

In the intertestamental period, the Books of Maccabees have a number of references to Asia and India. In these writings, Asia was used as a way of highlighting the might and dominion of the Seleucid empire:

> They also had defeated Antiochus the Great, king of Asia, who went to fight against them with one hundred twenty elephants and with cavalry and chariots and a very large army. He was crushed by them. (1 Macc. 8:6 NRSV)

> Then Ptolemy entered Antioch and put on the crown of Asia. Thus he put two crowns on his head, the crown of Egypt and that of Asia. (11:13 NRSV)

> Then Trypho attempted to become king in Asia and put on the crown, and to raise his hand against King Antiochus. (12:39 NRSV)

While the holy city was inhabited in unbroken peace and the laws were strictly observed because of the piety of the high priest Onias and his hatred of wickedness, it came about that the kings themselves honored the place and glorified the temple with the finest presents, *even to the extent that King Seleucus of Asia defrayed from his own revenues all the expenses connected with the service of the sacrifices.* (2 Macc. 3:3 NRSV; emphasis added)

Now Timothy, who had been defeated by the Jews before, gathered a tremendous force of mercenaries and collected the cavalry from Asia in no small number. (2 Macc. 10:24 NRSV)

When our expedition took place in Asia, as you yourselves know, it was brought to conclusion, according to plan, by the gods' deliberate alliance with us in battle. (3 Macc. 3:14 NRSV)

At a time when our ancestors were enjoying profound peace because of their observance of the law and were prospering, so that even Seleucus Nicanor, *king of Asia, had both appropriated money to them for the temple service and recognized their commonwealth*—just at that time certain persons attempted a revolution against the public harmony and caused many and various disasters. (4 Macc. 3:20 NRSV; emphasis added)

In the Book of Maccabees, there is a mention of an Indian mahout with Antiochus's elephants: "On the elephants were wooden towers, strong and covered; they were fastened on each animal by special harness, and on each were four armed men who fought from there, and also its Indian driver" (1 Macc. 6:37 NRSV).

India also appears as one of the limits of the Persian empire under Darius in the apocryphal Greek version of the Book of Ezra known as 1 Esdras. The passage runs as follows: "Now King Darius gave a great banquet for all that were under him, all that were born in his house, and all the nobles of Media and Persia, and all the satraps and generals and governors that were under him in the hundred and twenty-seven satrapies from India to Ethiopia" (3.1–2 NRSV).

Asia, in these writings, is perceived as a place full of cash and cavalry. India in the Hebrew scriptures and in the intertestamental writings is portrayed as a powerful nation that supplies forces for war, including trained warriors driving elephants. For the Selucid kings, elephants were an "important instrument of war" that they used in their campaigns. The Mauryan king Chandragupta gifted 500 elephants to Seleucus I (305–285 BCE) in exchange for a matrimonial alliance and the return of territories that were part of India.[2] There is also the record of Antiochus I receiving twenty Indian elephants sent by the governor of Bactria to the satrap of Babylonia, who dispatched them to Antiochus I to fight against the Ptolemies.[3] It was generally accepted that African elephants were "no match for the much fiercer Indian ones."[4] The mention of Indian mahouts and an Indian army as part of the Selucid international force attacking Israel reinforces the prophetic portrayal of the tiny and hapless nation of Israel faced with numerous and powerful enemies.

In the New Testament, however, under the Roman empire the picture is different. Asia is mentioned in the writings of Luke (Acts 2:9; 6:9; 16:6; 19:10, 22, 26, 27, 31; 20:4, 16, 18; 21:27; 24:18; 27:2), Paul (Rom. 16:5; 1 Cor. 16:19; 2 Cor. 1:8), Deutero Paul (2 Tim. 1:15), Peter (1 Pet. 1:1), and John (Apocalypse 1:4). The Asia mentioned here is Proconsular Asia—a Roman province that included the Western part of

Asia Minor and had Ephesus as its capital, now in Western Turkey. Proconsular Asia contained the seven churches of the Apocalypse (Rev. 1:11). Although the cities Jerusalem, Bethlehem, Antioch, and Armenia were all geographically in West Asia, culturally and politically they were part of the West.

Significant events of early Christianity took place in Western Asia—Bethlehem, Jerusalem, Ephesus, Antioch. It was in Antioch that the followers of Jesus for the first time were called Christians (Acts 11:23–26). Although major events of nascent Christianity played out in Asia, it was seen as a place to be avoided. The Acts reports that Paul and his companions traveled through Phyrgia and Galatia but the Holy Spirit kept them from preaching the word in Asia (16:6). The unknown author of 2 Timothy encapsulates the mood: "This you know, that all who are in Asia turned away from me" (1:15).

In the portrayals of the New Testament writings, Asia and Asians do not come across as attractive or appealing. They are portrayed here as disruptive, and Asia is seen as a hostile territory. For instance, in the trial of Stephen, Asians are seen as part of the Jewish orthodoxy who argue with him: "Then some of those who belonged to the synagogue of the Freedmen (as it was called), and of the Cyrenians, and of the Alexandrians, and of those from Cilicia and Asia, rose up and disputed with Stephen" (Acts 6:9). In another example of Asian hostility seen in Ephesus, the preaching of the new Christian movement creates a stir when it leads to a loss of income among local silversmiths. The chief instigator is Demetrius, who made silver shrines for the local goddess Diana. What is surprising is that just a few years earlier, the very same Ephesians had welcomed enthusiastically the message of Paul. The apostle taught for five hours a day in the rented school of Tyrannus in Ephesus (Acts 19:9). Now, a few years later, in a changed scenario, the same province had turned against him. Asians are thus portrayed as a people who are not reliable and who deserted Paul when he needed them most. Paul singles out Phygelus and Hermogenes, who failed to come to his rescue when he was in trouble with the Roman government.

There were exceptions. For instance, there was Onesiphorus, an Ephesian Christian who visited Paul when he was in prison and whom Paul praised for his kindness, courage, and hospitality. Another Ephesian, Tychicus of Asia, came to Paul's rescue. Paul then dispatched him to Ephesus in the hope that a native of that province might succeed in sorting out the troubles there (Eph. 6:21; also see 2 Tim. 4:12).

Tychicus is mentioned five times in the New Testament. A close reading of these passages will reveal two things. First, he simply accompanies Paul in his journeys. He is mentioned, with Aristarchus and Secundus of Thessalonica, Gaius of Derbe, and "Timothy, and Tychicus and Trophimus of Asia" (Acts 20:5), as one of Paul's companions on his travel to Asia. Second, he merely follows the orders of Paul and fulfills whatever is asked of him. Tychicus was sent to Ephesus twice. On the first occasion, he was sent to tell the Ephesian church how Paul was doing. Paul wrote to the Ephesians, "But that you also may know my affairs and what I am doing, Tychicus will make all things known to you" (Eph. 6:21). On the second occasion, Tychicus was dispatched to Ephesus to win back the rebellious Ephesian Christians (2 Tim. 4:12). The last time we hear of Tychicus, Paul has summoned him again for a visit. "When I send Artemas to you, or Tychicus, be diligent to come to me at Nicopolis, for I have decided to spend the winter there" (Titus 3:12). Paul asked Titus to come to him and was willing to send one of the two men, apparently to take over the work that Titus was doing in Crete. Again, it is apparent that Tychicus was willing to go wherever Paul needed him to go. Very little is said about Tychicus, except that he is a "beloved brother and faithful minister in the Lord" (Eph. 6:21; also see Col. 4:7). The impression that one gets is of an obedient and pliant Asian who had no voice or initiative of his own but who respected authority and faithfully followed orders.

While some Asians are portrayed as unquestioningly obeying authorities, others are seen as having authority and position. They are recognized as administrating agents of the imperial government and as the wielders of power. Colonialism creates and relies on a subset of a colonized population that forms a collaborating comprador class. Luke refers to a group of Asian chiefs—Asiarchs. The "chiefs of Asia" (Acts 19:31) were certainly wealthy and influential citizens who were elected annually to supervise and conduct religious festivals, especially the ritual concerned with emperor worship. Their responsibility included organizing games in their home cities. In the eyes of Christians, these Asiarchs were all pagans. Some were portrayed as friends of Paul, although their religious views differed fundamentally from those of the apostle. The idolatrous practices of these people went against the tenets of the gospel that Luke was trying to convey. What endeared Luke to them was their imperial connections. As officials of the Roman empire, they were jealous supporters of royal authority and showed intense loyalty to the emperor. It was these Asiarchs who were the officers of the imperial cult, but they did not find Paul a threat to the emperor. They saw to it that he and his traveling companions, Gaius and Aristarchus, were not exposed to the mob.

Going beyond the canonical books of the New Testament, one of the rejected writings of the early church, the Acts of Thomas, offers a prominent place to India, a site where the apostle Thomas was sent to evangelize. In the Acts of Thomas, an early third-century text, India features frequently. This was one of the many early church writings that was left out of the New Testament. In it, India is seen as fertile ground for evangelization long before the modern colonialism made it a prime target for conversion. The opening section of the narrative makes it clear that the reluctant apostle was forced to go to India: "I am an Hebrew man; how can I go amongst the Indians and preach the truth?... Whither thou wouldest send me, send me, but elsewhere, for unto the Indians I will not go" (Acts of Thomas 1). In the Acts of Thomas, one can glean at least three images of India. These negative images predate orientalist characterizations of India, which later became pertinent marks of colonial discourse. First, India is polytheistic and full of demons and idols. Thomas is portrayed as the one who rescues India from the demons, pronouncing their final destruction: "They also shall now be abolished, with their works" (Acts of Thomas 77). Second, India is full of poor people in need of aid and financial support. Thomas distributes the money given by the king to build a palace for the poor and the needy (Acts of Thomas 19). Third, it is an intolerant place. Thomas was killed for converting King Misdaeus's wives and a relative, Charisius. Interestingly, the Christ that Thomas presented to the Indians was not the one Paul portrayed in his preaching to the Gentiles—not a crucified savior but Jesus as a "teacher of the truth" (Acts of Thomas 79), who preached a life of renunciation and asceticism. What Jesus offered was not the Semitic prescription of redemption from sin but a "tranquil life without grief or anxiety" (Acts of Thomas 12), "free of care and grief and fear" (Acts of Thomas 28) and of "care and anxiety" (Acts of Thomas 77). In a sense, Thomas's Jesus seems to have recycled the message that the Buddha had preached to the Indians five centuries before.

To summarize, then, in the biblical writings, Asia does not fare favorably. It is seen as a troublesome territory to be avoided. Its people are complex. They are hapless yet helpful. As individuals they do not take any initiative, but as a group of people with power they are helpful to the apostle Paul.

An Indian God among Hebrew Deities

It may sound improbable, but there is also a possibility of a Hindu god featuring in the Bible. When King Ahasuerus, who ruled Persia, was enraged by his wife Vashti's refusal to show her beauty in his royal presence, the incensed king turned to the seven princes of Persia and Media (Esther 1:13, 14). As the text has it, one of them was Carshena, who could be the Hindu god Krishna, the prince of the Yadhava family.

There is a hermeneutics of omission at work in Eurocentric biblical scholarship when it comes to recognizing who Carshena was. Most Western commentators, so meticulous in explaining biblical texts line by line, take one of the following approaches: Some completely ignore this verse. Others blame the poor translation. A. W. Streane, in his Cambridge Bible for schools and colleges, claims that the name "evidently suffered much in transmission."[5] Some argue that the prince was from Africa, without providing any credible evidence for this suggestion.[6]

The possibility of the presence of Hindu deities cannot to be ruled out if one takes into account the geopolitical conditions of the time. Persia's connection with India is well recorded. Cyrus extended his conquest up to the border of India. The conquest of India by Darius, the father of Xerxes, is mentioned in Herodotus (iii:94–106; iv:44). Herodotus records that the Indian troops were part of the international composition of the army of Darius I and Xerxes and that they fought under the command of a Persian. Herodotus provides a description of the Indian soldiers: "The Indians wore garments made of tree-wool, and they had bows of reed and arrows of reed with iron points. Thus were the Indians equipped; and serving with the rest they had been assigned to Pharnazathres the son of Artabates" (vii:65). Indian bowmen were prized components of the armies of Darius and Xerxes.[7] These Indian soldiers along with their dress and military equipment might well have brought their gods and goddesses with them.

Then there was the case of two rebelling Indian chiefs who fled westward with their clans and established colonies in Western Asia near Vishap, on the western Euphrates, during the reign of Valarsbak (149–127 BCE). They founded a temple for the worship of Gisani (Krishna) and Demeter (Baldev).[8] Whether these gods were Aryan or Dravidian is a contested issue. The colony came to a violent end in the fourth century (CE), when St. Gregory, the illuminator, attacked these "pagans." The chief priest and his son were slain, their 12- and 15-cubit-high copper statues of gods were smashed, and the temples were raised to the ground. Churches replaced the temples and crosses were erected where the idols once stood. More than 5,000 "idolaters" were converted to Christianity, and 438 sons of the priests or temple servants who remained loyal to their faith had their heads shaved and were dispatched to distance places near the Caspian.[9]

The extension of the Persian empire up to India and the presence of a Hindu colony in West Asia point to the possibility that Hindu deities might have mingled with Hebrew gods. The Vedic deities such as Mithra, Varuna, and Indra were found in the north of Syria in the middle of the second millennium before the common era. These gods of the Rig Veda were known to the Hurrians and the Hittites. Stanley Cook, Regius Professor of Hebrew at Cambridge University, advocated a "vaster background of history and religion" for biblical religion, which would take into account "non-Israelite or non-Hebraic factors." "In the Mosaic Age," Cook claimed, "Varuna, the remarkable ethical god of ancient India, was known to north Syria."[10]

The reluctance on the part of biblical scholars to admit the presence of Eastern gods alongside the Jewish one could be attributed to either the conviction of Euro-American scholars that Christianity was largely influenced by Hebraic and Hellenistic cultures or the obsession of biblical scholars with the salvation history model, which prevents them from accepting any potential influence from Eastern religions.

Traveling Merchants and Importing Goods

The Christian Bible mentions not only the presence of Indians, Asians, and the possibility of a Hindu god but also the importation of Indian goods. The Hebrew scriptures record the celebrated visit of the Queen of Sheba meeting with King Solomon and showering him with gifts of a 120 talents of gold and a great quantity of spices and precious stones (1 Kings 10:10). It is believed that these articles must have come from India to Africa and then to the court of Solomon. The historical books of the Hebrew scriptures record that every third year King Solomon's ship together with King Hiram of Tyre's ships brought gold from Ophir; and from there they brought great cargoes of almug wood and precious stones (1 Kings 10:11; see also 2 Chron. 8:18). The exact location of Ophir has been a puzzle to scholars. The conjecture is that it must have been a place in India. This speculation, according to Max Müller, is not a modern one. His identification of Ophir with India was based on two factors. One is textual. Müller draws attention to the way the Vulgate translates Job

28:16: "It cannot be valued with the gold of Ophir (Sophir LXX) as *'Non conferetur tinctis Indiæ coloribus.'*" "In Coptic," Müller goes on to claim, "*sofir* is the name for India, the same word by which the LXX translated the Hebrew Ophir."[11] The other consideration is linguistic. The words used to describe the merchandise that Solomon's ship brought from Ophir during his reign, such as gold, silver, ivory, apes, algum trees, and peacocks, are foreign to the Hebrew language. Müller made a confident proposition: "I believe, by certain Sanskrit words which occur in the Bible as names of articles of export from Ophir, articles such as ivory, apes, peacocks, and sandalwood, which, taken together, could not have been exported from any country but India."[12]

The equivalent words for these commodities in Hebrew are strange to that language. The plausible etymology of these words, in Müller's view, is Sanskrit or other Indian languages, such as Tamil and Malayalam. Müller's conclusion is that if these languages were spoken in Ophir, it was a place situated somewhere "in India and accessible by sea."[13] There are other factors that support the theory that India is Ophir. The geographer Ptolemy places it at the mouth of the Indus. The coast around modern Bombay is identified as "sovira" in Buddhist literature. The Jewish historian Josephus identifies the biblical "sophir" with the Indian "Land of Gold."

THE IMPORTED ALMUG WOOD was used to decorate the temple and the royal palace that King Solomon built. Harps and lyres were also made from it for the musicians. As the text put it, "So much almugwood has never been imported or seen since that day" (1 Kings 10:12). These almug wood trees have been identified with sandalwood, the wood derived from the Sanskrit *valgu*. These trees were found in South India, mainly in Mysore, Coimbatore, and Salem districts. These must have been taken to Gujarat ports and from there transported to

Syria via Arabia.[14] King Solomon's throne was overlaid "with ivory and the best gold" (1 Kings 10:18). It is probable that some of the ivory might have come from India. The Hebrew word for ivory, *shen habbin*, is a translation of the Sanskrit *ibba danta*, meaning elephant's tooth. Indian textiles and scents also seem to have made their way into the biblical world. The book of Psalms (7:17) and the Song of Solomon (4:14) refer to the fragrant Indian wood called aloes (Hebrew *ahiliam*)—the term derived from the Sanskrit *agaru* from the cognates in Tamil: "All your garments smell of myrrh, aloes, and cassia, out of the ivory palaces, whereby they have made you glad" (Ps. 45:8 American King James Version). Another Indian article to reach the Hebrews was *sadin*—cotton cloth. Isaiah 3:23 refers to *sadin* for linen.[15]

Another article of trade that found its way from India into the biblical world was ebony. The earliest reference to it is found in Ezekiel, where it appears as a commodity in the trade of Tyre: "The men of Dedan *were* thy merchants; many isles *were* the merchandise of thine hand: they brought thee *for* a present, horns of ivory and ebony" (27:15). The view of Wilfred H. Schoff, who has written extensively on the trade and travel intercourse between India and Rome, is that "If the Oxford editor's identification of Dedan with the South shore of the Persian Gulf be correct, this passage indicates a steady trade in ebony from India prior to the seventh century BC."[16]

One of the ingredients of the sacred oil of the Hebrew priests is cinnamon, and this was brought by Arab merchants from India (Exod. 30). Sapphire, too, was procured from India. Srinivasa Iyengar's contention is that all the articles that Egypt got from India were also "imported into Palestine."[17] Indian animals and birds, too, feature in the Hebrew scriptures. The Hebrew word for peacock, *tuki*, and for ape, *kof*, both seem to be derived from and correspond to Indian words, *tokei* (Tamil), *ab (Sanskrit)*, and *kapi* (Sanskrit), respectively.[18]

Indologists and orientalists have all along acknowledged that there had been a periodic flourishing trade between India and the Mediterranean world, with various regions of India trading with various parts of the Middle East. There is evidence of contacts between the regions of Western India, which comprised Baluchistan, the coastal region of the Makran, and Sind, and the cities of Mesopotamia, which go back as far as 2800 BCE. The discovery of Harappan engraved seals in Sumer was proof that there had been commercial contact between Harappa, in the Indus Valley civilization located in Punjab and Sind, and the cities of Sumer. Typical Indian objects have been found in Sumer. These objects, including cylinder seals, inlay work, and "a scratched representation of a humped bull," were characteristic of Harappa.[19] The presence of a variety of finished ivory objects, such as combs, anthropomorphic and zoomorphic figurines, rings, and rods, discovered in Mesopotamia, suggest that they were from the East and presumably from India.[20] These discoveries point to the fact that there was a flourishing trade between India and Mesopotamia. There was also the presence of Tamil traders at the Red Sea ports and even in Alexandria. The recently discovered Ostracon inscriptions discovered at Quseir al-Qadim near the Red Sea, and written in Brahmi characters, refer to two Tamil names—Catan and Kanan—indicating the possibility of trade.[21]

The volume of trade between Rome and India in the time of Augustus was similar to the trade between Europe and India during the colonial period. Warmington, who has studied the commercial transactions between Rome and India, has observed that it was one-sided—contrary to popular expectation, more trade flowed from India to Rome than vice versa. The amount of commercial goods imported from India was so great that the Roman empire was "unable to counter balance the inflow of Indian products by a return of imperial products."[22] The Romans, in order to offset the trade balance, even coined false money, thinking that the Indians would not be able to distinguish between genuine Roman money and the counterfeit version, but, as Srinivasa Iyengar commented, the "Tamils proved to be too shrewd, for the silly experiment was not repeated."[23]

Traveling Stories

Along with Indian wares, Indian wisdom and folktales probably reached the Mediterranean world. One story that found its way into the Hebrew canon is popularly known in biblical circles as Solomon's judgment. This is the story of a king who was trying to solve a dispute over the ownership of a child claimed by two women. This story was used to illustrate the astuteness of King Solomon and is often claimed as an apotheosis of Jewish wisdom. But the story is not unique to the Jews. There is a comparable Buddhist version in the Tibetan translation of the Buddhist Tripitaka. On comparing the stories, Max Müller wrote that he felt a "certain shudder" when he read the decision of Solomon to divide the child in two (1 Kings 3:25), whereas he found the Indian tale "showing a deeper knowledge of human nature, and more wisdom than even the wisdom of Solomon."[24] In the Buddhist version, it was not the king but a wise woman called Visakha who came out with this extraordinary solution: "What is the use of examining and cross-examining these women? Let them take the boy and settle it among themselves." The king appeared to be frustrated with the quarreling women and was found be helpless and did not know what to do. It was at this point that Visakha offered the amazing resolution to the dispute by asking the mothers to solve it between themselves. When the women were trying to get hold of the child, the child was hurt in the ensuing struggle and began to cry. Thereupon, one of the women let it go because it was hers and she could not bear the agony of the child. Along with peacocks, ivory, sandalwood, and apes, these stories also must have traveled from India. Müller wrote: "We seem perfectly within our right when we look upon the numerous coincidences between the fables of *Aesopus* and the fables occurring in Sanskrit and Pali literature as proving the fact that there was a real literary exchange between India, Persia, Asia Minor and Greece beginning with the sixth century BC."[25]

The story of Abraham pleading for Sodom (Gen. 18:17–33) looks at the outset like a Jewish tale. Irving Wood, who studied the folktales in the Hebrew scriptures, was of the opinion that once verse 22, which acts as a link with the previous narrative, is removed, the tale is "independent and complete." The Jewish influence further diminishes when verses 18–19 are taken as part of the later prophetic phraseology.[26] Once you isolate the story from national interest and the traditional concepts of Jehovah, it is, as Wood argued, more about the greatness of Abraham than about the compassionate nature of God. The ethical nature of a God who sets aside punishment so easily at the request of a human being was, in Wood's reckoning, "hardly the God of the prophets." Such a god is a god of the folktale "from ancient India." Wood wrote: "The primary purpose of the tale is not to teach about God, but to tell a story about a hero, who was so great that he could get what he wanted from God himself. As a prophetic teaching, it would be immoral. As folk-tale it is not."[27]

There is another Indian story, known as "The Blind and the Lame," that found its way into the Apocryphal book of Ezekiel.[28] G. F. Moore points out that in the Sankhya text, the Indian parable seeks to convey a simple philosophical query: How can contrasting entities like *purushsa*, the self, which has intelligence but no power of its own to act, and the body, which has the energetic power but no intellect, cooperate?[29] This parable explains how the keepers of the king's garden, a lame man and a blind man, who were helpless and impotent, collaborated and managed to get out of the forest with the lame man riding on the shoulders of the blind man. Moore is of the view that this story is "ultimately of Indian origin."[30]

The New Testament, too, contains stories that have parallels in the East. One is the Johannine narrative of the woman caught in adultery (John 8). In the Buddhist Jataka version, the king was encouraged by the Buddha to forgive his unfaithful wife and her lover. The king followed the advice of the Buddha and told both his wife and her lover, "Commit not again such an evil deed."[31] This recalls the Johannine version, where a woman caught in adultery was brought before Jesus and he uttered similar words.

How these stories found their way into the biblical world remains a mystery. Jataka Tale 339 talks about the natives of Baveu, which is probably Babylon,[32] bargaining with Indian merchants for birds that were foreign to them—royal peacocks and crows. As the Jataka Tales originated in India, there were contacts between India and Babylon from the second millennium, and Thundy claims that "it is more than likely that India must be the source of these tales."[33] These stories, of course, are not mere reproductions from one cultural and religious context to another. They differ in details, execution, and purpose, but the main thrust and moral remain the same.

Tamil Poetry and Jewish Love

There is a possibility that one of the books of the Hebrew scriptures, the Song of Solomon, might have been influenced by *Aham* poetry, a poetical tradition of the Tamils. Tamil *aham* poetry is about the sexual conduct of a hero and heroine toward each other in the private and public domains. It is about "love in all its varied situations: pre-marital and marital; clandestine and illicit; conjugal happiness and infidelity; separation and union."[34] Chaim Rabin, who first mooted the idea, claimed that it was "possible to suggest that the Song of Songs was written in the heyday of Judean trade with South Arabia and beyond (and this may include the life time of King Solomon) by someone who had himself travelled to South Arabia and to South India and had there become acquainted with Tamil poetry."[35] Rabin's assumption was that this unknown traveler might have borrowed the recurrent themes and some stylistic features from the Tamil poetical form and, like all good borrowers, adapted it to suit the Jewish context. An example of this was that he had lengthened the short poems into a long dialogue, although one can see marks of the shorter Tamil form in the Song of Solomon.

In studying both the Tamil and Hebrew texts, Rabin concludes that there are features in the Song of Songs that have parallels only in the Sangam poetry of the Tamils. Rabin identifies three important characteristics of Song of Songs: first, the primary and proactive role given to the woman. The woman is not only the "chief person," but it is she who expresses her love. There are fifty-six verses in which the woman's voice is heard, whereas only thirty-six verses are devoted to the male character. There is also a marked difference between the way the lovers reveal their feelings. While the man mainly describes the beauty of the woman, the woman on her part expresses difficult and intricate human emotions.

Second, nature provides the backdrop against which love and the conjugal life in all its variety occur. The natural landscape not only supplies the similes but also provides the locale against which the emotions of the lovers are enacted. Whenever an actual physical fulfillment is hinted at, it is the natural setting, such as the forest (1:16), high rocks (2:14), and flowering vineyards (7:13–14), that provides the location, or such actions are couched in agricultural similes, like fertilization of the date palm (7:9). Such an embracing of nature was in contrast to the Jewish prophetic attitude, which is unfriendly and at times hostile to the natural world.

Third, the woman expresses her longing for a lover who is far away, and she fears that such a longing is immoral and will result in loss of respect. This would involve her being disrobed, punished, and shamed by the watchman. More important, she asserts her chaste and pure status. According to Rabin, these three characteristics are found only in "one body of ancient poetry" and that is "in the Sangam poetry of the Tamils."[36] Rabin substantiates his claim by showing philological similarities between the Song of Songs and the Tamil aham poetry. Peter Craigie, who is skeptical about seeing easy parallels, has pointed out that the similarities between Hebrew and Tamil traditions are not limited to love poetry alone. There are other examples of similarities that may be accidental, or coincidental, or archetypical human experiences that need not "indicate historical connections," which weakens Rabin's case. Craigie illustrates his point by showing common features found in the religious experience and an awareness of holiness in the writings of the Hebrew prophet Isaiah and the Tamil poet Appar. Although such similarities diminish Rabin's case, Craigie concedes that such anomalies do not disprove Rabin's main thesis. Craigie credits Rabin with providing historical, philological, and literary data that are "sufficient evidence to formulate the hypothesis."[37] Abraham Mariaselvam, in his study of the Song of Songs and the Tamil aham poetry, has shown the presence of Tamil words in the Song of Songs. He has identified the following as Tamil loan words found in the Song of Solomon: *nērdĕ* (1:12; 4:13), *ahālot* (4:14; see also Ps. 45:9; Prov. 7:17) *karkom* (Song of Sol. 4:14), and *qāneh* (4:14).[38] Mariaselvam recommends a more detailed study of both these literary types but is of the view that the "*probability* of the influence of Tamil aham poetry on the Song of Songs seems to be on a firmer ground."[39]

Asian Author?

The authorship of the Book of Revelation remains a puzzle. Of all the New Testament books, the Apocalypse of John is regarded as the Asiatic book of the Bible, and of all New Testament writings it gives the greatest possible attention to its Oriental provenance. The most popular suggestion, that John the Presbyter might have been the author, was first proposed by Austin Farrer. This speculation has spawned a number of theories regarding the identity of the author. One identifies the Presbyter John as an Asian king—Prester Chan who was driven out of his kingdom by the Tartars and was later wrongly regarded as an African king.[40] Leaving aside the claim for the imaginary empire, Presbyter John, simply as a bishop of Ephesus, was the superintendent of the earliest outpost of Christianity. As Swete put it, "the Apocalypse of John is clearly a product of Asian Christianity, and the purpose of the book cannot be understood without an effort to realize the position of Christianity in the cities of Asia during the first century of our era."[41] Biblical scholars have made a career out of speculations and conjectures. There is no harm in adding one more.

Alien Concepts and Passages

There are theological ideas and passages in the New Testament that have no obvious Hebraic or Hellenistic origin or roots. These concepts are not inherently part of Jewish or Hellenistic tradition. Some of them could have easily been traced from beyond the Mediterranean and possibly from India. One such example that does not fit in easily with Jewish and Hellenistic thought patterns are the phrases in James "the tongue is a fire" and "the cycle of nature" or wheel of birth (3:6). The Buddha's comparison of the sense organs to a flaming fire is found in his early sermons. In his sermon on the burning, the Buddha declares that all sense organs are on fire: "The ear is burning, sounds are burning.... The nose is burning, odours are burning.... The tongue is burning, tastes are burning" (Mahavagga 1:21, 2–3). The Buddhist saying is similar to the one found in James: "And the tongue *is* a fire, a world of iniquity: so is the tongue among our members, that it defileth the whole body, and setteth on fire the course of nature; and it is set on fire of hell" (James 3:6). For Nicol Macnicol, the Scottish missionary in India, the Indian case is further strengthened by James's use of the phrase "burns up" or "consumes." His contention is that those who are familiar with Indian *tapas* (*tap* is to burn, *tapas* meaning a burning or fiery discipline) know that it is a "means towards the destruction of the whole world of iniquity of *karma* thus causing the weary wheel to cease to revolve."[42] Just as the Bhagavad Gita speaks of the sacrifice of *jnana* (knowledge) as binding people to the wheel of rebirth (4:10), the author of James's epistle denounces *sophia* as a human product that is "earthly, sensual, devilish" (3:16). Richard Garbe, too, concurs with Macnicol that the expression is "so specifically Buddhistic and so generally Indian that it is difficult to account for it in any other way than by Indian derivation."[43] The other phrase, "cycle of nature," has no discernible Jewish background. It suggests a revolving wheel of birth and rebirth and the successive transmigration of soul, and it sounds Buddhistic.

Another passage that sits uncomfortably with Jewish thinking is the Pauline statement about self-mortification: "And though I bestow all my goods to feed [the poor], and though I give my body to be burned, and have not charity, it profiteth me nothing" (1 Cor. 13 AV). Paul may be alluding to an event that happened in 20 BCE, when an Indian, in order to make a spectacular show for the Athenians and for the emperor, immolated himself. He leapt on the fire with a smile on his face and a girdle around his loins. This event was commemorated by an inscription on his tomb. This man was one of the eight Indians who brought gifts from an Indian king to Augustus. Strabo (c. 63 BCE–21 CE), the Greek geographer, philosopher, and author of six books on Asia in Greek antiquity, reproduced the words of the inscription: "Zarmanocheges, an Indian from Bargosa, having immortalized himself according to the ancestral customs of his country, lies here."[44] Zarmanocheges is a mangled translation of his Indian name, Sramanacharya. "Archarya" could have meant he was a Buddhist priest. Bargosa refers to the commercial port on the Narmada river in central India. In a culture where communication was through orally mediated stories, Paul might have known about Archarya's stunning death and similar suicide stories. Three hundred years previously, another Indian, whom the Greeks called Kalanos and who accompanied Alexander the Great in 325 BCE, underwent a similar voluntary death. He was the king's eulogist. The cause of his death was not entirely clear. Strabo reports that when Kalanos became sick and refused to listen to his king, the seventy-three-year-old put an end to his life by lying on a golden couch on a pyre. These events were accompanied by an elaborate ceremony and caused a sensation that must have remained in the popular imagination for a long time.

Then there are passages in the New Testament that advocate severe ascetical practices and avoidance of sexual contact. The author of 1 Timothy fulminates against those who advocate an ascetic lifestyle. Two sources of human enjoyment come under attack—sex and food. The anger of the author is directed against those "forbidding to marry and commanding to abstain from meats," as these activities, according to the author, were created by God "to be received with thanksgiving by them that believe and know the truth" (4:3). Such teachings, in the view of the author, come from "hypocritical liars" and "have consciences seared with hot iron." The question, then, is where did these hypocritical liars receive their teaching? Extreme forms of asceticism were foreign to Judaism, and there was no evidence of them in the new Christian movement. Celibacy for the sake of the Kingdom was recognized by both Jesus (Matt. 19:12) and Paul (1 Cor. 7), and both remained celibate. But the avoidance of marriage was encouraged not because it was seen as the ideal spiritual state but for the sake of mission. The exact nature of self-restraint expected is not clearly outlined by the author of 1 Timothy, but one can figure out from the epistle that it is about teetotalism—"Don't drink only water. You ought to drink a little wine" (5:3)—and about meat eating (Rom. 14). Judaism prescribes abstention from certain foods, but this is based on the notion of pollution paired with purity. Paul's letters document the fierce debates surrounding meat offered to idols. Paul's position is clear. He encourages Christians to eat meat because "nothing is unclean by itself" (Rom. 14:14), but at the same time, he cautions those who abstain not to judge those who eat (Rom. 14:3; 1 Cor. 10:29–30).

There were also in the second century Christians known as "Encratites" (literally abstainers), who refrained from marrying, from eating animals, and from drinking wine. But the extreme self-control they advocated has no Judaic or Christian roots. Their teaching resonates with that of the Indian asceticism where such self-restraint was seen as a true mark of spirituality. These Encratites were, in Clement of Alexandra's view, influenced by Indians who lived a frugal life with no roof over their heads, abstained from marriage, lived on nuts, and drank water from their hands (*Stromata,* Book I, Chapter xv). The third-century theologian Hippolytus of Rome (170–236) confidently made the claim that the opinions of Encratites, "have been formed not from the Holy Scriptures, but from themselves, and the Gymnosophists among the Indians."

A further example of foreign ideas from beyond the Mediterranean finding their way into the New Testament were concepts such as incarnation and the virtue of poverty. These concepts are fairly alien to the basic tenets of Judeo-Christian thinking. The interpretation by early Christians of Jesus as an Incarnation (Avatar), especially in the writings of John, has its roots in the Hindu and Buddhist traditions. The concept of an incarnate god or god in human form is integral to Eastern faiths, including Hinduism. According to R. C. Amore, who has done extensive study in this area, it was the "Buddhist avatar model" that helped the writers of the New Testament "to transform the Jewish Messiah concept into a saviour figure that was understandable to the gentiles."[45] In Amore's view, it was such a creative absorption of the Eastern concept that saved the nascent Christian movement from extinction. It was this imaginative incorporation that helped early Christianity to compete successfully with a whole series of Hellenistic and Roman cults and to combat Mithraism and Iranian religions. Oddly, such an absorption helped Christianity to withstand the westward expansion of Buddhism itself.

There are broad teachings extolling the virtues of poverty in the New Testament that might have been influenced by the Buddha's teaching. Jesus's teachings, as Sedlar has pointed out, have a "moderately ascetic character."[46] Jesus called the poor and the hungry "blessed." In anticipation of the eschatological end of the world, Jesus advocated the ethics of poverty and the accumulation of wealth not on earth but rather in heaven, where "moths and vermin do not destroy, and where thieves do not break in and steal" (Matt 6:20). He also directed his followers to detach themselves from material goods because "where your treasure is, there your heart will be also." He invited his followers to imitate the ravens and the lilies of the field, which are not bothered about what to eat and what to wear. What Jesus preached about detachment, freedom from care and lust, resembles the life and practice of Jewish sects such as the Essenes and Therapeutae, who seem to have been influenced by Buddhist teaching. As Charles Eliot observed in his monumental three-volume work on Hinduism and Buddhism, there is no record of Christ having contact with these communities, but it is probable that their ideals were "known to him and influenced his own."[47] The difference between the gospel and the Buddhist instructions was that the Buddhist sayings applied to those who had chosen to leave home and renounce the "pleasures and responsibility of marriage and business in order to devote themselves to a spiritual path."[48]

Another Indian concept, not Buddhist but with roots in Hindu religious tradition, that might have entered the biblical thought world is the idea of the "Son of Man." Jesus himself used this title to self-identify. The image of the Son of Man as the divine mediator, passing judgment and ushering in a new age, was developed and prevalent long before the time of Jesus. His use of this title and the concepts that surround it are often traced back to the Book of Enoch. Rudolph Otto, however, identifies a number of characteristics associated with the Son of Man that had no Jewish equivalent. The idea that the Son of God is also a Son of Man is certainly not from Israel. Otto is unambiguous about "The figure of a being who had to do with the world, and who was subordinate to the primary, ineffable, remote, and aboriginal deity of high antiquity among Aryans." There no hints as to the "concrete figure" behind the text, but "it may be regarded as indubitable that the phrase 'this Son of Man' points back in some ways to the influence of the Aryan east."[49] The Son of Man as an elect one "in whom dwells the spirit of those who have fallen asleep" is not "recognizable," and "few would think that anything of this kind could enter the mind of an Israelite." Otto claims that the concept of a soul after death entering into its *ishta-devatā* goes far back into Vedic times and is very much rooted in the "Aryan soil." According to the Aryan belief, "the believer in Vishnu enters into Vishnu, indeed into Vishnu's (spiritual) body, not in order to be lost in it, but really in order to dwell in it."[50]

Another notion associated with the Son of Man that has no Jewish basis is the idea of the Son of Man and the risen righteous beings clothed with the garments of glory. This bodily transformation is found in Paul, where he speaks about the risen soul having not a physical but a spiritual body. But the metaphor, in Otto's view, has its origin in the East. The notion that, in the final age, the holy ones will be clothed with garments of splendor, is suggestive of the Indian *šuddhasattva*, the radiant body, which is made of the "element of the pure."[51] Otto poses the question, "whence came these ideas, of which neither the prophets nor the Old Testament as a whole had the slightest notion?," and he also provides the answer: "Far off in the Indo-Aryan East, we find the clearest analogy to the process described of spiritual ascent, of unclothing and reclothing."[52] Otto's observation is that these materials are found in India in the pre-Christian Kausitaki Upanishad. "That they shine through in our Book of Enoch is just as certain."[53] Aryan material was "taken over, shifted" and "adopted not without strain to Jewish thought."[54] Where the Jewish thinkers differed from the Eastern usage was in merging the role of the Son of Man with the political fortunes of the Jewish people and the gathering of the scattered tribes of Israel. While the mystic conception of the Son of Man might have developed from Eastern ideas, the messianic concept associated with the title is of Palestinian tradition.

Loan Words, Lonely Developments

The influence of Buddhism on the Gospel narratives—or as Garbe has termed it, the "loan question"—is a contentious one. Mainstream biblical scholarship still shies away from engaging with it. The generally dismissive tone was set by J. B. Lightfoot (1828–1889), one of the Cambridge Trio, who were at the forefront of biblical scholarship in nineteenth-century England. Lightfoot claimed that "resemblances prove nothing" and might be "explained by the independent development of the same religious principles."[55] Although recognizing that knowledge of the East was imperfect, he condescendingly rejected what he called "alien elements" influencing the primitive Christian thinking as "taking lessons from the Chaldeans, Persians, Brahmins, and others."[56] Such Eurocentric thinking is still pervasive in mainstream biblical scholarship.

It was Indologists and religious historians who first highlighted these parallels. At the risk of simplifying and flattening out the work of these scholars, I classify them under four competing categories:

Refuters. These are the scholars who reject outright any such borrowing.

Parallelists. These are interpreters who hold the view that the historical parallels are "mostly just" parallels and, like parallel lines, "never meet."[57] Any resemblance between Buddhist and Christian texts, as

Rhys Davids, who introduced Theravada Buddhism to the West, claimed, was solely due to the "similarity of the conditions under which the two movements grew."[58] The similarities in their teachings was due to the coincidental spiritual yearning of these two masters. A similar view was taken by S. Radhakrishnan, the philosopher president of India. He asserted that whether these religions were historically related or not, they were the "twin expressions of one great spiritual movement. The verbal parallels and ideal similarities reveal the impressive unity of religious aspiration. Buddha and Jesus are the earlier and later Hindu and Jewish representatives of the same upheaval of the human soul, whose typical expression we have in the Upanishads.'[59] The common elements are accidental, and these masters were acting out an archetypal human behavior, which is not limited to one religious tradition alone.

Christian advocates. These scholars represent Christian orthodoxy and claim that Christianity influenced Buddhism. Samuel Beal, a pioneer in translating the Chinese Buddhist literature, put forward the thesis that Asvaghosa, who was supposed to have written the first biography of the Buddha, must have been influenced by Christian teachings when he was in Parthia or Bactria around 70 CE and incorporated some of them into his description of the teachings of the Buddha.

Advocates of Buddhist influence. There are scholars who argue for some sort of influence of Buddhism on Christianity. They differ among themselves as to how deep they believe this impact was. Some restrict it to a mild exchange of nonessential and secondary materials. Albert J. Edmunds and Richard Garbe fall into this category. Edmunds, who was tireless in assembling a vast number of Buddhist-Christian parallels, prevaricated for most of the time but came to the conclusion in the later part of his career that the matching elements were more than coincidental. He reckoned that Christianity, which emerged much later, was influenced by a variety of sources, including the Old Testament, the Greek mysteries, the Philonic philosophy, and "Hinayana Buddhism."[60] In his study of the narratives of the infancy and the temptation of Jesus, Edmunds concluded that the Hellenizing evangelists, Luke and John, borrowed "some minor features from the Hinayana Nikayas, then in the ascendant."[61] In its formative years, Christianity, as a weaker sect, was faced with the formidable Buddhism of Asoka. This established Buddhism, with its settled Pali text, was aggressive and a force to reckon with, and at this stage the "loans went from East to West."[62] The borrowing, as Edmunds hastened to add, was limited to only a "few passages of minor import which found their way from organized and aggressive Buddhism into formative Christianity."[63] A similar position was held by Richard Garbe. While admitting that the "direct" influence of Buddhism on the Apocryphal gospels was "unmistakable," he conceded that only an "indirect reflection glimmers through the canonical writings."

Like Edmunds, Garbe was quick to add the rider that when Buddhist stories went through various stages of transmissions outside their Buddhist environment and were assimilated by the New Testament writers, they "lost their specifically Buddhist character" as a result of the "Christian genius."[64] Garbe also reassured his readers that such a borrowing was harmless and that the eternal value of Christianity would "suffer no injury from it."[65] On the question of Christian influences on the development of Buddhism, Garbe is again of the view that it was limited only to "non-essential particulars."[66] There are some among the advocates of Buddhism who go still further and argue that Christianity borrowed directly from Buddhism. The scholars who fall within this camp are Edgar J. Bruns, R. C. Amore, Elmar R. Gruber, and Holger Kersten. Instead of simply displaying the actual parallels, these scholars go on to demonstrate the historical possibility of Buddhist influence on Christianity. Bruns, in his work on John, has shown that that "Johannine thought is structurally closer to Madhyamika Buddhism than it is to either Judaic or Hellenistic categories of thought then current."[67]

It was told of Edmunds that he was hoping to find a proof text in the form of some Greek translation or revision of ancient Buddhist texts from the excavations among the ruins of northern Afghanistan. This did not materialize. Edmunds also had another wish. He expected future scholars to take the next step and look again at the "canonical Gospels and Nikayas."[68] This wish, too, has not been fulfilled. There is a deadly silence on the issue of borrowing in current biblical scholarship. One can adduce the following reasons for this. First, biblical scholars are no longer polymaths but have become extreme specialists of detail and are incapable of raising larger issues. They are obsessed with technical and narratival details of narrow biblical segments and are unwilling to engage with the wider hermeneutical landscape that goes beyond Judea. Second, there is the apathy and cynicism of biblical scholars who are brought up on a diet of modern historical criticism. One of the enduring results of historical criticism is the textualization of the truth. Too much weight is given to the words of Jesus and the Buddha in the redacted texts. Since their teachings have gone through various stages of transmission by their followers, biblical critics conclude that it is impossible to recover the actual words of these masters. Therefore, there is no point in such a pursuit. But these scholars are not shy of identifying the authentic words of Jesus, as the Jesus Seminar has shown.[69] Third, after years of projecting an abstract Christ of faith, current biblical scholarship has turned its energies to historicizing and humanizing Jesus and placing him within the context of his Jewish environs. In doing so, they have made him more Jewish than Jews in general. Any attempt to place him within a wider religious and cultural context that might diminish the distinctiveness of his teaching and personality will be seen as anti-Semitism.

Concluding Remarks

In modern times there has been a grudging acknowledgment that some of the key theological concepts of Christianity might have had their origin in Zoroastrianism. Thus, Judeo-Christian faith owed an intellectual debt to Zoroastrianism for such theological ideas as a universal god, notions of angels, Satan, heaven, hell, resurrection of the body, life after death, the final judgment, and the apocalyptic ending of the world.[70] As J. C. Hindley, the New Testament instructor at Serampore College, West Bengal, remarked, it was no longer possible to "relegate Zoroastrianism to the fringe of Christian interest."[71] However, the influence of Eastern religions on the formative years of Christianity has gone largely unacknowledged and unappreciated. Stanley Cook's observation is worth remembering: "Palestine itself, [as has been seen,] was never isolated; it was no purely 'Hebraic' or 'Semitic' land."[72]

The mainstream biblical scholarship that draws on the comparative resources of Near Eastern texts is hesitant to go further afield. Richard Garbe wondered why the scholars who were convinced of deep-seated Hellenistic influences on the New Testament were so reluctant to accept Eastern influence, and he asked of whom they are afraid. As Amore has observed, the "idea that the Jerusalem and Galilean areas were exposed to Eastern influence before the time of Jesus is not nearly so far-fetched as it might seem initially."[73]

There is a lack of enthusiasm on the part of mainstream biblical scholars to admit a reciprocal exchange between the Mediterranean world and India. This reluctance can be attributed to a number of factors.

First, the standard orientalist assumption prevalent among scholars is that it is the West that provides moral, intellectual, and cultural strength and not the other way round. Müller, who himself was sympathetic to mutual intellectual intercourse between East and West, at times betrays orientalist thinking and gender prejudice. For instance, in dealing with the parable about Solomon's judgment, Müller says that one is so accustomed to seeing it as an exemplary "representation of Jewish wisdom" that one would find it difficult to believe that the story had been borrowed from somewhere else. The Hebrew scriptures, too, he notes have played their part in perpetuating the myth of Solomon's wisdom: "The whole world sought audience with Solomon to hear the wisdom God had put in his heart." (1 Kings 10:24). Besides the standard marks of orientalism, Müller demonstrated his gender bias. The fact that in the Indian story the solution came from Visakha, a woman, was too much for Müller. It severely dented the wise-man image carefully created for Solomon. Müller dismissed Visakha as a "mere woman."[74] Although he had carefully demonstrated that Indian fables had made their way gradually into Persia, Lydia, Alexandria, Greece, and Rome, and to Europe more broadly,[75] Müller was unwilling to accept that Eastern thought might have influenced Christianity. His view was that "intellectual exchange between Asia and Europe was perfectly possible,"[76] and he called this transmission the "intellectual commerce"[77] between India, Persia, Egypt, Syria, and Greece. But he restricted this exchange to the secular moral stories of the Jataka Tales. Müller, who was so meticulous in showing how the

Greek fables were influenced by Indian Jataka stories,[78] was reluctant to accept Christian indebtedness to Buddhism: "I have been looking for such a channel all my life, but hitherto I have found none."[79]

Second, the Bible is very resolute in advancing the notion that Jews first and then the Christians were chosen as enduring witnesses among the world's nations to strengthen the sovereignty of the biblical God. This corporate vocation is expressed through most of the writings of both the testaments and prevents foreign connection or contamination.

Third, a great deal of historical proof and textual evidence is expected from Asian documents when no such demands are made on Western claims. For example, no firm historical proof is offered for Peter's mission to Rome or the claim for an unbroken link between the archbishop of Canterbury and the early church. These events are upheld as authentically historical when the evidence is scanty and tenuous. There is no attempt to tread a middle path as has been done with the Gospel narratives. Similarly, when there is a reciprocal exchange, Western scholars are quick to point out the Sumerian influence on Tamil alphabets but do not give much weight to the claim that the Song of Solomon might have been influenced by Tamil aham poetry. What in most cases the biblical scholars tend to do is to repeat what the orientalists have all along done—they take cover under what Edward Said calls "academic security blankets," such as "history," "literature" or "the humanities," and they "conceal an often pompous scientism and appeal to rationalism."[80] In the case of biblical scholars, one could add to this list Christian orthodoxy. When biblical scholars feel that these borrowings do not serve their purpose, they resort to orientalist jargon as a way of avoiding the reality.

Fourth, for many scholars Christianity's dependence on Eastern faiths is seen as undermining its supreme status. Conventional piety and the unique revelation of the Christian religion hinder them from acknowledging influences.

Fifth, these early trade studies were undertaken at a time when India was a colony and there was an assumption fueled by the imperialistic thinking of the time that a subjugated nation was not capable of trading, let alone imparting its stories and religious ideas. Or, as Craigie put it, those biblical scholars who would have formerly been labeled as pan-"Babylonists" would be "shocked at the thought of turning to the Tamils."[81] Wilfred H. Schoff pointed out, "The truth is, that during the period between 50 BC and 100 AD approximately, India was a leading factor in the world's thought, industry, commerce, and wealth."[82] He held the view that the "spreading of ideas together with an exchange of goods" from India at that time "was not only a possible *assumption* but, a probable fact"[83] (italics in original).

Finally, it is worth reiterating that the cultural and commercial intercourse between the Mediterranean world and India was not as slight as once imagined. It was substantial and was not confined to material goods alone; metaphysical motifs, too, were transacted. To Charles Eliot, it was "clear that from 200 BC until 300 AD oriental religion played a considerable part in the countries around the Mediterranean."[84] He claimed that Egypt, Syria, and other Hellenistic states were "realties, distant but fabulous regions to the Indians of this period."[85] It was also probable that the missionaries of the Indian emperor Asoka reached Babylon and Alexandria. The accounts of Rufinus of Aquileia and Jerome, both third-century historians and theologians, attest to this. Arthur Lillie, who served in the British army in India and wrote on Buddhist influence on early Christianity, points out that Oxyrhynchus, a city in upper Egypt, housed "ten thousand monks and two thousand nuns. Another near Nechia, forty miles from Alexandria, had five thousand monks." He further cited

Philo saying that "in his day the forty-two districts of Egypt were full of them."[86] The presence of Indians at the great learning center of Alexandria, the second city of the Roman empire, is acknowledged by Ptolemy, Dion Cassius, and Chrysostom. In his oration on Homer, Chrysostom mentions the presence of Indians in the audience: "For I see in the midst of you not only Greeks, Italians, Syrians, Libyans, Cillicians, Ethiopians, Arabians, but even Bactrians and Scythians, and Persians, and some Indians who view the spectacles with you and are with you on all occasions" (Oratio XXXII).[87]

Chrysostom was also known to have heard of the Indian epic, the Mahabharata.[88] It is alleged that the guardians, auxiliaries, and craftsmen of Plato's *Republic* were based on the Hindu caste system.[89] Then there is the case of Indians visiting Athens and disputing with Socrates. Eusebius records an incident reported to him by a musician called Aristoxenus, pupil of Aristotle, arguing with Socrates. When these Indians asked Socrates to explain the purpose of his philosophy, his reply was that it was "an inquiry into human affairs." According to what Eusebius heard, one of the Indians burst out laughing and said: "no one could comprehend things human, if he were ignorant of things divine."[90] If Eusebius's report is true, then we must revise many of our fixed and predetermined notions about the intercourse between the East and the Mediterranean world in antiquarian times.

Although it has become an academic cliché, it is important to re-iterate the fact that cultures are connected and cultural products and ideas travel to and fro. The interconnected world is not a recent phenomenon. It was also so in the past, although with less intensity. The marks of civilization, such as art, philosophy, and science, are not self-contained autonomous entities. To borrow a phrase from Romila Thapar, they are a product of "maximum intermingling." To this list one could add sacred texts as well. In these days of identity hermeneutics, the purpose of this chapter is not to claim that Asia was part of biblical salvation history or to place the continent within biblical geography. Some ethnic groups, such as African Americans and Native Americans, have tried to situate themselves within the biblical world. Such a positioning of Asia would make biblical salvation history the norm with which the rest would have to fit. It would also deny the existence of other salvation models outside the Bible and in other Asian religious traditions. The sole purpose of this exercise is to show that there were cultural and religious exchanges between the biblical world and Asia, where merchandise and moral stories were freely borrowed and exchanged. No culture is pure; it draws on a variety of sources. Such a hermeneutical to-and-fro does not allow one religious tradition to have the final say or claim monopoly of a thought or a story. The idea is not to diminish the originality of a story but to underscore how by borrowing the story is enriched. As Jorge Borges put it, in a short story about a library, there are "interpolations of every book into all books,"[91] and they "differ by no more than a single letter, or a comma."[92]

2 Colonial Bureaucrats and the Search for Older Testaments

There were two prevailing perceptions among European orientalists, missionaries, and colonial administrators. One was that the salvation of Asia depended on rejecting its heathenish religious practices and idolatrous ways and embracing Christianity. The other involved a more cautious and conciliatory approach, seeking common ground as a way of wooing the natives, and did not see conversion as a holy warfare. John Muir (1810–1882), the Scottish Sanskrit scholar, exemplifies this latter position when he says:

> Would it not be possible to demonstrate to the Brahman that the facts which are recorded in the first books of the scriptures, are probably the foundation of his religion, and that the corruption of those truths may be severally traced to various periods of a comparatively late date? Might it not be shown that their belief in the incarnations of Krishna for instance, originated in the general expectation of the one incarnate God, who has now appeared among men and established a pure faith? Could not the imagined atonements of their self-inflicted tortures, be traced to the perversion of the great truth, that "with-

out shedding of blood there is no remission" but that a greater and more perfect dispensation now prevails?[1]

While these two perceptions prevailed, there was a third group, composed of colonialists and orientalists, who were promoting the idea that the older sacred texts and records of China and India contained the original, pure revelation and that this might improve the tenets of biblical religion and also provide an alternative to biblical revelation. More important, these interpreters believed that such a recovery of Asia's past could lead them to a reconstructed understanding of the origin of humankind and the development of religions and philosophies. Their task gained momentum and urgency when orientalists discovered that the Chinese and Indian civilizations were older than the Hebrew, thus diminishing the previously held claim that the Hebrew scriptures were the earliest instance of revelation. Linked to this was the idea that the Mosaic revelation contained only fragments of God's self-disclosure. Among these scholars, A. M. Ramsay (1686–1743), in a posthumously published book, argued that that the book of Genesis was "an extract and abridgment" of the creation story and that therefore we must search and "see if we can find any texts, to supply the want of the precious monuments that are lost."[2] He found these missing parts supplied by Chinese records. Ramsay claimed that "the five canonical books of China" contained "clearer revelations concerning the mysteries of our holy religion, than the Pentateuch, or the five canonical books of Moses."[3] For him, "Chinese mythology, or rather theology . . . [was] a key to all others less ancient, and more obscured by the succession of time."[4] Others, like John Z. Holwell (1711–1798) and Louis Jacolliot (1837–1890), found the answer in India.

This chapter deals with the work of Holwell and Jacolliot, how these two interpreters came up with their own chosen Indian texts as an alternative to the Judeo-Christian revelation and how they tried to prove that biblical religion stemmed from and was inspired by ancient Brahmanical texts. In looking at their writings, I hope to draw attention to their hermeneutical preunderstandings, the status and standing of the Scriptures in the service of their theological agenda, the place they accord to Christ, and how their quest for the original revelation almost displaced and denied any Christian claim for the Judeo-Christian tradition as a source for humanity's origin and development.

Administrators and Their Interpretative Aims

Before Holwell got embroiled in Indian religious texts, he came to prominence when he published his version of what became firmly etched in the imperial memory as the Black Hole of Calcutta. This appalling incident happened on the night of June 20, 1756, when British prisoners and others were incarcerated in a poorly ventilated guard room by Siraj Ud Daulah, the Nawab of Bengal. Forty-three prisoners died as a result of overcrowding and extreme heat, and Holwell, himself one of the survivors, provided a detailed account, though with what are now seen as exaggerated numbers (23 survivors, 123 dead), in his *A Genuine Narrative of the Deplorable Deaths of the English Gentlemen and Others Who Were Suffocated in the Black Hole.* Holwell's embroidered account of the event became part of the imperial mythmaking and was later challenged by India nationalists such as Subhas Chandra Bose.

Holwell, born in Dublin, pursued a career as a surgeon in the East India Company. Tiring of constant traveling as a company servant, he was about to quit his job when he was offered a post as surgeon at Dacca. There he improved himself in the "Moorish and Hinduee tongues." He succeeded as principal physician and surgeon to the presidency, was elected an alderman on the mayor's court, and briefly acted as governor of Bengal. What is important to our purpose is Holwell's claim that he lost important ancient Hindu texts during the incident of the Black Hole. Among these were "two very correct and valuable copies of the *Gentoo Shastah*" and the translation he made of these, on which he spent eighteen months. The Hindu shastra that Holwell referred to here is named by him *Chartah Bhade Shastah.* Whether this was a genuine text or a forgery by Holwell is a matter of dispute among Indologists.[5]

The dedication page in the second volume of *Interesting Historical Events* gives a clue to Holwell's interpretative aims with this text: "My intention was to rescue the originally untainted manners, and religious worship of a very ancient people from gross misrepresentation." He meant to *"revive* and *re-establish* the *primitive truths* which constituted the ground work of the first universal religion."[6] In Holwell's reckoning, the ancient religion of Bramah was the *"most ancient* and, consequently *most pure"* of religions.[7] He did not want to look at the religions as they then appeared but as they really were "at their first promulgation."[8] Holwell's rescue mission was not restricted to recovering the original teachings of the Brahma but had an additional purpose, namely, to rehabilitate Christianity and guide it back to the pure primitive truths enshrined in the Hindu shastra.

Howell came up with his own text, what he called the *Chartah Bhade Shastah,* which he alleged was not only as ancient as any written work on divinity but also a much better work than the books of Moses, for it contained the *"one unerring original faith"* and "true originals"[9] and was not "copied from any system of theology."[10]

It was to the ancient Brahmins that Brahma was to declare "the divine stamp of God."[11] This self-disclosure of God happened in India because the Hindus, not the Israelites, were the chosen people of God. It was to the Hindus that God revealed not only the "real state and condition of man" but also the doctrines of the existence of one eternal God and temporal and future reward and punishment. It was from this text that other cultures stole their ideas. Howell asserted that the mythology and cosmogony of the Egyptians, Greeks, and Romans were "borrowed from the doctrines of the *Bramins*" and that these other cultures had even copied "their exteriors of worship, and the distribution of their idols, though grossly mutilated and adulterated."[12] It was the Brahmanical religion that manifestly carried the divine stamp of God. Holwell went on to claim that this *Chartah Bhade Shastah,* a contentious text, could act as a catalyst to reform Christianity.

Louis Jacolliot was a French lawyer who was part of the imperial magistrature and worked variously as an imperial prosecutor in Pondicherry and an imperial judge in Chandernagore in French-controlled India. Later he had a brief stint as an imperial magistrate in Tahiti, where he was involved in endless disputes with the colonial authorities, church figures, and Christian missionaries.[13] It was in Chandernagore, less than two years after arriving in India, that Jacolliot wrote *The Bible in India.* He subsequently became a prolific author. He had mustered enough Sanskrit to do some casual translations of the Laws of Manu. He was not seen as an academic in the mold of Max Müller. He made use of a text called "Agrouchada-Parikchai," which appears to be a patchwork drawn from the Upanishads, Hindu law books, and Masonic texts.

Jacolliot's hermeneutical object was very simple and straightforward, namely, to show that European civilization, its religion, its gods, and its legends, had come from India after passing though Egypt, Persia, Greece, Judea, and Italy. He boldly claimed that India became real to him when he listened to recitals of the ancient poems at the feet of

Brahma and understood the Laws of Manu when dispensed under the porches and pagodas. It was then that India appeared "to me in all the living power of her originality—I traced her progress in the expansion of her enlightenment over the world—I saw her giving her laws, her customs, her *morale*, her religion to Egypt, to Persia, to Greece and Rome—I saw Jaiminy and Veda Vyasa precede Socrates and Plato, and Krishna, the son of the Virgin Devajani (in Sanskrit, *created by God*) precede the son of the Virgin of Bethlehem."[14]

Jacolliot's interpretative enterprise starts with the presupposition that India was the "world's cradle" and as such had bequeathed the legacy of its language, laws, morals, literature, and religion to humankind. It was Manu, the Indian lawgiver, who was seen as having inspired Egyptian, Hebrew, Greek, and Roman law, and it was "his spirit [that] still permeates the whole economy of our European laws."[15] India was the "mother of the human race."[16] The ancient India was "initiatrix of all the civilizations of antiquity."[17] The Vedas were seen as the oldest work and one of the oldest testimonies to human life. Biblical concepts, including the unity of God, the Trinity, creation, original sin, and redemption, were all products of India—"a high philosophic and moral civilization."[18]

However, the India that Jacolliot looked on as a beacon of purity was not contemporary but ancient India. Jacolliot carved up Indian history into three neat phases: The first was the period of Manu and the Vedas—the period of Indian primeval wisdom. This was the moment of "brilliant civilization,"[19] the "period of living power and her originality" and "was the epoch of greatness under the regime of reason."[20] Whether this India existed or not is a moot point, but it was this imaginary India that Jacolliot admired most. This initial period of "primitive vedism" was replaced by a second era, which was dominated by priests and kings. This was the period of Brahmanism, when the priests gained the upper hand. They became the preservers and codifiers of laws and made the study of these texts the privilege of their caste, and thus they were able to control both kings and the masses. It was also during this period that the "priest shuts himself up in dogma and mystery, professing himself the sole guardian."[21] The "simple and pure worship of primitive revelation and of the Vedas" was substituted by numerous gods, saints, and mediators who transacted between the divine and the creatures. It was during this period that the great migrations took place toward the West, to escape from the tight hold of the priests. The third period was that of invasions and domination of India by foreigners, first by the Moguls and then by English merchants.

Jacolliot believed that his task was to return to the first India, which he imagined as the "fountain head," the source of all poetic and religious traditions of the ancient and modern world—the worship of Zoroaster, the symbols of Egypt, the mysteries of Eleusis, the priestess of Vesta, Genesis and the prophecies of the Bible, the morals of the Samian sage, and the sublime teaching of the philosopher born in Bethlehem. Jacolliot firmly believed that modern spiritual ideas could add nothing to the metaphysical conceptions of the ancient Brahmins. He substantiated this by citing the words of Victor Cousin to illustrate his point: "The history of Indian philosophy is an abridged history of the philosophy of the world."[22]

The Christian Bible as a Pale Imitation

Holwell did not hesitate to acknowledge the divine and canonical status of the Hindu scriptures, a status that, later, Max Müller, as an expert on Indian textual matters, was reluctant to acknowledge. Holwell believed that every Christian owed to the Hindu scriptures a "degree of veneration,"[23] and he worked out his own canonical hierarchy. At the top, carrying the "divine stamp of God," was the *Chartah Bhade Shastah of Bramah* (literally, the four scriptures of the divine words of the mighty spirits), the oldest Hindu scriptures, which Brahma revealed to the ancient Brahmins. These were the "first written manifestation of . . . [God's] will."[24] They were "original and not copied from any system of theology."[25] These scriptures, which according to Holwell originated precisely 4,866 years before, were "preached to the delinquents, as the only terms of their salvation and restoration."[26] An additional reason for conferring a primary status on the ancient Vedic text was that it contained what Holwell saw as predetermined elements of divine revelation that were not *"from our own Scriptures."*[27] The *Chartah Bhade Shastah* contained such essential points as metapsychosis, the existence of the angels, their revolt and ejection, the coeval creation of angelic and human spirits, their apostasy, and their degraded and probationary existence on the earth. In other words, what Christians call original sin, "erroneously imputed to us from Adam,"[28] was seen as having sprung from a much older, Vedic, source. Another important motive for granting a pivotal position to the ancient Brahmanical texts was that they approved vegetarianism, a cause that Holwell enthusiastically promoted. These Vedic texts endorsed a strict obedience to the first injunction and law of God, "thou shalt neither kill, nor eat thy fellow creatures of the brute creation." This "positive injunction" against the killing and eating of animal beings was "delivered by the mouth of and scriptures of Bramah."[29] The next in Holwell's canonical pecking order was the law of Moses, and the last in the line was the teaching of Christ enshrined in the Gospels, which were meant for the Jews, the Gentiles, and the pagan world. It was in the Gospel dispensation that what was hidden from generation to generation—the mystery of life and future state of human life—was made manifest. Only these writings—*Chartah Bhade Shastah,* the Law of Manu, and the Gospels—in Holwell's opinion, had the "signature of divine origin," because they were "plain, simple, and positive, not disguised by mysterious, allegories, etc."[30] For him, "the first and last revelation of God's will, that is to say, the *Hindoo* and the *Christian* dispensation, are the most perfect."[31]

Holwell did not care too much for the entire New Testament. He was unequivocal in rejecting the writings of apostles and disciples, which he regarded as trying to make doctrines out of Jesus's words since his ascension. The stupendous example of Jesus's life and teaching needed no dogmas to prop up and give credence to his achievements. Jesus himself would "disown'[32] these dogmatic formulations when he returned to the earth.

Holwell accorded scriptural authority only to the four Gospels, which record the words that "fell from the mouth of *Christ himself*," although Howell had doubts about the early sections of the Gospel of John. These utterances of Jesus were the only *"standard of our faith and sheet anchor of our hope."*[33] The paraphrases, exposition, and visionary doctrines of the apostles and the disciples had to be rejected. The dispensation that fell from the mouth of Christ himself was alone seen as the "most perfect, sublime, yet plain system of divinity and morals" promulgated to humankind, and it expressed rudiments of God's love, repentance for sin, mutual love among human beings, and, more important, "a proper faith and reverence for that *divine being,* who was delegated from the presence of God to preach these primitive truths as necessary."[34] Holwell treated the writings of Paul as "reveries." He found the "mission of Moses" depicted in the Hebrew scriptures as glaringly incompatible with the Bramah, except for a shared monotheistic understanding of God. Holwell did not hold the prophets in much esteem. As he put it, he was reluctant "to pay compliment to the veracity" of the prophetic writings. He also pointed out that Moses, Isaiah, Jeremiah, Samuel, and other Hebrew prophets who claimed to represent God went beyond their remit and introduced qualities to God, such as revenge, wrath, hatred, and violence, which "exceeded their commissions and humanized their God."[35] Of all the ancient Hebrew personalities, for Holwell Daniel stood out as exemplar. This was because Daniel exemplified the two pet causes that Holwell espoused—vegetarianism and teetotalism. Daniel's refusal to eat meat and drink wine, in Holwell's words, exhibited to "mankind a fine lesson." It was not clear from the text what made Daniel refuse the food from the royal kitchen. Did the food not meet the dietary standards of Judaism? Were they given foods forbidden in the Torah, or were the meat and wine first offered to idols before they were handed out to Daniel and his young companions? Holwell does not dwell on these complicated issues. To him, what counted most was Daniel's rejection of slaughtered flesh and intoxicating drink.

Unlike Holwell, who had his own canonical hierarchy, which placed the ancient Hindu texts at the pinnacle, for Jacolliot the ancient Vedas had "incontestable precedence over the most ancient records." These antique Sanksritic texts, which, according to the Brahmins, contained the "revealed word of God," were "honoured in India long before Persia, Asia Minor, Egypt, and Europe, were colonized or inhabited."[36] Not only the shastras but also the Laws of Manu were established during the Crida Yuga—the first age. Jacolliot was unequivocal about the finality of the Hindu revelation and its preeminence among revelatory traditions: "The Hindoo revelation, which proclaims the slow and gradual formation of worlds, is of all revelations the only one whose ideas are in complete harmony with modern science."[37] He was dismissive of both the Hebrew and

Christian disclosures as revealing "nothing."[38] For him, there was "no other revelation"[39] except the one revealed to the Indian sages of the past "from which sprung all others."[40] Jacolliot adduced another reason for the superiority of the ancient Brahmanical texts—the high esteem in which women were held. The Vedic woman was "free, chaste, and devoted, reigning in the hearts of her husband and her children," whereas biblical women were concubines, slaves, and prostitutes. Had Moses had the courage to introduce these values to the Hebrews, there would have been a revolt because the Israelites had a low view of women. They had the habit of making excursions into neighboring territories to procure virgins and did not hesitate to sell their daughters if a good price was found.

Jacolliot's conviction was that the Christian Bible was the "falsified and ill-executed cop[y]"[41] of the Vedas and the other written traditions of the Hindus. As far as he was concerned, the Christian Bible was not an original book. None of the morals or customs enshrined in the pages of the Bible were its own. They were all borrowed or copied from the writings of the most ancient civilization—India. The Christian Bible was "hurriedly written without order and without connection."[42] Primarily, the Christian Bible was an abridgement of the ancient sacred books. Jacolliot was convinced that the Christian Bible "constantly copie[d] passages"[43] from the books of Manu and the Vedas.

Basically, Jacolliot doubted the authenticity of biblical stories. He saw the history of the patriarchs and of Joseph as fictions invented by Moses. In his opinion, they belonged to an Egyptian tradition picked up by Moses with a view to making the Hebrew people part of the providential mission of God and claiming for his ancestors the status of the chosen of the Lord. The source for the Deluge was the Hindu epic the Mahabharata. Similarly, the apocalypse predicted in the

Book of Revelation was based on the return of the ten avatars and their combat with demons before the great destruction—*maha pralaya.* The figurative style of the book, featuring animals and elements, and, above all, its darkness are in the "characteristic cloudy spirit of the East."[44]

The life of Jesus recalled by the evangelists was essentially "a tissue of apocryphal inventions" intended for popular imagination and to establish the basis for the new religion. The evangelists were in effect "impostors" whose aim was to keep the memory of Jesus alive and to gain new converts. To achieve this and to attract attention, the Gospel writers added miracles and wonders to the story of Jesus that went against natural law and rational thinking. Knowing well how the Jews were susceptible to the supernatural, the apostles "re-originated" the incarnation of Christ and came up with the idea of the Virgin Birth and the divinity of Christ. Jacolliot advanced another reason that the apostles added miraculous elements to the life of Jesus. The supernatural events were "posterior invention"[45] because of the failure of the Jews to recognize Jesus as the much anticipated Redeemer. Jacolliot concluded that the Gospel accounts were myths based on the mythology of ancient India.[46]

Besides doubting the authenticity of the biblical narratives, Jacolliot treated them as distorted accounts of the Vedic and Brahmanical records. For instance, in his account of the Adam and Eve story, the blame is put on the woman. This, in Jacolliot's view, was a distortion of the fall of humanity.

While Holwell found that the Bible discouraged murder, especially the killing of animals, for Jacolliot the Bible was "full of hecatombs and human sacrifices, and the book itself is written with blood."[47] Jacolliot found that there were parts of the Pentateuch, with their violence and destruction, that were out of place in the Bible, and his fervent hope was that these aggressive chapters would be replaced with the "rightful teachings of the Vedas." He declared that in vain had he searched in the pages of the Hebrew Bible for a hopeful sign or a gleam of a future. All he noticed was debauchery, massacre, "sacrifices of oxen, dismal superstitions, and streams of human blood poured forth in the name of Jehovah."[48] For him, the morality of the Bible was summed up in the verse from Numbers where Moses says, "why have ye saved the women and the children? Slay therefore all the males amongst the children, and the women who have been married. But reserve for yourself all the young girls who are virgins" (31:17). For the faithful, it may be the "supreme law, the work of wisdom," but to others it is a code of "truculent superstitions." Masses of people bend their knee before it without "examination or comprehension."

Jacolliot enumerates a number of parallels between the Hebrew scriptures and India's sacred books. One such was the Indian sacrifice story of Adjitgarta, which provided the model for Abraham. Adjitgarta, like the Jewish patriarch, was childless, and when he was blessed with a son, Vishnou (Isaac), Adjitgarta was asked to sacrifice his son but was prevented by God at the last minute. In another parallel story, Saul consults the witch of Endor on the eve of the battle of Gilboa. This was an import from India, which has a tradition of women priestesses. The social manners and customs found in the Hebrew scriptures were also seen as drawn from India—for example, the remarriage of widows to the brother or a relative of the deceased husband. Illustrative of this custom were the stories of Onan marrying Tamar, the widow of his brother, and Boaz marrying Ruth, the wife of Mahlon. Such practices, according to Jacolliot, did not have any precedent in the books of the Hebrew scriptures. This Hindu practice was "rational and logical" because it "protect[ed] the interests" of both the dead and the biological fathers, and moreover it assigned "a religious motive for an act otherwise incomprehensible."[49]

Jacolliot claimed that the early church borrowed a number of insights from the ancient Indian scriptures. The life of renunciation and contemplation was alien to Jesus and early Christianity. Cenobitic life was unheard of in Judaism and in paganism. It was the resurrection of the Brahmanical idea that led to the introduction of monasticism among the early Christians. Jacolliot quotes from Manu, the Hindu lawgiver, in support of a life of poverty. For example: "Let him preserve absolute silence, even when in the villages begging nourishment for his perishable body."[50] It was these Brahmanical principles that produced Christian ascetics such as Simon Stylites. India and its philosophical and theological traditions were the precursors of Moses and Christ. For Jacolliot, the foundations of Christian theology were "incontestably acquired" from India.[51] Stated differently, the inspiration for Jehovah came from Brahma, Moses was based on Manu, and Krishna provided the archetype for Christ.

Besides cultural insights, the nascent Christian church took over a number of rituals, including baptism, ablution, anointing with sacred oil, purification of the newly born by water, and sacraments such as confirmation and the holy communion. These were all adopted from various customs of the ancient Brahmins. Jacolliot illustrated this with appropriate texts from the Vedas. For the rite of confirmation, one of the seven sacraments of the church, he found a parallel from the Atharva Veda (Book of Precepts): "Whoever shall not, before the age of sixteen, have had his purification confirmed in the temple by unction of holy oil, by consecrated investiture, and the prayer of the Savitri, should be expelled from the midst of the people as a despiser of the divine word."[52] Jacolliot argued that the sacrifice symbolized in the mass was nothing other than the Hindu sacrifice of Sarvemeda, where Bramah sacrifices his son, who came to earth to die for the salvation of humankind.

Although Holwell and Jacolliot were dismissive of the Hebrew scriptures, Holwell made use of them to advocate for vegetarianism. In his idiosyncratic theological scheme, the fall of humankind was caused by humans mindlessly butchering and killing animals. This malevolent act, according to Holwell, was the *"one of the great roots of physical and moral evil in the world."*[53] The animal kingdom was not created for consumption. For Holwell the dictate of Moses was unmistakably clear: "And God said, Behold, I have given you every herb bearing seed, which is upon the face of all the earth, and every tree, in which is the fruit of a tree yielding seed; to you it shall be for meat" (Gen. 1:29). Genesis recommended that humankind not eat meat because the animal salts and juices *"inflamed the state of the human body,"* which then gave birth to "a train of monstrous, unnatural, violent, and consequently ungovernable passions, as lusts of every kind and species, ambition, avarice, envy, hatred, and malice, etc."[54]

Destabilizing Moses

Although the emerging biblical criticism of the time was starting to cast doubt on the authorship of Moses, Holwell and Jacolliot worked on the then prevalent premise that it was Moses who wrote the first five books of the Bible. Both found the dispensation of Moses to be restrictive and limited. Jacolliot spoke for both when he opined that Moses was "incompetent" and was incapable of the "task of regeneration."[55] Holwell wrote that Moses's dispensation was a "very imperfect one" on several counts. Moses's inadequacy had largely to do with Holwell's understanding of the doctrine of the creation of humanity. Seen from this perspective, he found that Moses's activities were restricted to one tribe favored by God and that he was disturbingly silent about such primitive truths as the existence and fall of the angels. There was an additional reason for the adverse portrait of Moses. Holwell condemned Moses for allowing animal sacrifices. The killing of animals, as far as Holwell was concerned was the original sin humanity had committed. Because it was Moses who encouraged cruelty to animals, God deprived him of the honor of leading his people into the land that was promised to him.

Moses's mission, too, was, in Holwell's view, flawed. Although his dispensation contained both spiritual and temporal aspects, "the spiritual sense was hidden" and was "imperfect."[56] In Jacolliot's writings, Moses emerges as an unoriginal person who recycled other peoples' ideas and gave the impression of being a hard-hearted legislator. According to Jacolliot, in effect Moses borrowed ideas from the ancient Vedic texts. He had been initiated into sacerdotal education in Egypt, in the "splendours of Hindu deism"[57] and Vedism, but abandoned these and embraced the ritualistic practices of Brahminism that emerged later.

In Jacolliot's opinion, Moses "obtained his traditions of Genesis," patriarchal narratives, purity regulations, and so forth, "from the sacred books of Egypt, which themselves were but a rescript of the Vedas and religious beliefs of India."[58] Among the cultural norms Moses borrowed were restrictions on certain animals considered impure; the belief that defilement resulted from contact with the dead; the practice of sacrifices, such as offerings of sheep, goats, and doves, and the immolation of oxen; ceremonies such as offering flour, bread, and oil; purification rites after childbirth; sanitary laws that had to be observed by men and women; marriage rules governing the priests;

and the idea that there were defects that excluded some priests from officiating. Jacolliot asserts that Moses "copied these antique traditions word for word" and that his borrowing echoed "the sublime breathings of the primitive and unabridged Veda."[59] He provided narrative parallels from Manu and other Hindu texts to demonstrate how the Hebrew scriptures were dependent on Oriental religion. His conclusion was that, compared with the "grandeur of idea and dignity of thought" found in the Hindu scriptures, the Hebrew Bible was an "inferior" product.[60]

Moses was not only a pale imitator but also an initiator of the idea of an angry God. He felt the need to give a more threatening role to God and turned Jehovah into a jealous deity, athirst for human sacrifice. Moses did this in order to control, chastise, and calm the Israelites, for whom the language of reason was ineffective. Revealing his disgust for the Jews, Jacolliot claims that Moses was forced to come up with his severe picture of God because of the "degraded moral condition of the Hebrews."[61] Moreover, it was impossible to convert these "quondam slaves of Pharaoh into respectable people,"[62] and further, they were "stupefied by servitude."[63]

Jacolliot found Moses's dispensation lacking important theological insights. For instance, the idea of a redeemer was totally absent from Moses's thinking. Jacolliot's conclusion was based on two factors. First, there was no mention of it in the Genesis story. Second, Moses would have found it difficult to discover anything that, "distinctly or indistinctly, plainly or figuratively," could refer to a redeemer. It was the prophets who learned about this tradition, which was bequeathed by India. However, Jacolliot acknowledged that it was Moses who first introduced the idea of monotheism into biblical thinking. Echoing the view of Renan, Jacolliot saw biblical monotheism as a defect in Israelite thought. Unlike the thinkers of the time who viewed monotheism as an advance on the polytheistic ideas of Israel's neighbors, Jacolliot, following Renan, felt that, "far from being an improvement," the idea of monotheism spawned bigotry and privileged status. This "all powerful and protecting God, supreme giver of all good, image of power and of goodness,"[64] was "wrathful, sanguinary, and destroyer of nations."[65] The idea of a single God leads to a "theocratic *regime*."[66]

In contrast to some orientalists of the time, Jacolliot and Holwell ruled out any possibility of biblical thinking influencing the ancient world. For them, it was a case of Brahmanical customs, creeds, and ideas transforming biblical teaching. On the question of who influenced whom, Holwell and Jacolliot were unanimous. It was the ancient Brahmanical texts that provided the ingredients of biblical religion. Their reasoning, however, was based on different presuppositions. Holwell emphasized the fact that India existed as a nation "separate and unmixed," "more ancient than any other,"[67] and "eminently distinguished in the most early known times."[68] Moreover, Egypt, in Holwell's view, was "little known to the world,"[69] and it was the Egyptians who pilfered and borrowed the fundamentals of the *Chartah Bhade Shastah*—monotheism, immortality of the soul, general and particular providence, the future state of reward and punishment, the fall of the angels, and the transmigration of souls. Holwell ruled out the possibility of Indians borrowing from other nations on the grounds that the Brahmanical notion of pollution-purity prevented the Brahmins from crossing the sea. While admitting the possibilities of navigation, Brahmins could not have traveled to Egypt or Persia because they were dissuaded from sea travel.

Jacolliot's refusal to accept the possibility of biblical faith having any impact on the religions of the East was based on his sheer anti-Israeli feelings. His reasoning was that this "petty people," brutalized by servitude and influenced by their desert traditions, had neither "the idea nor the time to acquire a taste for great things."[70] A degenerate race like the Jews were incapable of anything. Compared with the Brahmins, the Semites lacked philosophy, arts, literature, and science. Jacolliot commented that "no people of earth have done so little, produced so little, thought so little."[71] Throughout the text, Jacolliot calls the Jews pariahs, outcasts. This view was in keeping with the anti-Semitism of Renan, whom Jacolliot cites in his book. Essentially, it meant that, in contrast to the Aryans, the Semites had no scientific or artistic originality. They had not produced any national epic or mythology. They were incapable of thinking abstractly and had shown no aptitude for managing great states or leading military operations. Jacolliot was convinced that Judaism, with its "train of superstitions, immoralities and atrocities," could not be the "guardian of primitive revelation, and the inspirer of modern intelligence."[72] Could Judea claim these? Jacolliot wondered. As he put it, an insignificant page of Vyasa or Plato, or the most simple tragedy of Sophocles or of Euripides, or a broken arm of the statue of Phydias or a sculpture of Dahouta was more instructive than anything that was to be found in the Bible.

Jacolliot's claim was that Europe had all along borrowed from other cultures. European poets had copied from Homer, Virgil, Sophocles, and Euripides; Western philosophers had drawn inspiration from Socrates, Pythagoras, Plato, and Aristotle; historians had modeled their work on the writings of Titus and Tacitus, orators on Demosthenes and Cicero; physicians studied Hippocrates; legal codes had been transcribed from Justinian's laws. Just as Europeans had been inspired by the Greeks and Romans, India, with its brilliant 6,000 years of civilizational history, had made an impact on Egypt, Persia, Judea, Greece, and Rome. Jacolliot contended that if we acknowledge that modern India had borrowed and was inspired by other cultures, why not "continue the same logical argument, and accept India as the initiatrix of ancient peoples?"[73]

Begotten Christ and a Krishna Clone

Holwell saw Christ as equivalent to what he called the Hindu Birmah. The Birmah was understood in a figurative sense, the "first of the three primary created angelic beings," other two being Vishu and Shiva. This Birmah, for Holwell, was the Indian or rather preexistent incarnation of Christ as God's "chosen vehicle of his incarnation."[74] For Holwell, Birmah and Christ were one and the same individual and the "first begotten of the father," who "most probably appeared at *different* periods of time, in *different* parts of the earth, under *various* mortal forms of humanity."[75] Birmah represents what the Brahmins call "the first great attribute of God, his *power of creation.*"[76] Christ was not God but a *"distinct created being.*"[77] Jesus declares and maintains "the unity and supremacy of God"[78] and his own subordination. The divinity of Christ was "ill-founded" and not *"the true doctrine of the New Testament.*"[79] For Holwell, Jesus was basically simply a human being, a *"mere enlightened man,*"[80] who did not "deify himself."[81] Jesus's powerful cry on the cross was seen as an indication of his human nature. Holwell offers a series of quotations from the Gospels to prove Jesus's dependence on God and his human limitations. One example is recorded in Matthew. Jesus says of the Judgment Day: "But of that day and that hour knoweth no man, no not the angels of heaven, *but the Father only*" (Matt. 13:32; emphasis in original). The task of Christ was not to announce anything new but to restore once more the primitive truths that were revealed by Brahma.

For Jacolliot, the story of Jesus was mostly a reworking of the story of Krishna. To him, Krishna was the "messenger of God, the promised of God, and the sacred." Throughout his book, Jacolliot chose to call Krishna "Christna." This decision, he claimed, was based mainly on grammatical reasons rather than on any resemblance between the two names. His argument was that the aspirate of the Sanskrit *Kh* is translated better by *Ch.* In any case, the word *Christos* is Greek in origin, and most Greek words, in his view, were borrowed from Sanskrit. Jacolliot's supposition was that the name *Christos* was part of the scheme devised by the apostles to "construct a new society on the model of primitive Brahmanical religion."[82]

Jesus was born into an "unintelligent" and "little cultivated class," but he was able to rise above his station. He could spearhead a moral revolution because he had learned, from the East, wisdom reserved in the sacred books for long ages for those to be initiated. Between his twelfth and thirtieth years, Jesus had studied and meditated in Egypt, perhaps even in India. He and his disciples drew inspiration from this primitive spring. While retaining the Hebrew tradition, Jesus "purified it" with the help of Christna, the Hindu reformer.[83]

Jacolliot highlighted a number of events surrounding Jesus's life that had precedents in Krishna's. These resonances, in his view, demonstrated how a number of Puranic and Vedic passages percolated into the biblical narratives, which were all either plagiarized or adopted or patent imitation.

First, both redeemers were born of virgins. Both mothers—Devaki and Mary—conceived by divine intervention, and despite their motherhood, both women remained virgins. The son of Devaki was named Christna and later his disciples gave him the title Jezeus, which meant pure essence. The son of Mary was called Jesus or Jeoshuah, but later his disciples named him Christ.

Second, there was the massacre of innocents. The order of the evil king of Madura to kill all the newborn male children on the night Krishna was born was renarrated by the Gospel writers. In the Gospel version, King Herod embarked on a similar sinister action. Both kings had the same fear that they would be usurped by the newly born divine child.

Third, the story of the anointing of Jesus was the revival of the story of Nichdali and Saraswati. In this Indian story, these two women approached Krishna with the intention of adoring him; the onlookers disapproved of such an action. In the biblical narrative the woman came up to Jesus and the apostles repulsed her. In the Vedic story, the women anointed Krishna; in the Gospels, the same act was ascribed to Mary Magdalene. The moral of both stories is the same—the weak and helpless are received by the Lord. The only difference between the stories is that in the Hindu version those of the lowest class are virtuous and honest and come to seek redress for their barrenness, whereas the biblical narrative is about pleading pardon for sins.

Another similarity is found in the Transfiguration of Jesus. Krishna appeared before his shaken disciples, who were alarmed by the army sent by Kansa, the tyrant of Madura. This appearance of Krishna was "logical and comprehensible" and restored the diminishing power of Arjuna and the other followers of the Hindu redeemer. No reason was given for the Transfiguration of Jesus. More confusingly, the disciples who witnessed the event were forbidden from talking about it. This prohibition allowed the disciples to fabricate the event later.

Jacolliot's Jesus is an attempt to understand the pivotal figure of Jesus without acknowledging his roots in Judaism. Basically, for Jacolliot, Jesus replaced and reignited Krishna's philosophical teachings, and his appearance on earth was the same as the Hindu incarnation.

Mary revives the figure of Devaki, the mother of Christna; Herod is the carbon copy of Kansa; the Jordan plays the part of the Ganges; the holy water succeeds the water of purification; baptism, confirmation, ordination of priests by tonsure, and consecrated oil are all modeled on or resemble Hindu practices.

Krishna came to preach charity, love, self-respect, faith in the creator, the immortality of the soul, liberty to people, and free will. He also forbade revenge, commanded that good should replace evil, and denounced tyranny. He consoled the weak and sustained the unhappy and the vulnerable. As Jacolliot put it, Krishna "lived the poor and loved the poor." He lived a life of chastity and charity. He was the greatest figure of ancient times, and it was he who inspired Christ at a later period, just as Moses was inspired by the work of Manes and Manu.

Both Holwell and Jacolliot agreed on one aspect of Christ, that he did not come to purify or fulfill the expectations of Judaism. In Jacolliot's view, Krishna did not incarnate himself to establish a new religion because Brahma could not destroy what was revealed and declared good. Krishna's chief task was to usher people to uncorrupted faith recorded in the ancient Vedas. Jacolliot assigned a similar role for Jesus. Jesus appeared on earth not to reform Judaism but to "recall" human beings "to the simple and pure faith of the first ages."[84] The mission of Christ, according to Holwell, was to confirm "the authenticity and divine origin of the *Chartah Bhade Shastah of Bramah*" and to "revert to their original dignity and angelic source."[85] Ultimately, it was about restoring primitive truth and recreating the primitive age.

To sum up their Christological quest, Jacolliot's and Holwell's defined hermeneutical aim was not to search for the historical Jesus—a quest vigorously pursued at that time—but to seek the origin of his teaching and look for clues and traces behind Jesus's religious pronouncements. The Christ they came up with was completely contradictory to the prevailing notions of Christ propagated by the missionaries of the time. In Jacolliot's and Holwell's reckoning, Christ was not a majestic hero but a fumbling and stuttering human being.

Reflections: Holwell and Jacolliot and Their Oriental Mannerisms

The hermeneutical enterprise of Holwell and Jacolliot was a reversal of that of the missionaries and orientalists. A perception among some missionaries was that the Indian sacred scriptures were derived from the Bible. The observations of some of the Jesuits who traveled through India in the early part of the 1700s typify this position. In his letter to the bishop of Avranches, Father Bouchet confirmed what the bishop had written in his *Book of Evangelical Demonstration.* In it the bishop claimed that the "Doctrine of Moses had penetrated as far as India."[86] Firsthand experience in India further helped Bouchet to validate his bishop's assertion that the "Indians have taken their religion from the Books of Moses and the Prophets."[87] Bouchet's contention was that the "People of India, formerly, in all likelihood Christians . . . [had] fallen again long since into the darkness of Idolatry."[88] In the rest of his letter, Bouchet impressed the bishop with a list of biblical ideas, events, and personalities that provided ingredients for the ancient Indian Puranas and Vedas. The Jewish Miriam becomes the Indian Lakshimi; Abraham's wife Sarah becomes Saraswati; and Job provides the model for the Indian Harichandra, who, like his biblical counterpart, had to undergo a test of character. More important, Bouchet confidently claimed that at least three of the Vedas derived from the Christian Bible. The Rig Veda "resembles the first chapter of Genesis," the Sama Veda aspects of the Exodus, and the Atharva Veda others of Leviticus and Deuteronomy. Bouchet boldly informed his bishop in France that the law books of the Brahmins "are an imitation of Moses' Pentateuch."[89] Holwell and Jacolliot for their part spent their energy in the opposite direction, showing that the theological substance of the biblical books was supplied by the ancient Hindu Vedas.

The hermeneutical enterprise of Holwell and Jacolliot went against the dominant thinking of the orientalists of the time. While Jacolliot appreciated the literary output and the profound knowledge of orientalists such as William Jones and Henry Thomas Colebrooke, he found that their work lacked "exactness of expression." His assessment was that these orientalists were overtly obsessed with the text, which prevented them from comprehending the symbolic sense of poetic chants, prayers, and ceremonies, and they "thus too often ... [fell] into material errors, whether of translation or appreciation."[90] To understand India, all the knowledge acquired in Europe, according to Jacolliot, came to "nought." Those who studied India would have to relearn just as the child learns to read, for the benefit is so great.

For much of the nineteenth century, orientalists and biblical scholars were preoccupied with the New Testament's connection to Judaism and relationships to Near Eastern cultures. Holwell and Jacolliot spent their energies on texts originating far beyond the Euphrates and ideally beside the Ganges. They were trying to construct a textual East as a way of distancing the Semitic and Hellenistic influences of biblical religion. Invoking selective ancient Vedic tradition provided them with an easy escape route from Jewish and Hellenistic thinking. They had another important agenda—finding a model for a universal society after the chaos and confusion caused by the Tower of Babel. They were in a sense, to use an analogy from

Edward Said, spiritual heirs to the knights-errant bringing back to Europe a sense of holy vocation as it was once ordained.

While orientalists and missionaries were trying to situate Asian religions within the biblical chronology and theological framework, Holwell and Jacolliot turned their attention in the opposite direction, by trying to prove that it was the ancient Brahmanical texts that inspired and instigated the emergence of the biblical testaments. Their interpretative exercise goes beyond the traditional sources of knowledge for the origins of humankind—Near Eastern cultures and chronologies. This meant they depended less and less on classical, conventional, and biblical sources. In a sense, their attempt was not to discover, recognize, and understand the East as the "Other" through the usual Judeo-Christian religious practices but to understand and enhance biblical faith through the Brahmanical "other"—in other words, to present the concept of Christian salvation as having emerged from Vedic thought.

Both exhibited the standard marks of orientalism: They argued for a Vedic golden age and subsequent corruption by a priestly class and advocated the rescue and recuperation of ancient Brahmanical texts; they privileged Sanskritic writings and favored texts as the ultimate depository of truth; and they depicted contemporary India as corrupt and depraved. Holwell described Hindu contemporaries as being as "degenerate, crafty, superstitious, litigious, and wicked a people as any race of beings in the known world."[91] Whereas the ancient Brahmins were "an ornament to the creation,"[92] the present-day Indians were seen as "very defective, fallacious and unsatisfactory."[93] In the rhetoric of orientalism, the work of Holwell and Jacolliot could be termed the "idealization of the primitive."

Both Howell and Jacolliot were involved in classic acts of colonialism—taking over other peoples' texts and beliefs, emptying them of their content, and redeploying them with theological and ideological elements of the domineering culture. Another colonialist act was to see themselves as rescuing the hapless natives from their own ruthless tyrants. The tyrants they confronted were the wily priests who had manipulated the people for their own advantage. Another mark of colonialism was that of the weaker culture borrowing from the stronger. In their case, it was the biblical culture benefiting from pristine Brahmanical culture.

Jacolliot and Holwell replaced Hebrew, Greek, and Latin with Sanskrit as the vehicle for divine communication. In Jacolliot's view, Sanskrit was the most irrefutable and simplest evidence for the Indian origins of European races. Recovery of the Vedas perpetuated the notion of Sanskritic India, thus erasing other language traditions. The insistence of Holwell and Jacolliot on a revelatory role for Sanskrit overlooked the fact that the divine revelation could just as well have happened through another language of India, such as Tamil, which has its own Vedas.

Both exercised the standard authority of the orientalists—the advantage of knowing vernacular languages, although their grasp of Sanskrit was questionable. Both dismissed the idea that they were like travelers trudging through the empire interested only in external things. Holwell complained that travelers observed superficially and described to their readers condescendingly how Indians worshiped stone idols. Had these travelers taken the trouble to learn the language, they would have understood the "mysteries of theology" that lay behind the words and actions of Indians. Jacolliot, too, disapproved of the work of colonial travelers, arguing that they looked only at the surface and lacked the necessary knowledge to appreciate India's past splendor. Travelers were easy victims of ignorance. Both Holwell and Jacolliot claimed their legitimacy from the forceful fact of actually residing in and being truly in existential contact with the Orient.

Although both men were engaged in the orientalist pursuit of recovering the ur-Vedic text, which would provide all the answers to the mysteries of life, their mission was slightly different from that of other orientalists. One reason was that they used these primordial, immaculate, autochthonous Brahmanical texts to clean up awkward or objectionable elements of Christianity. In effect, what they did was to replace one set of stereotypes with another: the mythless, unphilosophical Semites with the myth-creating, literarily active, and philosophically inclined ancient Brahmins. Holwell and Jacolliot employed Vedic wisdom to castigate the institutionalized form of Christianity—the Anglican Church in the case of Holwell and the Roman Catholic Church in the case of Jacolliot. Holwell found the Thirty-Nine Articles "unintelligible" and in need of correction.[94] Jacolliot saw the Roman Church as the enemy of liberty, modern intelligence, freedom of thought, and civil independence.

Holwell and Jacolliot perpetuated the orientalist notion of the primal purity and immaculacy of ancient narratives—Brahmanical texts and to some extent the Gospels, which enshrine the words of Jesus. These pure and simple Hindu and Christian texts were subsequently made unintelligible and complicated by Brahmin priests and the Christian apostles—and later by the institutionalized church. Holwell wrote that when we compare the original, august, and simple doctrines of the ancient Brahmins with the doctrines of those who followed them in priesthood, one could see how these successors had mutilated the sublimity and purity of the original message of Bramah. Similarly, the plain and comprehensible words of Jesus were turned into the doctrine of the Trinity and the Apostles' Creed by those who styled themselves saints and church fathers, with a view to "cover, obscure and hide the True God from the people."[95] Holwell even suggested that the Apostles' Creed should be corrected. In his assessment, these were "inflamed mistaken zeal and doctrines never dictated by their divine master."[96] Jacolliot, too, held a similar view about India—that an earlier, original, and untainted tradition had been made to look profane by the subsequent Brahmanical priests. Jacolliot saw Christianity undergoing a similar pattern from purity to decay. He alleged that Jesus had preached pure and simple morals that he learned from fifteen years of study of the Vedas. Then his disciples, in order to win converts, added miracles and supernatural events to the subsequent narratives of Jesus's life, and they fabricated dogmas, such as the doctrine of the Trinity, which they borrowed from the theology of the East. Later the Christian priests respectfully adopted Brahmanical rituals and rites. As they then went on to collude with the rulers of the world and carried on to rule the world "by confiscating the idea of God for [their] own profit," Jacolliot claimed, "the purified religious ideas" of Christianity had been "sacerdotalized." The Christian priest replaced "My kingdom is not of this world" with "The entire world is our kingdom."[97]

Howell and Jacolliot vigorously defended and rescued Indian philosophies, mythologies, and especially Brahmanical tenets, which in certain European circles at that time were ridiculed and treated condescendingly. Both sought to rectify this one-sided defamation of India. Holwell rejected the warped perceptions of India by both ancient authors, such as Arrian of Nicomedia, and modern writers, such as John Locke, Lord Shaftesbury, and David Hume, as "defective, fallacious." When the Roman Catholic Church stigmatized the doctrines of the Brahmins, Holwell shot back with the telling remark "their own tenets were more idolatrous than the system they travelled so far to arraign."[98] Holwell claimed that the India he found was both politically and commercially "superior to us."[99] Jacolliot poured scorn on those of his fellow French scholars who laughed at the chronologies of the Indians despite the fact that India, as he claimed, had a million years of history, richness, and productivity, in contrast to the French, "who had made a little world" for themselves "dating from scarce 6,000 years" and believed in a world created in six days.[100] He characterized France as a "country of superficial spirits and of inconsiderate affirmations."[101]

The method used by both Holwell and Jacolliot could be described as a form of history of religion—an emerging discipline at that time—which enabled them to propose a radically revised message of the Bible that drew sustenance and substance not from Palestine or Mesopotamia but specifically from India. The message of Jesus was seen not as fulfilling God's promises and the prophecies of the prophets but as replicating West Asian and especially Indian ideas and expectations. India and West Asia provided an alternative to the geographical locations of the Bible. The ancient Brahmanical texts, they thought, would replace the Hebrew scriptures, which were nothing but an eclectic choice of verses from the Vedic literature that supported and enforced their already decided theological agenda. Like any passionate interpreter, they unashamedly delved into the ancient sources to prove their pet theories and ideas.

Both exhibited anti-Semitism. Whereas Holwell was mild in his pronouncements, Jacolliot was venomous. He had hardly anything positive to say about the Jews. He considered the Hebrews as the refuse of Egypt's criminal class. He even ridiculed their claim as God's chosen people. The Hebrews boasted of themselves as the only people of God, but the examples they displayed for their neighbors betrayed and contradicted their chosen status. They showed duplicity and cruelty, and in God's name they exterminated the occupants of the lands that they desired to seize for themselves. As a people, Israelites were the "most scorned of antiquity." The adjacent nations knew about their servile origins, and when slaves were required these nations knew where to procure them. The Israelites were a people "begotten of rapine and murder, who only knew how to live by murder and rapine."[102] They were basically a violent people. They picked the pockets of the Egyptians before leaving that country, continued their pillage and plundering of countries, and tested the patience of the people until they were severely punished and reduced to servitude. Jacolliot's attempt to show common beliefs and practices between Vedic and biblical narratives effectively demoted Judaic ethics and prophecy, the two characteristics in which the ancient Jews traditionally outclassed other nations and cultures.

Along with anti-Semitism, both Holwell and Jacolliot were engaged in Brahmin-bashing. They blamed the contemporary Brahmin priests for the corruption of the Vedic faith while exonerating the ancient Brahmins as innocent and immaculate. It was the later Hindu priests who in their craving for power polluted the pure teachings of the Vedas and drifted from them. For Holwell, the difference between the ancient Hindus and the Hebrews was that when both deviated from the primitive truths, the former were enslaved at home, whereas the latter were driven from home and taken into captivity.

What Holwell and particularly Jacolliot did was to displace the Jews from center stage. Jacolliot's mission was to expose the Jews as imitators of the Vedic Aryans. The Jews should not be given credit for their influence over Europe. Jacolliot was part of the tradition that idealized the ancient East, especially Vedic India, as the source of all cultures. This was a time when German and French romantics looked East for spiritual and intellectual inspiration and rejuvenation. They were fascinated with India, and this prompted some of them to see Christianity as a derivation from Aryan mythologies, so that the honor should not go to the Jews or their book. Jacolliot boldly asserted: "No, we shall not go to these people in search of the origin of our beliefs and of our philosophic and religious traditions, and it is not from this book, the Bible, that will emanate the new faith of modern nations."[103] Jacolliot's writings were antinarratives, constructed chiefly to make the Jews secondary and to sideline them in history and achievements. His desire to find the origin of humanity simultaneously knocked the Jews from their pedestal and dismissed their ideals.

Both Holwell and Jacolliot set out to erase the identity of the Jews and then reintegrate them by subsuming them under the ancient Brahmins. Their achievement was to bring to the fore some troubling analogous ideas, concepts, and narratives from the East, which questioned the Christian claims to orthodoxy and the uniqueness of biblical revelation. They further challenged the idea of the Semitic region as a unique locus of God's revelation. They drew attention to biblical religion's debt to other Eastern religions.

Both placed the Christian Bible alongside other sacred scriptures and treated them all as instances of divine revelation. They presented other scriptures, in their case ancient Hindu texts, as challenges to the authority of the Christian Bible. For them, it was not the Bible that questioned the authority of other sacred scriptures but the opposite. Their hermeneutical strategy was in contrast to what Max Müller advocated: "Yet if we wished our own religion to be judged, we should wish it to be judged by the New Testament. It is but fair, therefore, that we should judge other religions according to the same rule."[104]

I conclude with a concern and a hermeneutical task. The concern is that, at a time when there is controversy over India's past, culture, and identity, the investments of Holwell and Jacolliot in a Vedic India could well be manipulated by Hindu fundamentalists for purposes other than those shared by these two authors.

Whatever the motives of Holwell and Jacolliot, their idea of circumventing the Judeo-Christian route to discerning the divine could be suggestive for Asian interpreters. I believe that too much emphasis and weight have been accorded to the Judeo-Christian revelation. Christian interpreters have looked both at revelation from the perspective of Christ and at Christ from the perspective of revelation. Holwell and Jacolliot invite Asian interpreters to look beyond the traditional notion of God's self-disclosure through a Semitic idiom and heritage. This leads to a related point. Until now, Asian theologians have devoted their energies to translating Semitic idioms in order to communicate with Asian sensibilities. C. S. Song advocated that if Asia was to be a "theatre of God's direct redemptive operation," then Asian nations should go through experiences similar to those that were "unique to Israel." He urged "Japan, China, Indonesia and so on" to go through "their own experiences of exodus, captivity, nation-building, rebellion against heaven."[105] Song's appeal implies not only that the religious experiences, redemptive acts, theological ideas, and insights of the Semitic imagination set the standard for God's self-disclosure but that other nations also will have to replicate them in order to be part of salvation history. More critically, all other revelations will have to be measured against biblical revelation. Instead of endlessly reconceptualizing biblical tenets to suit Asian realities or ceaselessly seeking for Asian counterparts for biblical personalities and historical events, I would suggest that Asian interpreters, and for that matter interpreters from other cultures also, should look for the ongoing human-divine tensions in Asia, or in their indigenous cultures, and see how these engagements match, illuminate, and enlarge or subvert and supersede the biblical revelation and narratives.

3 Enlisting Christian Texts for Protest in the Empire

Asian biblical interpretation is often viewed as a tame affair. It has frequently been criticized for not producing the sort of vigorous hermeneutical debates that mark such high points of Western biblical interpretation as inerrancy of the Bible, authenticity of the Virgin Birth, or the historicity of the resurrection. However, because Asia has a different reception history of the Bible, these Western disputes are not really an appropriate way of judging the quality and content of Asian biblical interpretation. Asia has its share of biblical controversies, but unlike the Western debates, which were marked by questions posed by the Enlightenment, secularization, or denominational differences, Asian disputes were of a different kind and conducted under the rubric of national struggle and national identity in colonial and postcolonial contexts. These textual confrontations indicate that the "natives" were not mere hapless recipients of the white man's book but active producers of interpretation. More to the point, these Asians used the very tool supplied by missionaries and turned it against them. What this chapter aims to do is to highlight three textual controversies that occurred in Asia during the colonial period.

Bengali Babu, the Baptist Missionary, and Their Biblical Battles

Probably one of the earliest textual confrontations in Asia was between the Bengali Rammohun Roy (1772–1833) and the Baptist missionary Joshua Marshman (1768–1837). Roy was not the stereotypical native. He was by birth, background, and education many stations above his Baptist adversary. He was proficient not only in Sanskrit, Persian, and Arabic but also in the biblical languages. His pioneering efforts in interreligious matters prompted Monier Williams to call him "the first earnest-minded investigator of comparative religion that the world has produced." Roy was very supportive of missionary work and was one of the signatories to a request addressed to the Scottish General Assembly to send more missionaries. Before he produced the controversial text in question, he used to attend the Bible translation sessions of the Serampore Baptists.

The text that provoked controversy was Roy's *Precepts of Jesus: The Guide to Peace and Happiness. Extracted from the Books of the New Testament, Ascribed to Four Evangelists* (1820). Ironically, it was published by the press owned by the Serampore Baptists. This truncated version consisted largely of the ethical teachings of Jesus found in the Synoptics and a few passages from St. John's Gospel.

Roy's *Precepts* followed the tradition set by Tatian (185 CE) in his *Diatessaron*, the first harmonized version of the Gospels. Unlike Tatian, Roy's ambition to compress the four into a single gospel was not spurred on by the duplications and inconsistencies found across the Gospels. Raised on different and often contradictory versions of the Ramayana and the Mahabharata, Roy would not have been unduly troubled or bewildered by such discrepancies. He saw his task as seeking the "purest principles of morality"[1] and weeding out all the "falsehood ... common to all religions without distinction."[2] Roy was an "equal-opportunity" cleanser of religious texts. He had engaged in this type of purification with his own Hindu texts. He was involved in a similar enterprise with Islamic texts. His tract *Tuhfat-ul-Muwahhidin* (A Gift to Monotheism), like most of his rereadings, was not anti-Islamic but an account of the fallacy of dogmatism prevalent in all religions. Whereas Tatian was trying to rearrange the Gospels, starting with the prologue of John, and stuck to the historical and chronological order of the fourth Gospel, Roy simply followed the canonical order of the Gospels. His selection moved from Matthew to Mark to Luke, and as an afterthought he added John—the Gospel he found most difficult to comprehend. The selections from the fourth Gospel were in line with Roy's hermeneutical agenda. One passage, John 4:23, lends support to Roy's lifelong battle with all religions including his own—not least in regard to his detestation of idol worship: "But the hour cometh, and now is, when the true worshippers shall worship the Father in spirit and in truth: for the Father seeketh such to worship him. God is spirit, and they that worship him must worship him in spirit and in truth." The inclusion of the episode of the woman caught in adultery was to support Roy's contention that forgiveness could be achieved without an atoning death—a sore point for his missionary opponents. Another Johannine passage that found its way into the *Precepts* to reinforce Roy's singular hermeneutical aim of putting the Gospel into action was "love one another as I have loved you."

Roy did not provide any critical notes or alert readers to potential parallel passages in the Gospels. It took another two decades for biblical scholars to advance the thesis that Mark might have been the source for Matthew and Luke. Whereas later biblical scholars would use Gospel harmonies to determine the historical accuracy of Jesus's life, Roy was consumed by the message of Jesus himself and especially his ethical teachings. Roy was ruthless in weeding out genealogies, historical incidents, biographical details, supernatural events, miraculous stories, and doctrinal teachings. He was clear as to why these passages had to go—because historical incidents were liable to be doubted and disputed by free thinkers, while the miracles carried "little weight" among Indians fed on the heavy diet of the supernatural deeds of their own gods and goddesses. The doctrines the missionary cherished, such as the Trinity, were unscriptural and later additions. In his correspondence with missionaries and to his well wishers, Roy tirelessly repeated that "the idea of a triune-God, a man-God, and also the idea of the appearance of God in the bodily shape of a dove, or that of the blood of God shed for the payment of a debt, seem entirely heathenish, and absurd."[3] Moreover, the doctrine of the Trinity was not an essential article of Christian faith "until the commencement of the fourth century." It was introduced by the political "authority of a monarch,"[4] indicating that its doctrinal approval was achieved not solely on the basis of its scriptural strength but on the authority of ruling powers.

Roy's chief aim was to rectify the message misperceived by the missionaries and rescue it from doctrinal entanglement. Roy saw his task as to purify what he called "popular corruptions of Christianity."[5] He wanted to come up with a Christianity that was not "encroached upon by human opinions" but "sought to attain the truths of Christianity from the words of the author of this religion."[6] Roy believed that the essence of the Gospel was expressed mainly through the moral teachings of Jesus. It was not Jesus's divine personality or saving power but his ethical principles that were crucial for Roy. The picture of Jesus that emerged in the *Precepts* was that of an exemplary moral guru. This did not mean that Roy disregarded the person of Jesus. As the exegetical exchange progressed between Roy and Marshman, it became clear that for Roy Jesus was more than an ethical thinker. Jesus was the "esteemed saviour" who fully instructed people in "Divine will and law, never before so fully revealed"[7]—a process that started with Moses: "It is true that Moses began to erect the everlasting edifice of true religion, consisting of a knowledge of the unity of God, and obedience to his will and commandments; but Jesus of Nazareth has completed the structure, and rendered his law perfect."[8] In Roy's view, Jesus was the "Redeemer, Mediator, and Intercessor with God, in behalf of his followers."[9] Roy was intent on avoiding the presentation of Jesus in Hindu garb as another divine avatar, which some missionaries were keen on. Such an attempt at the separation of Jesus the divine incarnation from his ethical precepts went against the theological views of the missionaries.

The Baptist missionaries were committed to an evangelical understanding of Christology that placed much emphasis on salvation through the saving blood of Christ. They felt that Roy's construal of Jesus was weak in this regard, and therefore a strong stance had to be taken. John Marshman's response took the form of a series of theologically dense rebuttals, reiterating the traditional position, in the Baptist magazine *Friend of India*, later published under the title *A Defence of the Deity and Atonement of Jesus Christ in Reply to Ram-Mohun Roy of Calcutta* (1822). Marshman's argument was that the Bible at its core is a doctrinal depository of the basic tenets and foundations of evangelical Christianity, such as the atonement, the doctrine of the Trinity, and the divinity of Christ. In his desperate defense of these jewels of evangelical doctrine, Marshman asked what the Gospel was without these dogmas.[10] He searched throughout the canonical texts for traces of the evangelical teachings. He tried to present early evidence of the Trinity even in improbable books such as Judges and Isaiah. "When stripped of those doctrines," Marshman lamented that the Holy Scriptures became "a stone of stumbling, and a rock of offence."[11] He was appalled by the figure of Jesus projected by Roy and accused him of reducing Jesus to a "level with Confucius or Mahomet" and of seeing him "as a teacher and founder of a sect."[12] In Marshman's view, Roy had come up with a supine image of a teacher "who cannot search the heart" and a savior who did not warrant submission.[13] The ensuing exegetical battle was tedious and torturous. Roy's response was a series of four appeals to Christians.[14]

A close look at the debate will reveal that both Roy and Marshman agreed on the authority of the scriptures and both used the same King James Version to validate their case. For Roy, the appropriate stance toward the Bible was not veneration but a proper investigation with the help of reason. He had no qualms in deleting narratives that went against rational thinking. For Marshman, the scriptures were "divine oracles" and "Divine Writings," and as such, "the authenticity of its narratives and the reasonableness and importance of its doctrines"[15] should not be doubted. Moreover, the scriptures had grand designs, and the doctrines embedded in them strengthen their textual coherence; thus, one cannot pick and choose as Roy had done. Roy and Marshman were convinced of the significance of Jesus for salvation, but the similarity ends there. They differed in their views on how salvation was to be attained. For Roy, it was not about atonement for sin but simply enacting the words of Jesus in daily life. For Marshman, it was a total surrender of one's life to Jesus because Jesus had sacrificed his life for the salvation of humankind. Therefore, the person of Jesus was more important than his moral teachings. One was about the enactment of the ethical precepts, and the other was about understanding and responding to the doctrines. Instead of answering back, Marshman, at a loss for words, cited the Psalmist: "if the foundations be destroyed, what shall the righteous do?"[16] Roy and Marshman were speaking from two different cultural and theological perspectives and as a result were failing to communicate.

Roy's intention had never been to undermine Christianity or, as he put it, "to oppose any system of religion much less Christianity," but he was himself hurt by the "indiscrete assaults" made by Christian writers on Hindu religion—a religion that had been venerated from generation to generation. He found missionaries and other Christians lacking in charity. He reminded them of the biblical verse "Do unto others as you would wish to be done by," implying that "if you wish others to treat your religion respectfully, you should not throw offensive reflections on the religion of others." He took a similar position in the *Tuhfat*, his tract on Islam, where he concluded with the words of Hafiz, the Persian mystic poet, when the Sufi master told his fellow believers that there was no sin except injuring one another. It is in this context that one needs to note a sharp exchange between Roy and Marshman over the colonial term "heathen." Throughout the controversy, Marshman kept on calling Roy a "heathen." This caused much irritation to Roy. The trouble was that they understood the term differently, one in an evangelical and the other in a colonial sense. Marshman defended himself by saying that anyone who did not believe in the divinity and atonement of Christ and the authority of scriptures, in his view, was a heathen, irrespective of religious and racial background or social status. Roy, in contrast, understood the term in its prevalent colonial usage, which implied that a native was incapable of making any intelligent contribution. Whatever his defense, it was thoughtless on the part of Marshman to call Roy a heathen, for he knew well that Roy was an articulate scholar and a religious reformer who had waged endless battles with his own Brahmin pundits about the unsavory aspects of Hinduism. Roy found the use of the term "unchristian." He retaliated by asking the public to read his writings and decide who was the heathen.

There was an interesting postscript to the debate. Although the missionaries were anxious that the *Precepts* might injure their program of conversion in India, the text was in fact influential in helping one prospective Hindu convert make a final decision in favor of Christianity. Pyari Mohan Rudra, who came from an old, landed, aristocratic family of Bengal, was struck by the "sublimity of the teachings of Jesus and the perfection of his character" found in Roy's booklet, which led him to read the original Gospels in the New Testament.[17] As a result, he later became an Anglican minister and was involved in important pastoral and educational work. Ironically, the only convert that the Baptist missionaries claimed to have had at this time—Krishna Pal—later lapsed. Rudra's conversion would have brought a wry smile to the face of Roy. Although Roy believed that Christianity properly inculcated had a "greater tendency to improve the moral, social, and political state of mankind, than any other known system," he never envisaged that India would embrace the Christian faith. When a Harvard professor, Henry Ware Sr., had asked him "Whether it be desirable that the inhabitants of India should be converted to Christianity?," Roy's answer was: "I am led to believe, from reason, what is set forth in scripture, that 'in every nation he that feareth God and worketh *righteousness* is accepted with him,' in whatever form of worship he may have been taught to glorify God."[18] Roy's choice of Gospel material further hints at his views on proselytization. He omitted Matthew's missionary command (Matt. 28:16–20) and the rare incident of Jesus's encounter with the Gentile—Syrophoenician Woman/the Canaanite woman (Mark 7:25–30; Matt. 15:21–28). He did, however, include Matthew's version of Jesus sending out the apostles. Those familiar with the text will know that the disciples were sent out not on a universal mission but with the specific task of seeking out only the lost sheep of the house of Israel.

For Roy, the whole dispute was about authority and knowledge. He was convinced that Marshman was not presenting well-reasoned arguments but asserting the power of a conqueror. As he put it, Marshman's interpretation was elevated by "virtue of conquest." The exchange between Roy and Marshman was not distinguished for its exegetical brilliance. What was important was the cultural context—the colonial milieu in which the controversy took place.

Divine Mandate and Christian Mandarin

The second instance where the Bible became the focus of a significant controversy in Asia was in connection with the Taiping Rebellion (1850–1864). Both the rebellion and the controversy were initiated and guided by Hong Xiuquan (1814–1864), who lived among the rural population. He was a teacher who had the advantage of being familiar with both the Chinese classics and the Christian scriptures. His reading of the Bible provided resources for him to resist the oppressive forces of the day—repressive Manchu rule, feudal Mandarin practices, and intervening foreign and missionary intruders. The story has it that, after failing the civil service exam three times—an exam based on Chinese classics, which was a sure route to government posts—Hong had a series of strange visions and mystical experiences in which he was taken to heaven and commissioned by God to exterminate evil and save the righteous. "Evil" included the Manchu dynasty, the magical rites of Taoism, Buddhist idol worship, and veneration of saints in Roman Catholicism. It was by sheer accident that Hong came to see the intricate connections between his visions and mystical experiences and his commissioning by the biblical God and embracement of Christianity. This happened when his cousin Li Chung Fang drew attention to a book Hong had read nine years previously and had totally forgotten. To Hong's great surprise, the contents of the book seemed to authenticate the visions he had been having. This corroboration further reinforced the idea that the divine assignment he received was genuine and that the God who placed such a task on him was Shang-ti, whom this books announced. The book from which Hong learned Christianity was a tract titled *God's Words to Admonish the Age,* consisting of sermons, biblical citations, and general principles about religion, compiled by a Chinese convert called Liang Afa, a printer by profession. By combining in his message the popular Chinese concept of the heavenly God, his vision of Christianity, and Confucian principles, Hong was able to strengthen his antifeudal and anti-Western goals.

Hong's vision had serious hermeneutical and political implications. In these mystical trips to heaven, he was supposed to have met with God and Jesus. These heavenly visitations led Hong to believe that he was the son of God and the younger brother of Jesus. Hong described God as a "man, venerable in years, with golden beard and dressed in black robe," who offered Hong a sword to "exterminate the demons,"[19] and that God was willing to offer further help to purge all the evil forces: "Take Courage and do the work; I will assist thee in every difficulty."[20] While Hong was in heaven, God asked him to look down from above. Hong could not believe what he saw—the decadence and wickedness of humanity—and he was speechless. The old man also decreed that "all men ... [should] turn" to Hong and "all treasures ... [should] flow" to him. In his vision, Hong also saw a man of middle age whom he called the elder brother (i.e., Jesus), who went with him on his mission to exterminate the evil spirits. Hong also saw in this vision both the old man and the elder brother rebuking Confucius. The old man rebuked Confucius for his muddleheaded teaching, while the elder brother reprimanded him for writing "bad books for the instruction of the people" and because his "younger brother" (referring to Hong) had been "corrupted by reading" his books.[21] At first, Confucius tried to argue but then became speechless and seemed ashamed and guilty. When he tried to escape, he was chased and captured by the angels and ordered by God to be whipped. What these mystical experiences confirmed in the mind of Hong was that the condition of China was hopeless and that the situation was ripe for God's intervention. His belief was that he was chosen to do for China what Jesus had done for the West. Hong's mission on earth was to rid China of evil influences, which included the Manchus, Taoists, Buddhists, Confucians, and Westerners.

Hong's hermeneutical enterprise had largely to do with tampering with biblical texts and making marginal notes in them. Unlike many resistance movements, Hong and the Taiping rebels did not see themselves as the new elect of God, nor did they claim any new covenant with God. This may be due to the book that influenced Hong: Liang Afa's *God's Words to Admonish the Age* did not refer to God's special call to the Jews. Hong firmly believed that, as a younger brother of Jesus, he had a commission from God to slay the demons and restore the Chinese to the worship of the true God—Shang-ti—a practice that had been in existence even before the time of the Chinese philosophers. Hong's hermeneutical program of back-to-the-one-true-God was based on the notion that the Chinese in ancient times had known how to worship the true God before Taoists, Buddhists, Barbarians, and the devil himself perverted their minds. Hong said to his followers: "Throughout the whole world there is only one God.... The

Chinese in early ages were looked after by God. . . . They walked in one way. . . . Ming of the Han was foolish, and welcomed the institutions of Buddha; he set up temples and monasteries, to the great injury of the country."[22] In Hong's view, in the classical period monarchs venerated the true God, Shang-ti, but China's rulers had since deviated from the worship of the true God. Examples of this deviation included sacrificing to "Empress Earth," honoring shamans, searching for Buddha's bones, and sending people to India to get Buddhist books.[23] God, though angry, had out of compassion chosen Hong to deliver the Chinese from "the devil's grasp, and lead them about to walk again in the original great Way."[24] Since the emperor had assumed the title reserved for God, he must be challenged, condemned, and made to repent.

What Hong did with the Bible was equally radical and amazing. His explanatory notes came to be known as the Taiping Bible. The fullest version contained only the first six books of the Hebrew scripture, whereas the New Testament, which Hong called the Former Testament, was complete from Matthew to Revelation. The marginal notes were numerous and need a close reading. For our purpose, they are significant for six things.

First, these notes reflect Hong's monotheistic ideals. These were largely influenced by Hong's reading of the Hebrew scripture and especially of the first three of the Ten Commandments, with their prohibition of the worship of idols and blasphemy. Hong took such prohibitions as a biblical censure of the imperial cult and the authority of the emperor. It was the third commandment that implicated the imperial system in the sin of blasphemy. To this commandment, which read "Thou shalt not take the name of the Great God in vain," Hong added, "whoever takes God's name in vain or rails against Heaven offends against the Heavenly Commandment." The accompanying poem that he penned further reinforced the accusatory tone toward the imperial power and the fate that awaited the emperor and those complicit in the entire imperial system:

> Our exalted Heavenly Father is infinitely honourable,
> Those who violate the proper boundary and profane his name
>   seldom come to a good end.
> If unacquainted with true way, you must awake;
> Those who are wantonly irreverent, their crime is boundless.[25]

In a culture dominated by the imperial cult and altar sacrifices, Hong and the Taipings could condemn with apparent ease the religious images and cultic practices of the dynastic rulers. Hong's convictions led him to ask his followers to destroy the idols and remove the tablets of Confucius in schools. He and his followers openly castigated the Buddhist deities and Confucian practices. One of the idol-smashing expeditions was to Guangxi, Kwangsi. At a temple in Xiangzhou Hsing-Chou, Hong ordered four of his men to "dig out the eyes" of an idol, "cut off its beard, trample its hat, tear its embroiled dragon gown to shreds, turn its body upside down, break off its arms."[26] Hong also offered rewards and punishments for those who kept or broke the Ten Commandments. Those who followed the commandments were "raised from a low to a high station," and likewise those who deviated from them were degraded from a "high to a low station and reduced to mere husbandry."[27]

Second, Hong appropriated biblical narratives to suit his politics and theology. He was clear about the atrocities inflicted on the land both by foreign invaders and by China's own rulers. In Hong's view, evil had pervaded humanity, and he had the divine commission to destroy it. His rereading of the Parable of the Tares reflected the new mood and his mission: "The Father and the Great Elder Brother descend upon earth to slay the vicious and save the righteous, to gather the wheat and burn the tares. This has come true."[28] Similarly, his marginal note on Matthew 10:32–33 reinforced the idea that he had been given the divine task of rescue, to "exterminate the vicious and save the righteous."[29]

Third, these marginal interpolations fit in with Hong's views on Jesus. His explanatory notes make it clear that he believed that God and Jesus have separate existences and that Jesus should not be confused with God. For Hong, Shang-ti was the supreme God. Hong was attracted to the notion that God and Jesus were two different entities, and he configured a Jesus without traditional divine attributes. This was in contradiction to the missionary preaching of the day. Hong was tireless in his efforts to deny that Jesus was God. There are a number of instances where Hong makes his Christological position clear. His comments on Mark 12:29 reveal his mind: "The Great Elder brother stated quite clearly there is only one Great Lord. Why did the disciples later suppose that Christ was God? If he was, there would be two Gods. Respect this." His annotation on Acts 4:24 states, "That God is the Supreme Lord means that the Heavenly Father our Supreme Lord is God, not Christ is God." To reinforce his claim that God and Jesus are two persons, Hong cited Saint Stephen, whose vision of Jesus standing separately from God is recorded in the Acts of the Apostles.

Fourth, these annotations claimed biblical validation for the establishment of an alternative Heavenly Kingdom of Peace that confronted both the Manchu dynasty and Western intruders. The political ambition was amply evident when Hong challenged the emperor's authority in two ways. He identified the Christian paradise with his own Heavenly Kingdom in Nanking. His annotation on Acts 15:15–16 reads: "Now God and Christ have descended into the world, and are rebuilding the temple of God at the Heavenly capital of the Heavenly Dynasty." He identifies Nanking as an earthly "Small Paradise" as distinct from heaven as the "Great Paradise": "Small Paradise on earth is where the bodies give glory to God" (1 Cor. 15:45, 46, 49). The Taipings' Heavenly Kingdom thus became the New Jerusalem. Hong's marginal comment on Revelations 3:12 reads: "The New Jerusalem sent down from Heaven by God the Heavenly Father is the present Heavenly capital. This is true." The creation of the heavenly dynasty was the fulfillment of what Jesus had foretold in Matthew: "Thus the Great Elder Brother formerly issued an edict foretelling the coming of the Heavenly Kingdom soon, meaning that the Heavenly Kingdom would come into being on earth. Today the Heavenly Father and Heavenly Elder Brother descend into the world to establish the Heavenly Kingdom."[30] Hong's idea of a Kingdom of Heaven that is earthly and present here and now was in line with what biblical scholars of a certain generation used to call *realized eschatology*—the reign of God appearing in the present time. The messianic mission whereby Hong would establish this kingdom was foretold in the covenant that was made after the flood: "I am 'Jih' the sun, therefore my surname is Hung. The Father first made this sign, prophesying that he would send Hung Jih to be the sovereign."[31]

Hong also challenged the monarch's association with the divine and heaven, and he challenged as well the exclusive claim that only emperors could worship God. Hong democratized access to God. At a time when the Chinese "mind had been deluded" by the idea that only the monarch could "worship the Great God," Hong proclaimed the Great God as universal "Father of all." To reinforce this point, Hong tapped into the Chinese idea of filial piety: "If you say that monarchs alone can worship the Great God, we beg to ask you, as for the parents of a family, is it only the eldest son who can be filial and obedient to his parents?"[32] As Thomas H. Reilly puts it, "the imperial figure represented just one more idol to smash."[33]

Fifth, Hong's marginal comments demonstrate the type of disciplinary code that he was trying to impose on his followers. The way he annotated the seventh and tenth commandments hints at his puritanical intentions. Although the seventh commandment was about committing adultery, Hong expanded this to include segregation of sexes and prohibition of the "casting of amorous glances," "the harboring of lustful imagining," "singing of libidinous songs," and "smoking of opium." The additional prohibitions Hong lists for the tenth commandment include gambling, buying lottery tickets, and taking bets on who would succeed in the state examinations. All this serves to illustrate the strict, morally upright community that he was trying to forge.

Finally, linked to the above, Hong adjusted the biblical text to tally with his severe moral codes. He erased any moral blemishes associated with some of the biblical characters. For Hong, who banned any form of alcohol, the state of drunkenness ascribed to Noah and Lot's daughters was too much, and he left out any mention of this in his version. He also edited out Judah's incestuous relationship with Tamar. But the story that offended Hong most was that of Jacob. He found it difficult to accept on two counts—one was the duplicitous way Jacob secured his birthright, and the other was the damage it did to family values. Hong discarded these unappealing biblical accounts and rewrote them to suit his needs. In the rewritten version, Jacob does not make Esau sell the birthright but, as Spence puts it: "Speaking as a respectful younger brother, Jacob gives Esau a brief lecture on the need to respect his birthright, and then agrees to 'divide' it with him in exchange for the pottage that Esau craves."[34]

Besides these direct raidings of biblical texts, there are indirect allusions to the role the Bible played in the ideology of the Taipings. The followers of Hong shared everything, which resembled the practice of the early church reported in the Acts. The families retained the produce they needed, and the surplus was taken over by local officials to be used for general purposes. Although this model is found in the Chinese classical texts, knowing Hong's appetite for using biblical texts to support his cause and his utter contempt for anything official, his thinking could have been based on the Acts model. "The Land System of the Heavenly Dynasty" contains elements that resonate with the communal sharing depicted in Acts: "All the fields in the empire are to be cultivated by all the people alike. . . . There being fields, let all cultivate them; there being food, let all eat; there being clothes, let all be dressed; there being money, let all use it, so that nowhere does inequality exist, and no man is not well fed and clothed."[35]

Hong's use of biblical texts was probably one of the first instances where the Bible was deployed for political purposes in Asia. Hermeneutically, Hong stands within the annotating tradition that goes back to the Geneva Bible, where the Puritans used the margins to settle political religious scores and reinforce their strict moral behavior. There is one stark difference between the Puritans and the Taipings, however. Whereas the Puritans were antimonarchy and resisted the power of kings, Hong tried to take his place as the rightful king and projected himself as the chosen instrument of God. In sharing a perspective with the Puritans, Hong was able not only to read his political vision into the text but also to claim kinship with a Jewish God and his son, inserting himself into salvation history. His imperial lineage is evident in his conversation with his sister: "Sister, I am the T'ai-p'ing Son of Heaven."[36] His claim that he was "sent by

Heaven as the true ordained Son of Heaven to exterminate the depraved and preserve the upright"[37] further reinforced his royal aspiration. The biblical vision of paradise offered Hong the promise to overthrow all the oppressive forces—the empires and institutions that were a hindrance to his Hakka community, which led a life of struggle and uprootedness. Like all messianic movements, Hong blended both traditional texts and personal revelations to create his own vision for society. In doing so, instead of waiting for a messiah, he proclaimed himself as that messiah. However, the political momentum he initiated ended in failure, resulting in a heavy loss of life. What he failed to note was that the very Bible that provided him with creative impulses foretold not only paradise and bliss but also pain, defeat, and destruction.

Compared with Roy, Hong's interpretation contained much that was erroneous and blasphemous and little that was Christian. Even so, there was no ferocious attack on him by the missionaries. The only missionary who raised any issue with him was Joseph Edkins of the London Missionary Society. His dispute was largely to do with Hong's failure to apprehend "rightly the true Scripture doctrine of the person of Christ."[38] Hong's Christology, according to Edkins, resonated with that of Arius. Hong sent a terse reply saying that Arius was right. In fact, most of the missionaries secretly admired the audacious way in which Hong actualized the biblical idea of the Kingdom of Heaven on earth. His monotheistic values, his extraordinary hostility to the idols, and the fact that he used a foreign text such as the Bible to attack the falsehoods and errors in his own indigenous culture endeared him to the missionaries. Hong's willingness to replace the books of Confucius with those of the Bible as the text for the public service examination in the territories under his control was seen by the missionaries as an opportunity to evangelize

China. The fact that the Taiping children were made to learn by heart the Lord's Prayer and that the soldiers were required to memorize the Ten Commandments further impressed the missionaries. Thomas Taylor Meadows, a civil servant, could not hide his enthusiasm when he wrote: "If the Tae pings succeed, then 480 millions of human beings, out of 900 millions that inhabit the earth, will profess Christianity, and take the Bible as the standard of their beliefs; and these 480 millions will comprise precisely the most energetic and most civilized half of the human race."[39] There were more than 400 people involved in printing the Bible, and these bibles were distributed free. E. G. Fishbourne, the commander of the ship *Hermes,* visited Nanking and commented that the Taipings were the first government to implement the biblical religion on so "grand a scale."[40] Silvester Horne claimed that this "singular revolutionary movement" played an "even more remarkable" role than the noble work done by the medical missionaries.[41]

Not all Western missionaries were enthusiastic about Hong's interpretation. If there was criticism, however, it was limited. Only the Roman Catholic reaction stood out. Hong's disastrous interpretation was attributed to Protestant preoccupations—"the indiscriminate circulation of the Bible" and the "inalienable right of private interpretation."[42] Apart from minor dissatisfactions, the general view among Protestant missionaries was that, as long as the standard of faith of the Taipings was biblical, this would "do wonders for the spread of Christianity if rightly directed."[43] Instead of indulging "in an indiscriminate condemnation" of Hong and his followers "for mistaking the nature of Christianity," Joseph Edkins advised his fellow missionaries that they "ought rather to rejoice that they know so much better of it as they do."[44] The highest endorsement came from Griffith John of the London Missionary Society. He came to

the defense even of the atrocities of the Taiping rebels. These misdemeanors were no worse than those the British had committed in India. In his pamphlet *The Chinese Rebellion,* John wrote that he firmly
believed that the Taiping rebels were the "chosen instruments to re-
lieve China from the darkness and thraldom of idolatry and, in connection with foreign missionaries, to bless her with the light and liberty."[45] In the estimate of these missionaries, what Hong and his
followers lacked was the "enlightened prudence"[46] of Westerners.
The missionaries' admiration for the Taiping Chinese was for their
contradiction of the standard Oriental images. The Chinese, who
were hitherto seen as "slothful" and "sensual" and, as a nation,
"having only sordid aims in life,"[47] were now turned into a people
of bravery and discipline because they had taken up the religion of
the Bible.

It is interesting that the Chinese version of the Bible that Hong
used was Karl Gutzlaff's translation of the King James Version. One
of the stipulations of the 1611 translators had been that the new version should not contain any marginal notes. It was precisely Hong's
marginal notes that made the vernacular version of the King James
Bible come alive and turned it into a contested text in imperial times.

The Gandhian and His Bible

A third instance where the Bible provided the ammunition for an
exegetical engagement was when J. C. Kumarappa, an Indian Christian, confronted the English Anglican bishop of Calcutta, Foss
Westcott, at the height of India's independence struggle. This debate
is remarkable for the simple reason that the Bible, which was otherwise virtually absent from India's independence struggle, came into

some kind of prominence for a brief period. There were a number of reasons for this marginalization of the Bible. First, participation of Indian Christians in the independence struggle included a few leading figures, such as S. K. Rudra, K. T. Paul, and S. K. Dutta, and numerous lesser-known Indian Christians, and their organizations, with varying positions and motives, seem not to have been exclusively fashioned by Christian scriptural concepts and reasoning. Second, for many of the Indian Christians of that time, including Pandippedi Chenchiah and Vengal Chakkarai, their Christian identity was less dependent on or shaped by the truths enshrined in ancient texts, than by the claim of an experience of the risen Christ, which was central to their Christian life and praxis. Chenchiah and S. K. George made vague and limited references to the Exodus as a possible biblical model to apply against British rule, but they never spelled this out fully. Third, the Hindu text the Bhagavad Gita played a crucial role in the independence struggle. Although the struggle was fueled by secular ideals, Gandhi and other prominent figures who played a leading role made much use of this Hindu text so effectively that the British rulers banned it.

J. C. Kumarappa was a rare exception as an Indian Christian who not only joined the Indian freedom struggle but also employed the Bible to advance the cause of Indian independence. Yet he is hardly given any recognition in Indian Christian circles. His alienation from the mainstream Indian Christianity was due to a number of factors: his open identification with Gandhi and the Sarvodaya movement, his aversion to denominational Christianity, and his distaste for ritualized forms of Christian worship. To make matters worse, Kumarappa's criticism of his fellow Christians, who in his view were "following apishly in the footsteps of their imperial masters," did not endear him to his own community.[48] Another reason for his marginalization among Christians is that unlike most of the Indian Christians of that time, he did not make himself known to the Christian public by writing in Church periodicals such as the influential paper, the *Guardian*. Except for his correspondence with Bishop Westcott, which appeared in the *Guardian*, Kumarappa chose instead to publish in secular Gandhian journals such as *Young India* and *Harijan*. Interestingly, his books on theological issues were published by Navajivan Publishing House, which was the printing arm of Gandhi's work. Kumarappa was less interested in engaging in theological discourse than in the struggle for Indian independence and in working out an alternative economics for post-Independence India, especially one based on Gandhian principles.

The Bible, which was largely peripheral to the Indian independence struggle, came alive for a brief period in the 1930s. This happened at the height of the civil disobedience movement, when an interesting but short-lived exegetical exchange occurred between Kumarappa and Westcott, the bishop of Calcutta and metropolitan of the Anglican Church in India. The background to this was the brutality meted out to some Indian freedom fighters by the colonial police. These freedom fighters were protesting against the salt tax imposed by the British government. What upset Kumarappa was the savage treatment of these Indians, which consisted of extreme beatings and crushing of their testicles. In response Kumarappa wrote an open letter entitled "An Appeal to All Christian Workers and Missionaries." Kumarappa acknowledged that the Indian national struggle had only a limited appeal among Indian Christians, and not all were supportive of civil disobedience. But even among those who were skeptical, "there can be no difference of opinion" about nonviolence as a useful method, especially as it was "enjoined by their Master."[49] What he was trying to do was to impress on his fellow Indian Christians who were apathetic toward, and the foreign missionaries who were suspicious of, the Indian Independence movement that the nonviolent resistance adopted by the freedom fighters was integral to Christian tradition and based on the teachings of Jesus. He sent a copy of the letter with a covering note to Foss Westcott. In the covering note, Kumarappa expressed his concern that the police atrocities were causing serious harm to the image of the Christian church in India. As such, the bishop should make use of his influential office to register a protest and use his authority to urge the British government to be less violent toward the protesters and follow nonviolent methods, the very methods advocated by Gandhi and legitimated by Christ. Kumarappa reiterated the point he had made in the original open letter, that "nonviolence cannot be treated as a matter of policy. It is one of the basic principles inculcated and practised by Christ."[50]

Westcott, for all his Cambridge education, misread the letter and thought that Kumarappa was asking him to support the political aspirations of the Indian nationalists. In his reply, while supportive of Gandhi's social reforms, which, in his view, were in line with the teachings of Jesus, he did not hesitate to show his displeasure in a number of ways at the Mahatma's political engagement. First, he reminded Kumarappa that Jesus did not have any political ambition. The bishop cited the incident in St. John's Gospel (John 6:14–15): after the feeding miracle, the crowd was trying to make Jesus king so that, in Kumarappa's words, he "might lead them to assert their national independence and secure their freedom from Roman Rule,"[51] but Jesus withdrew to the hills. Westcott reprimanded Kumarappa for thinking that Jesus or his teaching provided any "warrant for the practice of civil disobedience."[52] Second, the bishop pointed out that disobedience went against natural law and this was not God's way of bringing changes. He asked: "can we expect that Jesus Christ who came to reveal the character of God would so utterly repudiate this revelation of God given us in nature?"[53] Much of the suffering in the world, the bishop reckoned, was caused by going against the natural law, which in most cases was done in ignorance, though he was quick to point out that "in the present civil obedience, there is no question of ignorance. It is deliberate and is intended to over-throw the Government."[54] Third, he cited Jesus and Paul as exemplars of obedience to the law. To strengthen his case, the bishop cited Jesus's words "Render unto Caesar the things that are Caesar's" and went on to say that far from being an agitator, Jesus encouraged his disciples to obey the Pharisees and Scribes: "Whatsoever they bid, that you observe." Moreover, the bishop showed his irritation at Kumarappa for using Jesus as an example and his teachings as a warrant for civil obedience. In the bishop's view, Jesus's nonretaliatory injunction was pronounced in the context of the state maintaining law and order. In a patronizing tone, the bishop accused Kumarappa of being ungrateful for the safe and stable government offered by the British.

Kumarappa's reply was vigorous and analytical. His rebuttal was mainly in the form of corrections to the bishop's factual and exegetical misunderstandings and assumptions. He pointed out that nowhere in the letter had he ever mentioned the phrase "civil disobedience," nor had he canvased the bishop to support the political cause espoused by Gandhi. All that he wanted from the bishop was that he should use his influence to advise the government to employ less aggressive measures toward the political campaigners. The methods exercised by the colonial rulers were inhuman, and an opponent such as Gandhi deserved better treatment. No gentleman or, for that matter, anyone who claimed to follow the "Prince of Peace" could tolerate such "brutalities and torture." Kumarappa also made it clear that he was not making any reference to the current political situation but only reiterating the importance of using the principle of nonviolence in resolving disputes. Kumarappa did not hesitate to remind the bishop that when it suited the British, the national interest came first rather than upholding the Christian principle of nonviolence: "You remember how during the World War practically every pulpit was turned into a recruiting sergeant's platform and every church service ended with that morbidly narrow nationalistic song 'God save the King' which embodies the 'tribal God' idea of King David."[55] He accused the bishop of mimicking Peter in denying the basic principle of nonviolence.

Kumarappa was a layman, but he was able to take on the bishop's interpretation of the Bible. He reminded the bishop that biblical interpretation has always been a selective process and that British church leaders and missionaries had "misled" the congregations committed to their charge. When it suited them, they had "torn from the context" the teachings of Jesus, had "twisted passages," and had selectively quoted to meet their national needs during World War I.[56] Kumarappa questioned the bishop's claim that Jesus did not entertain political aspirations. Using the same Johannine passage the Bishop had quoted, he reminded the Westcott that Jesus withdrew to the hills not because he had no political aspirations but because the people misunderstood his role. From "purely selfish motives" after the miracle, the crowd mistook him for a temporal king who could satisfy their human needs. Then Kumarappa challenged the bishop's citation of Jesus's words about obeying the Scribes and Pharisees, thus equating them with a colonial bureaucracy. He conceded that these sayings were from Jesus but urged the bishop to see them in their context. As long as the Scribes and Pharisees upheld the Law of Moses, Jesus urged his disciples to follow them. But this was not a slavish obedience as the bishop implied. Had the bishop looked at

Matthew 23 carefully, where this utterance is found, he would have noted in that same chapter, warnings and curses against the Scribes and Pharisees: "Woe unto you, ye blind guides"; "Beware of the Scribes and Pharisees." Kumarappa also pointed out that "meekly" following the Scribes and Pharisee was not enough; one had to go beyond the Scribal and Pharisaic expectations and excel: "Except your righteousness shall exceed the righteousness of the Scribes and Pharisees, ye shall in no case enter the kingdom of heaven" (Matt. 5:20). More important, Kumarappa pointed out to the bishop that Jesus himself did not always strictly followed the prescription of the Scribes and Pharisees. His violation of the Sabbath laws was a clear case of breaking the injunction. Kumarappa's inference was that when immoral and human-made laws like the salt tax and excise policy are imposed by the British government, "the righting process will lead to a disturbance of the peace."[57]

The epistolary exchange between Kumarappa and Westcott was a relatively minor affair compared with the prolonged and intense earlier nineteenth-century hermeneutical battle between Rammohun Roy and John Marshman. There was not much to-ing and fro-ing between the Indian nationalist and the English ecclesiastic. The brevity of this dispute was largely due to the Christian press not wishing to prolong the controversy. It felt that such intrachurch infighting would not be helpful to the political peace process that was being initiated at that time.

Like Rammohun Roy, Kumarappa was a formidable opponent. He was both privileged and highly educated. The bishop, with his third-class degree in the natural science tripos at Cambridge, was no match for him. Neither man was a trained biblical specialist, so their textual analysis is likely to be dismissed as amateurish by professional scholars. Both showed a broad commitment to the Bible and its civilizing influence. Both affirmed that the Bible possessed crucial religious insights, but where Kumarappa differed was that he could not follow its teachings uncritically. For him, the four Gospels formed "some of the most human documents setting forth the life and teachings" of Jesus.[58] He had a modernist understanding of the Bible—its message could be deciphered and applied to contemporary cultural and political needs. In order to have any cultural influence in India, the Bible must reflect peoples' aspirations. Westcott, in contrast, believed that the Bible's message was universal and therefore was not bound by any contextual constraints. This debate was basically about the sense and significance of a religiously authoritative text in a politically charged situation.

Besides using the Bible to confront the bishop, Kumarappa mined the Bible to enhance his political ideas and profitably employed it as a tool for critiquing the institutional church and the religion of the missionaries. The passage he chose in support of civil disobedience was "the Sabbath was made for man," which he saw as the slogan for resisting state-made rules. When the situation demanded, Kumarappa claimed that the Bible authorized direct action against "man made codes of law." He used biblical images very creatively, either to expose the hierarchy of the British government or to shame the institutional church. He equated government bureaucrats with the Pharisees and Whitehall mandarins with the "Herodians." He compared imperialists and capitalists to "Cain people" who "feel no responsibility towards their own neighbours."[59] He warned that the practice of corban should not be used as an excuse by consumers. Just as the practice of corban was invented to avoid parental responsibility, consumers should not abrogate their responsibility to probe by whom and under what conditions goods were being produced. If these goods were manufactured by slave labor, then consumers were party to slavery, and if the goods were made in an oppressive political context, the consumers participated in this. He likened the imperial ambitions of European nations and Japan toward countries including India, China, Abyssinia, and Czechoslovakia to the parting of Jesus's garments and casting lots on them. Kumarappa did not spare his own Christian community. He used the image of crumbs falling from the master's table to shame the dependency culture and obsequious nature of Indian Christians.

Concluding Remarks

There are differences between these three interpreters—Rammohun Roy, Hong, and Kumarappa—as to what motivated their expository activity. Hong viewed his task as a divine mission. His revolutionary but ill-fated vision was fueled by a potent mixture of messianic fanaticism and anti-Manchu nationalism. His self-belief was that as a younger brother of Jesus, he was charged with bringing divine light to China and the world. He envisioned his mission as similar to the one Jesus performed for the West—to bring people back to the great and supreme God whom once they had followed. He told the missionaries: "I am the one saviour of the chosen people."[60] Roy and Kumarappa were not deluded enough to make such a claim as Hong did when he said, "God has revealed to me through these visions that I am the full brother of Jesus, the second son of God. Therefore, I am in a position to receive and interpret his message directly; I am one of the Godhead."[61] Roy and Kumarappa saw their exegetical enterprises as existential responses to the inappropriate and at times arrogant and graceless interpretations of some of the missionaries. These two Indians were largely provoked by the colonial assumption that the uppity natives should be taught a lesson. A crucial difference was that while Hong found the biblical texts themselves problematic and in need of correction, Roy and Kumarappa were not uneasy about the texts per se but were troubled by the interpretations advanced by some of the missionaries.

Unlike Roy and Kumarappa, Hong did not have any bruising exegetical exchanges with a missionary opponent. The manner in which the disputation was carried out was also different. There was no direct one-to-one battle such as between Roy and Marshman or between Kumarappa and Westcott. In Hong's case, it was done indirectly. Questions were sent to Hong, and answers were mediated later in the form of communications or edicts. Whereas Roy and Kumarappa were vigorous in their defense and explanation of their theological stance, Hong did not answer his critics but simply restated his already declared positions based on his visions and reading of the scriptures.

Unlike Roy and Kumarappa, Hong was highly idiosyncratic in his interpretation. His monotheistic god had a wife and children. The wife was "exceedingly gracious, beautiful and noble in the extreme." This god had a son whose wife was "virtuous, and very considerate."[62] She was constantly exhorting the elder brother (i.e., Jesus) to be consciously and intentionally active. To the horror of the traditionalists, Hong used the model of the Chinese family to interpret the Trinity. He explained that the three persons of the Trinity were just like members of a Chinese family—the father being the head and the other two being subordinate to the father.

Roy and Hong approached indigenous texts differently. Hong seems to have been antagonistic toward Chinese texts. He approved only the two testaments of the Bible and the proclamations he compiled, and he rejected the works of Confucius, Mencius, and various philosophers and schools of thought. He dismissed all these as "the devilish books and heretical theories, [that] must be burned and eliminated and no one permitted to buy, sell, possess, or read . . . , or punishment shall be levied."[63] In contrast, Roy was tireless in his attempt to demonstrate that the Hindu Vedas were as pristine as the biblical texts. Just as he was trying to get rid of some dogmas of Christianity and Islam, he was engaged with Hindu texts to try to rediscover monotheistic elements enshrined in them in order to demonstrate that these were on a par with biblical texts.

As to his use of scriptural texts, Roy was very conservative in comparison to the other two. He simply ignored the materials that did not suit his hermeneutical aims and patched together the sayings of Jesus to illustrate the ethical content of the message. He did not make any attempt to alter or amend any of the sayings of Jesus. In his debate with Marshman, Roy made it clear that he never "expressed least doubts as to the truth of any part of the gospels."[64] Hong and Kumarappa were adventurous in that they altered, added to, and in the process almost rewrote the biblical narratives. Unhappy with the way some of the missionaries were engaged in evangelical activity in India, Kumarappa changed the wording of Jesus's charge to his disciples. The original commission read: "Go not in the way of the Gentiles, and into any city of the Samaritans enter ye not, but go rather to the lost sheep of the house of Israel." Kumarappa rewrote these words of Jesus to remind the missionaries of their task in their own countries: "Go not to the distant parts of the world to those to those professing other religion, but go rather to your own neighbours and teach them the right path."[65] Similarly, Jesus's weeping over Jerusalem was rephrased to indicate what the European nations were doing to the colonies: "O Europe, O Europe, ye that suppress meek and mild nations and live on their life blood, ye that controvert and distort my teachings and thereby exploit the ignorant, how often would I have gathered thy children together, even as a hen gathereth her chickens under her wings, and ye would not! Behold your countries are left unto you desolate."[66] Kumarappa often placed these rescripted verses within quotes to give the resemblance of their being part of the original sacred writ.

Hong was more daring in dealing with the text than Kumarappa. He worked on the assumption that God revealed to him that the New Testament contained "erroneous records"[67] and needed correction and that he was appointed to rectify these textual glitches. In his meeting with Edkins, he told him that "The Father gave forth the scriptures, and whatever faults there are in them, he has commanded me to correct them, and publish them to the world in their amended form." Then he went on to say that this task was being undertaken on behalf of the father: "The books you present to me, I, for the Father receiving, will correct, struggling in the Father's behalf."[68] While Roy and Kumarappa were simply dealing with the biblical narratives, Hong was bold enough to change the name of the New Testament. He called it the Former Testament and designated his own writings the True Testament. The change of title had a double implication. One was to remind the missionaries that God's communication to Hong was recent and hence more trustworthy than the ancient documents the missionaries brought to China, and the other was to let the missionaries know that they were expected to revere and teach the new fount of revelation, rather than instruct the Chinese with old truths. Hong saw this task as being done on behalf of God. His audacious rewritings were intended to reinforce the moral purity he was demanding from his followers.

All three—Roy, Hong, and Kumarappa—saw Jesus as a human being with a divine mission. Roy detached Jesus from the New

Testament's doctrinal trappings and projected him basically as a moral instructor whose teaching was "more likely to produce the desirable effect of improving the hearts and minds of men of different persuasions and degrees of understanding."[69] Roy effectively erased the plural and often contradictory pictures in the Gospels and depicted a single Jesus whose teachings were worthy of imitation. Roy's Jesus was an artificial creation in which the religious hero of one religion was borrowed to reinforce the religious morality of another religion. For Kumarappa, Jesus was a true struggler for freedom. In his view, Jesus's whole life was a "continuous fight against usurpation and unreasoning authoritarian rule and a heroic attempt to assert the divinity of man and the absolute supremacy of the Spirit."[70] Kumarappa also used Jesus as a convenient benchmark to differentiate between the religion of the missionaries, which was "smug, selfish, and individualistic," and the personal religion of Jesus, which, as a "social order,"[71] resonated with the Hindu idea of the joint family system, with all its shortcomings.

For Hong, Jesus was God's firstborn and Hong's "uterine brother." He said nothing about Jesus's early life or ministry. Hong's writings contain only a few facts about Jesus's life—the reasons for his appearance on earth, his birth, the manner of his death, his resurrection, appearances to his disciples, and his ascension. Apart from reference to sacrificing his life for the remission of sins, Hong ignores for the most part Jesus's parables, his teachings in the Sermon on the Mount, and the way he addressed ethical issues. Hong also provided additional material about Jesus. Jesus was part of the celestial family, with a spouse who was "kind" and "beautiful"[72] and constantly urging restraint. The Jesus we encounter in Hong's writings is one who is easily enraged and who has to be pacified by his wife. Hong's selection of material on Jesus was chosen for how it would establish his own place in the Taiping hierarchy and to furnish an authoritative precedent for his actions.

Ultimately for Roy, Hong, and Kumarappa, the validity and the potency of the text lay in the enactment of its precepts in life. All three saw in their own way how this was put into practice. While the Baptist missionaries were keen on getting the biblical doctrines correct and held the view that salvation was dependent on believing them, Roy was not bothered with these aspects of the biblical teachings but was interested in observing the teachings of Jesus as he understood them. He drew to the attention of his missionary opponents the many passages, and especially the parable in Matthew 25, that indicated that the judgment would not be made on the basis of "dogmas and histories" or founded on belief in the divinity of Jesus but would be made on the basis of human beings fulfilling their "civil duties."[73] For Kumarappa, it was a question of applying biblical ideals to economics. It also meant taking Jesus seriously and leading an austere life and being less greedy and less avaricious. He put together a selection of the sayings of Jesus as marks of ideal living: "Heal the sick, cleanse the lepers, freely ye have received, freely give. Provide neither gold, nor silver, nor brass in your purses, nor scrip for your journey, neither two coats, neither shoes, nor yet staves: for the workman is worthy of hire."[74] For Hong, the ultimate realization of Jesus's word was the establishment of the Heavenly Kingdom on earth. In the application of the texts, Hong and Kumarappa were political, and they put them to use effectively to affirm an anti-imperial stance. They were able to use the text to challenge the reigning powers of their day. Roy's usage was largely cultural and religious. He was more interested in introducing a moral element into everyday life than in engaging in anticolonial struggle. Although he supported and celebrated the liberation of South American countries from colonialism, Roy did not envisage political freedom for India.

As a result of the interpretative adventures of these three, the biblical narratives do not remain the same. In their hands, the Bible in the end emerges as a different book. All three come out with different forms of the text. Roy's *Precepts* hints at a gentler and kinder form of Christian message. Kumarappa's tone was teasing and sarcastic. His mock rewritings puncture the pomposity of the missionary interpretation. Hong's reconstructed text brings out a harsher and a meaner version of biblical faith. With the absence of Jesus's love commandments, the Golden Rule, and any reference to the Sermon on the Mount and with the emphasis on the strict observance of the Ten Commandments, Hong's biblical vision paints a cruel and ruthless biblical religion.

All three men both play fast and loose with and honor the Bible. They confound and enrich it. Particular passages are identified to suit special purposes. What all three agreed on was that if the "foreign" book had any relevance to Asia, it had to be revised and altered. The book, once held as God's unalterable oracle, now invited correction and amendment. Roy and Kumarappa would not have hesitated to agree with Hong: "Those books are neither polished in literary terms nor are they fully complete. You must all consult together, and correct them so that they become both polished and complete."[75] Of course, Roy and Kumarappa would have differed as to how to go about this task.

4   A Buddhist Ascetic and His Maverick Misreadings of the Bible

Asia has produced a number of Hindu and Buddhist interpreters who challenged both colonial rule and the colonial version of their indigenous faith. One of them was Anagarika Dharmapala (1864–1933), a Sri Lankan Buddhist revivalist, who taunted Western missionaries and the British administration. He was one of the "exotic" Orientals, along with Swami Vivekananda, P. C. Mozumdar of India, and the Japanese Zen master Soyen Shaku, who drew much attention at the Parliament of Religions at Chicago in 1893.

Dharmapala, whose original name was Don David Hewavitarane, like many Ceylonese in colonial Ceylon went to a Christian school, where he was forced to attend church services and recite and memorize texts from the Bible. In keeping with the colonial practice of the time, his education was largely dominated by Christian principles that showed little respect for the Buddhist dharma. The words of the warden of his college to young Dharmapala were indicative of this aggressive mood: "We don't come to Ceylon to teach you English, but we come to Ceylon to convert you."[1] Dharmapala was educated both by the Roman Catholic fathers and Protestant missionaries. He spent two years in a missionary boarding school run by the Anglican

Church Missionary Society in Kotte, then St. Benedict's College in Kotahene, St. Thomas's College in Mount Lavinia, and the Colombia Academy. At school, he was daily fed with biblical stories and he became familiar with a number of biblical figures, including both well-known characters, such as Adam, Abel, and Elijah, and less prominent personalities, such as Shadrach, Meshach, and Abednego. He claimed to have memorized the books of Exodus, Numbers, Deuteronomy, Joshua, the four Gospels, and the Acts. He used to read the Bible four times a day, so much so that his leather-bound bible was falling apart. Reminiscing on his early life, Dharmapala said that he became a biblical critic when he was at school. At twelve he began to question the Bible. One of the verses that he could not morally come to terms with was Psalm 19:5, which read "the sun as bridegroom coming out of the chamber and rejoiceth as a strong man to run a race."[2] He nowhere explains his problem with this verse.

Dharmapala recalled a number of incidents during his boarding school days that made him consider the unsuitability of Christianity. One was the violent action of his teacher. While young Dharmapala was trying to read a Buddhist pamphlet on the Four Noble Truths one Sunday, his teacher aggressively took the copy away from him and threw it out of the window. Another incident that horrified Dharmapala was seeing his teacher, a Christian preacher to boot, shooting a bird. He was appalled at the killing of an innocent bird, and his immediate reaction was that this was not "the religion for me."[3] Another major irritant was the constant ridicule he had to put up with about his Buddhist faith. Christian priests used to taunt him by telling him "Look at your mud image. You are worshipping clay." He was also disturbed by the behavior and lifestyle of the Christian priests. Their wine-drinking and meat-eating habits, especially consuming pork, did not endear them to him. There were trivial annoyances as well, as when he was asked to kneel before the bishop Hillarian Sillani and kiss his ring, although no such respect was shown to Buddhist priests who visited his school.

Dharmapala's attraction to Buddhism was in one sense accidental. On his way to St. Thomas's College in Colombo Academy, he had to pass through a Buddhist temple. It was the priest of the temple who introduced him to the work of the Theosophical Society and the two important personalities associated with its work—Colonel Henry Steele Olcott and Madame Helena Blavatsky, whom Dharmapala described as the first Europeans not to attack Buddhism. Besides these foreigners, there were two Buddhist monks—Venerable Hikkaduwe Sri Sumangala Thera and Migettuwatte Sri Gunananda Thera—who played a critical role in shaping Dharmapala's spiritual life. These two erudite monks used their vast knowledge and oratorical skills to challenge the Christian supremacy. There were a series of Buddhist-Christian debates at that time in small towns such as Gampola and Beddagama, which culminated in the now famous Panadura debate, where these two Buddhist monks played an important role. As a ten-year-old, Dharmapala himself witnessed these religious confrontations and later commented that Gunananda "supplied the oratory" and Sumangala "furnished him [Dharmapala] with the scholarly material and references."[4] Ironically, it was reports of these debates that alerted the outside world that Buddhism was robustly alive in Sri Lanka, not dead as the missionary press claimed. They attracted the attention of Colonel Olcott and persuaded him to come to Sri Lanka. Dharmapala's meeting with Olcott and Blavatsky, his denunciation of the life of a householder in favor of an austere ascetic life, his embrace and championing of Buddhist causes, the development of his unique sense of patriotism, his eventual disagreements and fallout with his one-time admirer Olcott, and the severance of his connection with the Theosophical Society are all well documented elsewhere and there is no need to rehearse them here.[5]

This chapter is largely concerned with an often-overlooked aspect of Dharamapala's work, namely, the numerous biblical citations in his writings. It demonstrates how his depreciatory reading of the Bible helped him to deal with the defamatory propaganda of Christian missionaries and to offer the Buddha's teaching as universal, scientific, and humanistic and, more important, to show how it deserved to be accorded a rightful place among the religions of the world. This chapter also discusses how Dharmapala's highly disparaging comments on Christianity, and the elevated form of Buddhism he constructed, helped to counter both Western hegemony and any threat posed to the Sinhalese by other communities in Sri Lanka.

Before we look at Dharmapala's interpretative practices, we need to remind ourselves of the historical background against which he undertook his hermeneutics. Dharmapala's hermeneutical activity should be seen against the anti-Buddhist feeling prevalent at the time at home and, to some extent, abroad. Besides holding onto the standard negative aspersions about Buddhism, some missionaries and Christian theologians predicated its eventual demise. Spence Hardy, a Methodist minister, who worked in Sri Lanka for many years and wrote many books on Buddhism, plainly confessed that the main aim of his study was to "expose the more prominent errors of Buddhism."[6] He was relentless in his attempt to show that the Buddha's life was a "myth," his teaching was a "mass of error," his morals were "imperfect," and his religion had no "substantiality."[7] Hardy earnestly hoped that just as the old idols of Europe—Jupiter and Mars, Woden and Thor—vanished, so would the Buddha. He confidently predicted that the Buddha would disappear, the *viharas* (Budhist temples) would be "deserted, the dagoba [Buddhist monument] unhonored, and the bana [preaching of Buddhist text and commentaries] un-read" and that in every household an altar would be "erected to the Lord God of heaven and earth."[8] John Henry Barrows, who came to prominence for organizing the Parliament of Religions in Chicago, and who invited Dharmapala to attend the meetings, found that the message of the Buddha was a "strange mingling of humanitarianism and scepticism."[9] He asserted that Buddhism, like all other religions, would "ultimately [be] displace[d]" all its "best ideals and aspira-tions" fulfilled in Christianity.[10] According to Barrows, there were "elements of the Gospel scattered and imperfect in all the religions," and the Buddha and his law were, like "Plato and his philosophy, and Moses and his priesthood," playing the role of "school-masters lead-ing to Christ."[11] Predictions of such a doomed scenario were not confined among foreigners alone. Even Sri Lankans joined in. James de Alwis, a reputable scholar, in one of his writings in 1850 predicted that "before the end of that century Buddhism would disappear from Ceylon."[12] It was against such a hostile imperialist-missionary ideol-ogy that Dharmapala waged his own vitriolic hermeneutics against Christianity and colonialism.

The Christian Bible Sponging on Adjacent Cultures

According to Dharmapala, most cultural material found in both testaments was basically borrowed from the nations adjoining Israel. He makes sweeping claims about how concepts, ideas, and stories from the nearby cultures were routinely annexed by the biblical writ-ers. He mentions a number of such borrowings. The Jews came to know of the creation stories only when they were taken captive to Babylon, and the biblical writers incorporated these stories into the books of the law after they returned to Jerusalem. The fact that there is no reference to the creation narrative in the books from Exodus to Malachi is an indication for Dharmapala that these creation myths were later additions after the exile experience. Similarly, the stories of the tall towers of Babel, which were originally used for astronomical purposes by the Chaldeans, were being ignorantly transmitted by the biblical writers as an example of people building a tower to reach heaven, so angering God and leading to God's cursing and causing the confusion of tongues. The story of the Flood was a belated incorporation. The stories of the Jewish ancestors including Abraham and Noah were based on Chaldean and Babylonian folklore.

The different characteristics of God depicted in the early chapters of Genesis were acquired either from the Chaldean teaching on the origin of the universe or from Egypt. The examples of such borrowings include a god who speaks, a god who creates human beings from the dust and makes them till the ground, a god whose spirit rests in the water, a god who is engaged with dragons, and a god who curses Cain and sends him away to a country where there are no inhabitants.

Biblical concepts such as the resurrection, the sonship of God, conflict between good and evil, the atoning power of the blood, and the father–son union were also acquired from neighboring cultures. The idea of sonship had its origin in Egyptian Osirism. Jesus learned the doctrine of resurrection when he was between thirteen and thirty years old and sojourning in Egypt. The dual conflict between God and Satan is straight from Persia. Jesus and Moses learned magic from Egypt. The blood of the sacrificial lamb that washes away sin is found in the Saivite form of Saktism, which speaks of the power of lamb or goat to cleanse people's sins. The Johannine saying "I and the Father are one" is similar to the Vedantic dogma of *aham brahmsmi.*[13]

The ethical and moral teachings of the Bible were collated from other cultures. It was the Babylonians who provided the initial ingredients for the Ten Commandments. The Sermon on the Mount echoes the Sutta Pitaka, the discourses of the Buddha. The Hebrew scripture, in Dharmapala's view, is a "record of savage immorality suited only to a low type of human society."[14] Its ethics encourage "unimaginable cruelty." An example of this is found in the Psalms: "Happy shall he be that taketh and dasheth thy little ones against the stones" (137:9). The ethics of the Bible stand in contrast to the sublime principle of the Aryan doctrine promulgated by the Aryan Teacher.

Basically, Dharmapala treats Hebrew scripture as the folktales of a nomadic people and he argues that the mythical stories of the Bible have "no scientific foundation" and are "unfit" for the advanced people of the twentieth century.

Demonizing the God of the Bible

Dharmapala engages in the standard Oriental practice of reducing and magnifying elements in a culture. The God of the Bible assumes diabolical proportions. Dharmapala depicts the biblical God variously as feckless, a monster, a deserter, and an absentee god. The God of the Jews is a warmongering God. Jehovah is the one who "loves blood" and has no compassion in his heart. Jehovah is portrayed as a kind of god who instigates the Jews to fight against other races: "And when the LORD thy God hath delivered it into thine hands, thou shalt smite every male thereof with the edge of the sword" (Deut. 20:13). The religion of the Jews is seen as purely a "fighting religion with Jehovah as the commander-in-chief."[15] The biblical God adopts all the "tactics of the military dictator."[16] Dharmapala calls the God of the Jews "the savage deity of Horeb."[17] This God is basically a "hill deity" known for his monstrous acts. Dharmapala claims that it was only after the Reformation that the God of the Bible changed character. This tribal god who became the guide of Protestant Christianity was "enthroned as the supreme God Lord of the World."[18]

Dharmapala's God of the Bible is a God who makes alliances with foreign kings and even with Satan and has no hesitation in handing over those of his own people who do not obey him. When the Jews become unmanageable, Jehovah is seen as a betrayer of his people. He is the one who changes sides and withdraws from the lives of the people, joining forces with the Babylonian king Nebuchadnezzar and sending his people into captivity. The biblical God does not stop at this. He is so angry that the Jews have left him for good that he destroys some of them. The God of the Bible is easily provoked when his chosen people honor other deities. His deep hatred is reserved for them when there is backsliding and they fail to listen to him: "Because they have forsaken me, and have burned incense unto other gods, that they might provoke me to anger with all the works of their hands; therefore my wrath shall be poured out upon this place, and shall not be quenched" (2 Chron. 34:25). It is the same deity that doubts the faith of his own people and hands them over to be harmed. Examples of such actions include permitting Adam and Eve, the first family, whom God blessed, to commit sin and allowing the innocent Job to be tormented by Satan.

For Dharmapala, the biblical God does not fulfill his promises. Those who arrived at the promised land were not the same generation that left Egypt and to whom God had given his word. The generation that reached Canaan was a new one and did not know who Yahweh was. Here Dharmapala contradicted himself. On the one hand, he acknowledged that the only achievement of the God of the Hebrews was to bring his people out of the house of bondage, but on the other, he blamed God for his failure to usher in the original recipients of his pledge.

The biblical God also takes a long leave of absence. Between the last book of the Old Testament, Malachi, and the advent of Jesus, God is missing from history. "For nearly 300 years, the history of Jehovah was a blank, before the advent of Jesus."[19] Dharmapala notes that this disappearance and reappearance enabled Jehovah to be theologically transformed into a mellifluous, more mellow figure: "Jehovah has disappeared and the God our Father came into existence."[20]

Dharmapala sees a God who sacrifices his son to save the world as "monstrously diabolical."[21] This was the same God who, a few centuries before, had prevented Abraham from sacrificing his son and now has adopted the very same method to appease his own anger. For Dharmapala, the biblical God was essentially weak and powerless. A sign of this powerlessness was that from the time of the Exodus to the Babylonian captivity, Jehovah and the prophets could not prevent the Jews from worshiping other gods.

Dharmapala occasionally resorts to mocking the biblical God. He ridicules the physical appearance of Yahweh. The God of the Bible lacked the "symmetrical features of a divine figure," and the biblical deity was only "represented by his back parts."[22]

For Dharmapala, the spirit of compassion is totally foreign to the biblical God. He lists a number of passages from the books of Exodus, Numbers, and Leviticus to support the cruel and vengeful nature of the Hebrew—Christian God. The God of the Bible is basically a belligerent God, "camouflaged as god of love," "the prince of peace."[23] The Hebrew God is an absolute autocrat whose main function is to send millions of people to an "eternal hell of fire and brimstone."[24]

Dharmapala's persistent question is how one can trust a God who could not protect his own people, who deserts them and inflicts all kinds of cruelty on them.

Monotheistic Monster

Monotheism comes under a fair deal of criticism from Dharmapala. His contention is that monotheism was one of the phases that humankind had to go through before reaching the idealistic stage offered by the Buddha. Humanity's yearning for spirituality began with animism, which was succeeded by polytheism, which gave way to monotheism, which in turn produced pantheism, which "culminated in the promulgation of the highest form of philosophy" in the teachings of the Buddha. For Dharmapala, Christianity was basically an Oriental Semitic monotheism. He viewed monotheism as "crude,"[25] "unscientific,"[26] "destructive,"[27] and inspired by fanaticism. Monotheism encourages animal killing, meat eating, bestiality, and alcoholism. As an example of bestiality, Dharmapala drew attention to the behavior of the Israelites after striking down the Philistines, when they "flew upon the spoil, and took sheep, and oxen, and calves, and slew *them* on the ground: and the people did eat *them* with the blood (1 Sam. 14:32; emphasis added). The classic instance of drunkenness was that of Noah, which provoked a family crisis. Monotheistic religion, in Dharmapala's reckoning, was invariably "bloodthirsty, despotic and cruel."[28] In contrast, the Indo-Aryan religions did not tolerate despotic gods. Rather, Buddhism advanced the notion of "super theistic transcendentalism" leading to the path of infinite wisdom and all-embracing love.[29] Monotheism fails to thrive in places that have strong philosophical foundations. China, with its deep philosophical heritage, found the idea of a monotheistic god of "no earthly benefit."[30]

Character Assassinations

For Dharmapala, all biblical personalities were tainted figures. The characters of the Hebrew scriptures beginning with Adam and Eve failed to exhibit a "high ethic in their life." The ethics of the twelve tribes of Israel was basically that of a savage tribe. Abraham did not lead an exemplary or truthful life. He told lies to save his skin and as a result the poor king Abimelch had to suffer by admitting Sarah to his harem. Dharmapala dismissed Jacob as a person who swindled his own brother and cheated his own father. The heroes of the Hebrew scriptures were all, in Dharmapala's reckoning, "veteran polygamists."[31]

The disciples of Jesus were dismissed as men of low intelligence and the riffraff of Galilee—the backwash of the barren portion of Asia. Dharmapala calls Peter "the bed-rock liar" and "a sneaking coward who denied his own teacher."[32] Dharmapala held Peter responsible for the death of Ananias and Sapphira—the couple in the early church who withheld a portion of their wealth instead of giving it to the common pool of the church. The sharing of wealth, according to Dharmapala, was a device manufactured by the church to boost its own financial resources.

Among the biblical personalities, only two characters come out positively. One is Moses, whom the people trusted. He was credited with discovering the deity in a desert hinterland in Horeb, and it was this deity who in turn appointed Moses as his agent. Had Moses not discovered the "Arabian Jehovah," Christianity would not have been in existence today. He showed himself as "a magician and was able to do things like a god."[33] It was Moses who found that the old ethic was untenable and not rational and altered it to reflect a more humane view. One of the changes he effected was that children should not be held responsible for their parents' misdemeanors. Moses was often seen as arguing with God about the difficulty of implementing some of God's commandments and about the damaging effect they had on God's reputation. God often listened and regretted his mistakes. In Dharamapala's view, Moses was a "kind of advisor" to God and not a "sneaking, snivelling hypocrite of the modern type of muddle headed panjandrums."[34]

The other biblical figure who is given guarded approval is the apostle Paul, who comes out slightly better than the other disciples. Paul is seen as an independent person who not only took on establishment figures but also came out with innovative theological ideas. He is seen as a person who opposed both Jesus and Peter. Paul is credited with starting the church for the Gentiles, which Jesus discouraged his disciples from doing. Paul initiated the inclusion of the Gentiles without any authority from Jesus. He challenged and crushed the personal disciple of Christ, Peter. Paul's letter to the Galatians was seen as an open rebuke to Peter. Paul's theology emerged out of his own imagination, and the Christ of whom he preached was a "spiritual ideal."[35] However, Dharmapala believed that the story of Paul's conversion was a "concoction of a later age."[36] Paul, too, had his blemishes. He suffered from "psychic hallucination," as was the case with another disciple, John.[37] The grudging admiration for Paul could be because Dharmapala saw himself as a latter-day reformer, like the apostle: "I desire to make an effort to reform Christianity just as Paul did."[38]

Jesus as a Hotchpotch Teacher

Dharmapala demystifies Jesus and portrays him as an ordinary, kind person but one who over the years was turned into a dominant figure by the ecclesiastical authorities. By pointing out that Jesus was the third child of Mary, Dharmapala makes him look like a regular member of the family, with no claim to uniqueness. He was a simple "ethical reformer" who became the "powerful despot" of the institutionalized church. Jesus as a religious teacher was a total failure, and he made no impression on people during his three years of ministry. The teachings of Jesus were fit only for the slaves: "my kingdom is not of this world"; "blessed are the poor; blessed are they that are persecuted for my sake"; "if thou will be perfect, sell all that thou hast and give to the poor." Only a few illiterate fishermen followed him.

Dharmapala identifies three types of Jesus—the Jesus of the Sermon on the Mount, "whose ideal is forgiveness and indifference to the things of the world"; the political Jesus, a despotic monarch who sends those who do not believe in him to eternal hell; and the Jesus of the fourth Gospel, who represents the Logos. The Jesus of the Sermon on the Mount was totally forgotten by the priests of the church. It is the political Jesus created by the Catholic Church that dominates the world today. Unlike the Buddha, Jesus was not a scientific or a philosophical thinker. He came to be worshiped because he claimed that he was the only son of God.

Dharmapala upholds and at the same time takes the sheen out of Jesus's teaching on the Mount for being unoriginal. His approval of the Sermon on the Mount is based on two factors. First, he finds it real because Dharmapala sees himself as having embodied its precepts in his own life. "To me," he wrote, "the Sermon the Mount [was] very practical, and I [had] been a world wanderer for forty years with no place to call my own, with only one desire and that [was] to be selfless and to work for the welfare of all beings."[39] Second, his approval is based on the fact that the Sermon on the Mount was drawn from Eastern religious teachings. Dharmapala claimed that the kindness advocated by the Sermon on the Mount was influenced by the Buddha. The ethics enshrined in the Sermon on the Mount are seen as evidence of Jesus being influenced by Buddhists and the Hindu Vedanta. The perfect moral code found in the Sermon on the Mount is similar to the one expressed in Buddhist texts such as the Sutra Nipta and Anguttpa Nikaya. Jesus taught a "hotch potch mixture of Judaism, Brahmanism, and Buddhism."[40] Dharmapala declared that if the Sermon on the Mount was removed from the Bible, biblical religion was about "vengeance without any hope."[41]

Dharmapala found Jesus's ethics "unworkable" and full of "inconceivable ideas" for the followers of Christ to put into practice. One such unpractical idea was found in the story of Jesus urging the rich man to sell everything to follow him. This criticism was based on Dharmapala's procapitalist view rather than the egalitarian message of the parable. Jesus, in Dharmapala's estimation, was a man of limited experience who had no understanding of the suffering caused by war. Dharmapala did not hesitate to point out how different and how reasonable Buddha was in dealing with his devotees and how he offered a "range of human possibilities" for his devotees to uphold. The impression one gets in reading Dharmapala's view of Jesus is that "the life of the Nazarene Jew was not of cosmic usefulness."[42]

Gospel Parables as Unpalatable

Of all the teachings of Jesus, his parables come under the most severe ridicule. In Dharmapala's assessment, the parables about the mustard seed, the sower, and the wheat and the tares were all "absurd."[43] These parables, according to Dharmapala, showed that Jesus was a man of "limited knowledge."[44] He dismisses the parables that had agricultural images as having been told by a person who had no experience of cultivation. He pointed out that the parable of the sower was shot through with ignorance (Mark 4:1–9; Matt. 13:1–9; Luke 8:4–8; Gospel of Thomas 9). His contention was that no one in Asia would go sowing in barren ground. Moreover, no wise farmer would allow both the wheat and tares to grow together.

Besides his accusation that Jesus's parables are illogical, Dharmapala perceives the characters in them as being largely ill mannered and destructive. He finds Matthew's parable of the laborers in the vineyard (Matt. 20:1–20) economically irrational. In this parable, where the householder treats those who went to work at the eleventh hour and those who labored all day as equal and pays them the same amount, Dharmapala's view is that the householder's action goes against all justice. He sarcastically calls the decision of the householder "divine socialism."[45] Dharmapala also demonstrates how the immoral people in some of the parables are paraded as prime representatives of God. A notable case in point is the parable about a king who wishes to settle accounts (Matt. 18:23–34), which starts with an act of mercy and ends in revenge. In this parable, the king pardons a servant who owed him 10,000 talents. But the forgiven servant refuses to show a similar kind of mercy to his fellow debtor and subsequently is severely punished by the king. The message of the parable is that "the heavenly father shall punish those who do not forgive their brethren."[46] The inference is that the king's behavior is an inappropriate model for God. Dharmapala regards the parable of the man who planted a vineyard (Mark 12:1–12; Matt. 21:33–46; Luke 19:12–27, Gospel of Thomas 65) as a story of "utter foolishness." In this parable, every time the owner sends his servants to get some fruits of the vineyard, they are beaten up by the farmers, and finally when he sends his son, he too is killed. This parable, according to Dharmapala, contains two absurdities. One is the unwise action of the owner in sending his son alone, and the other is Jesus's promise that the Gentiles will replace Jews in the Kingdom of Heaven. Such a missiological forehadowing, in Dharmapala's view, further illustrates the limited knowledge of Jesus and the Jewish religious leaders, who failed to recognize that other people also have knowledge of salvation.

Another parable that receives Dharmapala's sharp rebuke is the parable of the ten virgins. He regards the savior's abandoning of the five virgins in this story as an example of the ineffectiveness of the Christian gospel. The very people who needed compassion were let down. He finds similar fault with the teaching of the Bhagavad Gita. He castigates Krishna in the Bhagavad Gita for saving the righteous and destroying the wicked, instead of saving all. His claim is that the Buddha would not have acted in such a mean fashion. Instead of casting the people away, the Buddha would have shown compassion for those wicked and sinful people. Dharmapala is keen to identify and expose the contradictory elements in the parables. In the parable of the talents, a man was punished for his inability to produce wealth, whereas in the case of the parable of the rich man, the rich young man was consigned to hell because of his ability to generate wealth.

Dharmapala's caustic comments on the contents of the Bible, the biblical god, Jesus, and the church, as pointed out earlier, have to be seen against the ferocious missionary preaching and propaganda at that time in Sri Lanka. His work was a counter to certain political and cultural forces. Aided by this cultural pressure, he proceeded to construct a fixed sense of dissimilarity between the West and Asia, Christianity and Buddhism. The result was to make the Christian religion look aged, degenerate, and vindictive, not vigorous, rational, and compassionate, as the missionaries wanted it to be.

Prettifying Buddhism

Against the backdrop of the hostile politics and polemics of the nineteenth- and early twentieth-century colonial context, Dharmapala and the other Buddhist sympathizers and reformers like him projected Buddhism as a scientific faith that championed the cause of rationalism and enlightenment. While scientific discoveries, especially those of Darwin, rattled the basic claims of Christianity and the veracity of the biblical records, Dharmapala was able to present Buddhism as a successful accomplice of science. Just as the Darwinian law of evolution revolutionized the illogical ideas of human beings, so had the teaching of the Buddha twenty-five centuries previously. Dharmapala argued his case thus: "And when Darwin shows us life passing onward and upward through a series of constantly improving forms towards the better and best, each individual starting a new existence with the records of bygone good and evil stamped deep and ineffaceably [with] the old ones, what is this again but Buddhist doctrine of karma and dharma."[47]

Dharmapala further claimed that "the noble eightfold path has in it the essentials of scientific analysis."[48] He reinterpreted some of the trickiest Buddhist doctrines in terms of Western psychology. For instance, the doctrine of rebirth was reconfigured as a mental state in which past lives are manifested as psychological phenomena in one's current life. Semitic religions, in his view, lacked the scientific background or psychology to meet the challenges of science. In promoting Buddhism as a scientific religion, Dharmapala not only countered the scorn and slander of Buddhism by colonialists and missionaries but also demonstrated its noble character and impeccable credentials. It was Buddhism that "moulded the destinies of the Indian nation in its brightest, palmiest and most glorious days."[49]

He portrayed Buddhism as a "new religion that teaches new things which the old god-believers had no conception of." Buddha was seen as the one who taught people to attain salvation without the help of angry, bloodthirsty deities and Buddhism as a religion of "psychological" sophistication and "internal development." In opposition to other faiths that depended on savior figures, Dharmapala promoted an unmediated religion. His contention was that there was no need to seek the help of the gods to get rid of anger, pride, jealousy, ill will, and ignorance, when the gods themselves were involved in and embodied these symptoms. For him, salvation was achievable by doing good deeds, such as abstaining from killing, stealing, indulging in sensual activities, and drinking alcohol. There is no need for a vicarious savior provided good deeds are done. This, according to Dharmapala, resonates with the teaching of Jesus (Matthew 7:21).

Dharmapala also constructed a Buddhism that was a very attractive religion catering to the stresses and strains of individuals rather than as a religion beleaguered with ritual, rules, and institutional influence and power. In his famous speech to the Chicago Parliament of Religion, he told the audience: "The Message of the Buddha that I have to bring to you is free from theology, priestcraft, rituals, ceremonies, dogmas, heavens, hells and other theological shibboleths.

The Buddha taught to the civilized Aryans of India 25 centuries ago a scientific religion containing the highest individualistic altruistic ethics, a philosophy of life built on psychological mysticism and a cosmogony which is in harmony with geology, astronomy, radioactivity and relativity."[50]

Dharmapala relocated authority from institutions to individuals and offered a religion without the burden of doctrinal and ritual trappings. He refashioned Buddhism as the only religion that appealed to enlightened people of all castes and creeds.

He projected a Buddhism as being peaceful and tolerant. While European and Muslim conquerors went about their business of ransacking other peoples' wealth and heritage, Buddhists, in contrast, conquered others with love. Dharmapala claimed that "without the sword in hand, the Bhikkhus by the force of Wisdom and mercy conquered the continent of Asia."[51] These Bhikkhus did not trample on people but morally persuaded them to get rid of their vileness and arrogance.

He presented Buddhism as replenishing the deficiencies found in other religions. For instance, the ethics of the doctrines of Confucius and Lao Tzu did not speak about the welfare of the people of China, but this was "supplied by the Indian Buddhist bhikkus who went to China in the fifth decade of the first century after Christ."[52] He did not provide any evidence for this.

Dharmapala, who was so sweeping in his claim that biblical religion freely borrowed ideas and concepts from the neighboring cultures, was very protective when it came to Buddhism, which was influenced by the Hindu Vedas and the Upanishads and the Kapila Sutras. His assertion was that had the Buddha simply rehashed the "brahmanical dishes," Buddhism would not have become the religion of Ashoka. Buddhism, in his view, was such a vigorous and puritanic faith that people who were effeminate and addicted to sensuality would have found it difficult to "adhere to its virile, purifying ethics."[53]

The reconstructed and elevated Buddhism of Dharmapala resembled that of the pioneering band of Oriental scholars who often postulated the idea that the early textual Buddhism was authentic and pure and that the corrupt, degenerate, and syncretic elements were later accretions. Like the national reformers of the time, Dharmapala's construction of Buddhism was, to borrow the words of Edward Said from a different context, "Romantic and even messianic."[54] For Dharmapala, recovering Buddhism was essentially a redemptive project.

Mahavamsa: A Contentious Reading

While Dharmapala disputes the historical authenticity of the Bible and ridicules its message, he accords a high historical status to the Mahavamsa, a Pali text that goes back to the third century BCE. The Mahavamsa, allegedly written by a Buddhist monk, is a mixture of fact and fantasy. It was turned into an authentic chronicle by Dharmapala. It was he who single-handedly made the Mahavamsa the fundamental text for modern Sinhalese identity. He invoked in particular two narratives from the text that have become the template for Sinhalese nationalism. One was a description of the battle between the Sinhala king Duttugamanu and the Tamil ruler Ellala, a classic clash between two communities. He immortalized Duttugamanu as a righteous king and a national hero who organized a great crusade to liberate Buddhism from foreign rule. Linked to this was the idea of brutal aggression as a way to settle the threat faced by the Sinhalese. Dharmapala called the Ellala-Duttugamanu battle the "first armed conflict." Such a communal reading still has serious ethnic ramifications for communal relations in Sri Lanka. "Let the *'Mahavamsa'* be a guide" was the call of Dharmapala during the colonial days when missionaries predicted that the Buddha would disappear from the island.

Second was the notion that Sri Lanka had a divine destiny as the chosen home of the *dhamma.* The island is entrusted with the historical custodianship of Buddha's teachings, so that the Buddhist dhamma had to be safeguarded even by force. It was Dharmapala who first mooted the idea that the island was exclusively chosen to preserve Buddhism and that it belonged absolutely to the Buddhists. To support such a claim, he cited the words that the Buddha himself was alleged to have spoken on one of his visits to Sri Lanka: "In Lanka O Lord of God, will my religion be established" (Mahavamsa 7:4). However, there is no historical evidence that the Buddha ever left his native India.

Dharmapala's reading of the Mahavamsa is a case of an Oriental reorientalizing the Orient by invoking the past glories of Buddhism and Sinhalese civilization and voicing a longing for the lost wisdom. Such a reading instilled among the Sinhalese a distinctive nationalist characteristic and an almost messianic identity and self-worth in the face of the indignity and constraint endured under British rule and Christian missionary influence.

Racial Slanders

There are racial overtones in Dharmapala's writings. What he expressed freely at that time would certainly land him in trouble with Britain's Race Relations Act (a series of provisions by the United Kingdom's parliament to address racial discrimination) for instigating racial hatred. In his view, the two great gifts to the world by the Semitic and the Anglo-Saxon races are alcoholism and bestiality. He describes the British as having "leprously white skin."[55] The English are "supremely selfish and full of arrogance."[56] They are victims of "thana (desire), and mana (pride)."[57] Dharmapala was relentless in challenging and demolishing the superiority of the English. He did this first by refusing to accept the British as authentic Aryans. He differentiated between two types of Aryan—spiritual and anthropological. The British, in Dharmapala's view, were not Aryans on two counts. First, they did not live in the territory known as Bharatvarsha (an ancient name for India), and second, they did not conform to the sacred law. Therefore, the British were essentially Mlechas (the term used by Brahmanical writers to describe those outside the caste system, Brahmanical rituals, and Sanskrit language). His other way of putting the English in their place was to compare the ancient glories of Sinhalese civilization with those of the English. His intention was to construct an image of the Sinhalese as the legatees of a glorious civilization. He wrote: "What other nation on earth is there which could boast of a history of the island, a history of the great line of kings, a history of religion, a history of sacred architectural shrines, a history of the sacred tree, a history of the sacred relics?" He further reiterated his point thus: "Under the holy influence of the Tathagato's Religion of Righteousness, the people flourished. Kings spent all their wealth in building temples, public baths, *dagobas,* libraries, monasteries, rest houses, hospitals for man and beast, schools, tanks, seven-storied mansions, waterworks, and beautified the city of Anuradhapura, whose fame reached Egypt, Greece, Rome, China, India and other countries."[58]

He missed no opportunity to remind the English that, like them, the Sinhalese were Aryans and that they possessed a long and glorious Buddhist civilization that could match the civilization of Europe.

The implication was that the English should treat the Sinhalese not as upstarts but as a noble race, who practiced a noble religion and had inherited a noble tradition. In place of the imperialist stereotype of the colored man as a heathen savage, Dharmapala reversed the alleged superiority of his adversaries, coming up with his own stereotype of the Englishman as uncouth. His message to the English was that the Semitic god they worshipped would not be able to save them and that their salvation lay in following the teachings of the Buddha.

Anti-Semitic remarks are rife in Dharmapala's writings. He calls the Jews a "race of cut throats."[59] Their savagery was inconceivable as recorded in the books of Exodus, Numbers, Leviticus, Deuteronomy, and Joshua. Jesus was not a pure Jew because he came from David's lineage, which was tainted with mixed blood—David's father Jesse was a half Moabite, and Solomon's mother was a Hittite woman. Jews, for Dharmapala, were essentially a mixed-blood race, the blood of Egyptians, Syrians, Chaldeans, and Hittites running in them. Muslims were also portrayed in an unfavorable light. They were described as "destructive hordes," who fought with "cyclonic fury."[60] Their "fiendish acts" included persecution of Zoroastrians; the annihilation of Christians in Alexandria, Asia Minor, and Turkey; and the destruction of the Alexandrian library. But Dharmapala was a multiracial abuser. He did not spare Africans or the Chinese. He described Africans as "the semisavage half-animal people of Africa."[61] He likened Satan to a Chinaman.

While Dharmapala cast aspersions on other races, he constructed an idealized and romantic picture of Sri Lanka and the Sinhalese. He repeated the endorsement in the book *Geography of Ceylon,* which painted the Sinhalese as "polite, kind to their children and fond of learning." It was Dharmapala who introduced the notion of the Sinhalese as a "superior race,"[62] a "refined people,"[63] a unique race who have no slave blood in them.[64] The Sinhalese were a "pure" and "kind-hearted" people "with noble traditions, a noble literature and a noble religion."[65] Dharmapala perpetuated the idea that the Sinhalese were pure Aryans of pure blood. He cautioned Sinhalese women against cross-breeding with other racial groups of the island. It was the Aryan Sinhalese who had made this island into a paradise before the foreign vandals destroyed its innocence and beauty. The Sinhalese were an independent people for nearly 2,538 years before the island was invaded by the Portuguese, Dutch, English, Muslims, and Tamils. He blamed foreign influences for the decadent state of Sri Lanka. Christianity and polytheism were responsible for introducing vulgar practices including animal killing, stealing, prostitution, licentiousness, lying, and drunkenness. The primeval forests of the island were destroyed by the colonial bureaucrats in order to grow cash-producing tea. In Dharmapala's view, the "sweet, tender, gentle Aryan children of an ancient, historic race were being sacrificed at the altar of the whisky-drinking, beef-eating, belly-god of heathenism." Dharmapala was able to create an imagined Sri Lanka that was "free from foreign influence, untainted by alien customs"; and "with a word of Buddha as their guide," the Sinhalese people were able to "live [a] joyously cheerful life in those bygone days." The message was clear: the dazzling days of Buddhism and the Sinhalese people existed when the island was free of foreigners, invaders, and usurpers.

Dharmapala and His Hermeneutics: Some Reflections

Dharmapala belonged to the group of reactionary Asian intellectuals of the time who were convinced that if Asians upheld fervently the beliefs and practices of their religious traditions, which were presumed to be healthier than those imported from the West, Asia would be powerful again. To Dharmapala, it was a question of recovering the pure message of the Buddha.

Dharmapala's work primarily revolved around three imagined and real enemies: the foreign invaders, ranging from Tamil kings and Muslims to European invaders; Christian missionaries and their imperialistic engagements; and the moral decadence of Christian Europe. All were hell-bent on destroying Buddhism. According to Dharmapala, the two Semitic religions that had emerged from Arabia—Christianity and Islam—were the cause of the retarded state of the larger part of Asia. Islam was responsible for the destruction of Aryan civilization, especially for destroying the beautiful Aryan architecture in India; and Christianity was instrumental in introducing evil practices such as slavery and initiating immoral habits among the suggestible suggestible population of Asia, such as arrack drinking and opium and ganja smoking. As a result, the Sinhalese had lost their "true identity" and had become a "hybrid" race.[66] In the days of the Sinhalese kings, Dharmapala asserted that no alcohol was sold, no slaughtering of animals was permitted, and there was no buying and selling of land, for the people held the land in common.

Dharmapala's severest criticism was reserved for the Christian missionaries, who were variously described as advance agents of the "European trader and whisky dealer."[67] Missionaries, in Dharmapala's estimation, were both political and commercial agents, representing Christian governments, capitalists, and traders. They were portrayed as "great enemies of Buddhism," as their main aim was to "distort and misrepresent the holy teachings of the great Aryan saviour."[68] All that Christian missionaries could offer were "the myths of Canaan and Galilee which had their origin in the backwash of Arabia."[69] The lifestyle of the missionaries, too, came under scrutiny. They were seen as enjoying a high life, which included driving cars, playing tennis, attending parties, and, most significantly, preaching a religion in which they did not believe. The delivery of their message of self-sacrifice to the Buddhist was like, as he sarcastically commented, bringing coals to Newcastle—pointlessly redundant. "In contrast to my wine-drinking, meat-eating and pleasure-loving missionary teachers," Dharmapala remarked, "the Bhikkhus were meek and abstemious. I loved their company and would sit quietly in a corner and listen to their wise discourse, even when it was far above my head." He was equally contemptuous of Christian theologians, whom he described as "half insane," "full of conceit," "rigidly dogmatic," and lacking in "sobriety."[70]

Dharmapala did not totally oppose missionary work. He encouraged a different type of missionary—the type with scientific knowledge who could teach about radioactivity and start technical industries that would be economically beneficial to the local people, rather than missionaries who preach "antiquated theological dogmas" that originated in the muddled heads of medieval priests. The money the missionaries spent on conversion, Dharmapala felt, was a total waste. Instead, he preferred that this money be used for opening technical and scientific colleges where "heathen" boys could learn something practical that could be useful for the community.

Dharmapala's hermeneutical object was blatantly obvious. He wanted to tell the missionaries and reassure his Buddhist audience that the God of the Bible had no special spiritual value for Aryan Buddhists. The deity proclaimed by missionaries "could never win the respect of the thoughtful, cultured races."[71] Christianity as a system was utterly "unsuited to the gentle spirit of the Aryan race."[72] Christianity for him was an "Asiatic and Arabian cult" and did not have any special merit, except for slaves and the starving poor. It was an "Arab religion which had its origin in the back parts of Horeb."[73] Christianity was essentially a religion for "helots and the poorer class of people."[74] For Dharmapala, Christianity was an Asiatic superstition that had been rejected by the civilized races of Asia long ago but enthusiastically embraced later by the "ferocious vandals" of North Germany and since then had became the religion of Europe. Once it had been established in Europe, Christianity lost touch with the poor and became the "religion of the diplomatic politician and the dogmatic ecclesiastic."[75] Modern Christianity was a "mixture of Osirism, Mazdeanism, Babylonian myths, and Buddhist ethics with a tinge of Vedanta."[76] He treated Roman Catholic Christianity as a "kind of rejuvenated Roman Jupiterism." The ceremonial customs observed in the Vatican were a pale imitation of "Oriental barbaric pomp,"[77] and the ceremonies of the Byzantine church were copied from the "Buddhism of Turkestan and Turfan."[78]

Dharmapala routinely made it clear to his readers that it was not Christianity that made Europe great but scientific advancement. He was relentless in showing that it was industrialization that had brought about change in the West. He cites Western authorities to support this claim. One was William Lecky, who, in his *Map of Life*, had shown that it was the strong sense of thriftiness, industriousness, and punctuality that contributed to the advanced state of the West and not Christian influence. The implication of this assertion was that it was not the teaching of Christ that was instrumental in making these countries dominant and influential but scientific know-how and secular values.

Dharmapala was firm in his belief that a religion that did not care for the individual, that preferred prayer to social action, promised life hereafter, and spoke of eternal damnation, was "unsuited for a civilized Aryan community."[79] As far as he was concerned, there was nothing that Aryan Asia could learn from the ethics of Semitic barbarism. He was relentless in restating that Christianity was unsuited to the gentle spirit of the Aryan race. His verdict on the Christian church was devastating: "The history of the church had been one of failure."[80]

For him, the Bible and Christianity had nothing new to teach, they were no longer a reliable source for morals, and as such they had to be rejected. He was persistently posing the following question: "why should the Aryan nations and the Aryanized races of Asia be inflicted with this tribal story of race of cut throats, who were advised to spoil the Egyptians of their gold and silver? . . . What high ethic could the Aryan people learn from this mythical story of tribal god, which knew no other people, except the Hebrew tribe that was in bondage?"[81] With the increasing political power that Europe exercised in Asia, Christianity could become the religion of Asia. His contention was that Asians would not listen to a creed that had "no high ethic or a rational psychology."[82]

Although Dharmapala berated the Jews, he did not hesitate to invoke the image of the suffering Jews to explain the plight of the ordinary Sinhalese under colonial rule. In effect, he transferred the calling of the Jews to the Sinhalese. Like the exiled Jews who were forced live in alien conditions and were ignored by their elite, the Sinhalese had become strangers and foreigners in their own country, neglected both by the British rulers and by the landowning and highly educated Sinhalese upper class. As had been his practice, he picked and mixed verses from the Lamentations of Jeremiah to demonstrate the plight of the Sinhalese: "He hath led me, and brought me into darkness, but not into light" (3:2); "He hath filled me with bitterness, he hath made me drunken with arrack and toddy" (3:15); "You have made us an off-scouring and refuse in the midst of the people" (3:45); "Our inheritance is turned to strangers, our houses to aliens" (5:2); "We have drunken our water for money; our wood is sold unto us" (5:4). These verses suggest that the Sri Lankans were exploited and that their own lands and cash crops were sold back to them by the British. Just as Kumarappa did with the text, Dharmapala recontexualizes Lamentations to suit the Sri Lankans.

It is ironic that Dharmapala, who wanted to treat the Hebrew scriptures selectively, appealed to these Hebrew images of suffering and victimization. In doing so, he was able to claim that the Sinhalese were an innocent people following the divine plan and absolved them of any wrongdoing and claimed a moral high ground.

In contrast to Hindu reformers of the colonial era, such as Swami Vivekananda and Gandhi, who were keen to promote Hinduism as a universal religion worthy to be followed by all peoples of the world, Dharmapala with his aggressive spirituality was trying to fashion a Buddhism that was nationalistic in its outlook and unique to the Sinhalese. For him, Buddhism was essentially an Aryan religion based on Aryan values, proclaimed by an Aryan and practiced by Aryans. As Dharmapala put it, the Buddha "inculcated lessons that are embodied in the principles of the Aryan code of Righteousness."[83] While Hindu reformers were seeking to find points of contact between Hinduism and Christianity to show the resemblances between these two religions, Dharmapala dogmatically claimed that if there were similarities between Buddhism and Christianity, Buddhism was the original source. Unlike other revivalists in the Asian religions who saw all religions as having a common foundation, Dharmapala privileged Buddhism as the supreme religion. He claimed very boldly that the Buddhists had a "spiritual inheritance superior to any other worldly legacy."[84] Only in the Buddha were "the highest ideal of absolute self-sacrifice, loving kindness, [and] charity" found. Buddha's teaching was "more definitive."[85] For Dharmapala, the Buddha dhamma is the "religion of religions."[86] He was categorical in his assertion: "In the Dhamma or Dharma is embodied all that is useful for salvation of all beings."[87] Dharmapala claimed that "the Buddha was requested by Brahma to save the world."[88] The Buddha was the only one who could pay homage to supreme truth (dharma).[89] Dharmapala wrote: "To say that all religions have a common foundation only shows the ignorance of the speaker. The Dharma stands unique on its own basis and it has no connection with the later 'isms' founded by enthusiasts and visionaries.... The Dharma of the Tathagatha, we emphasize, has no relationship with any other existing religion. Dharma alone is supreme to the Buddhist."[90]

Dharmapala's hermeneutical tactics were a reversal of the type of strategy employed by the Western orientalists of the time. Just as orientalists such as Jones and Müller tried to demonstrate how Hinduism had deviated from its original textual purity, Dharmapala was venturing to show Christians how they had diverged from the essence of the teachings of Jesus enshrined in the Gospels. For Dharmapala, such a core message was found in the Sermon on the Mount, which he routinely claimed was largely borrowed from the Buddhist dhamma. Dharmapala provided no evidence for this but asserted that the missionaries who were sent by the emperor Asoka were in the Mediterranean world before the birth of Christ, which must have helped to disseminate Buddhist ideas and doctrines.

His other tactic was to expose the gap between the biblical teaching and practical living of Christians. Like most national reformers of the time, Dharmapala was conversant with the Christian scriptures and doctrines, and he was able to use this knowledge with devastating effect. From a young age, Dharmapala had mastered the intricacies of Christian theology and the central message of the Bible and was well aware of the parallels between Buddha's teaching and that of Jesus. He marshaled this information to heighten the disparity between the textual teaching of Christianity and the actual practice of it on the ground. Dharmapala unashamedly exposed the blatant hypocrisy and the glaring gap between the ethical teaching of the Bible and the everyday lifestyle of missionaries and colonial government officials. In doing so, he was able to provide a catalog of failures to live up to the Christian Gospel. He was able to draw attention to the contradiction between Christian love and the violent slaughter of animals. When in the United States, he declared that the great slaughterhouses of Chicago were a disgrace and that a religion that encouraged such behavior was not worth following. The failure to obey and live by Christian precepts comes out clearly here: "Today England, the US . . . [are] sending shiploads of missionaries to China, Ceylon, India, Japan, Burma to convert both Buddhists and Hindus, backed by the capitalists and gun boats. They do not go obeying the command of Jesus who said, Heal the sick, raise the dead, provide neither gold or silver nor brass in your girdles, neither coats, neither shoes nor yet a staff. Matt. 10.9–11."[91]

Dharmapala's strategy could be called a hermeneutics of equivalent reprisal. It is a tit-for-tat approach, where one weakness is pitted against another. A series of accusations is set in direct opposition or competition. It is reciprocal retaliation. Dharmapala's anti-Christian pronouncements have to be seen against the religious and cultural politics of the time. If the missionaries called a Buddhist priest "brainless dolt,"[92] Dharmapala accused the missionaries who worked in Asia of being "utterly deficient in scientific knowledge"[93] and said that all that they could offer were myths originating from an Arabian cult. Whereas the Bhikkhus were "meek and abstemious," the missionaries were "wine-drinking, meat-eating and pleasure-loving."[94] If

Buddhist morals were found be deficient, Dharmapala provided a long list of moral lapses of Christianity. His list of Christian misdemeanors included the Inquisition, the slave trade, the annihilation of the Tasmanians, the introduction of opium to China, the destruction of the native races of Central America and of the native Americans, and the lynching of "helpless negroes" in the United States. These were the work of the "followers of Christ." If Christians ridiculed the Buddha for not being omniscient, Dharmapala's response was to draw attention to the ineffectiveness of Jehovah. A case in point was that the very God who blessed Adam and Eve failed to protect them from falling into sin. Much of Dharmapala's hermeneutics was argumentative, assertive, dogmatic, and moralizing.

Like Rammohun Roy, J. C. Kumarappa, and Hong Xiuquan, whom we encountered in Chapter 3, Dharmapala envisaged his task as reforming Christianity. His prescription was very simple—eliminate the Hebrew scripture and all those passages in the New Testament that depict Jesus as "quick-tempered and intolerant." He also wanted to discard the miracles that Jesus himself disclaimed as well as the prophetic writings because the law and prophets lost their theological purchase after the arrival of John the Baptist. Dharmapala fashioned himself as a modern-day Paul who wanted to reform Christianity from the outside. What he wanted to preserve in Christianity was the Sermon on the Mount, which had universal application and, more important, was in harmony with the basic teaching of the Buddha. To save Christianity, Dharmapala said he would like to infuse it with "new wine" and "new truth." The momentum for this reformation was provided by Buddhism. The Christianity that Dharmapala wanted to revive was an ascetic form, akin to that preached by the Buddha. Traces of this asceticism—involving renunciation, rejection of wealth, and humility—are found in the Gospels (Mark 6:7–9; Matt. 5:18–21, 18:1–6).

Jesus preached a "doctrine of utter renunciation of all things of this world," but the doctrine was later abandoned under papal authority, which became the "vehicle of ecclesiastical power."[95]

Just as the Western missionaries wanted to civilize the Orient, Dharmapala was on a mission to enlighten the Western "vandals" with Buddhist "truth." He was well aware of the ancient richness of his faith and its potential transnational reach. The hope of the Westerners depended on their accepting the Asiatic creed—the gospel of love and wisdom preached by the Buddha. Dharmapala was anticipating a time when Europe would listen to the message of the Buddha. He was resolute in his belief that the survival and relevance of Christianity lay primarily in recovering the essential principles of Buddhism—self-reliance, renunciation of sensual passions, freedom from dogmas, and good deeds. To this one could add "no priestcraft, materialism, or sheep theology."

Like the Indian reformers at that time, Dharmapala, too, was involved in resisting colonialism. The motive for this resistance was not simply political or economic but largely religious. For him, colonialism had to be resisted because it threatened the very existence and continuance of Buddhism and the traditional Sinhalese way of life. As he melodramatically put it, without Buddhism, death was preferable.

Finally, Dharmapala's hermeneutics is a prime example of how natives themselves not only are quite capable of representing themselves but also are equally competent in producing racist, jingoistic, colonialist, nativist, and supremacist theologies. His vehement sentiments were directed not only toward the Christian West but also unleashed toward his own indigenous neighbors, in this case Tamils and Muslims. His representation of the Bible and the Buddha and his rereading of the Buddhist text, the Mahavamsa, stand out as one of those dazzling moments of resistance in colonial history where the native elites who had gone through Western/Christian schools demonstrate the superiority of their cultural heritage through recourse to the standard categories of the colonizer. His was a prime example of a colonial who, in the process of resisting, absorbs the colonial ideology and in turn recolonizes his own marginalized neighbors and becomes part of the colonial project and ideology. A mimetic resistance can end up not only mimicking the empire but becoming a menace to indigenous minorities.

5   Paul the Roman in Asia

Paul was in a way a typical product of the empire. He was born to immigrant parents from Judea who settled in Tarsus, a city colonized by Seleucid and Roman rulers. A Pharisee, at the same time he received his education in the language of the imperialist. He acquired Roman citizenship. How he managed this is a mystery. He may have inherited it from his father or his grandfather for the distinguished services one of them must have rendered to the state. Paul traveled throughout the Roman empire preaching a new message—the Christ crucified—an amalgam that drew on the spiritual wealth of two contrasting cultures of the time—Hebrew and Hellenic. He offered this message to both Jews and Gentiles or to anyone who cared to listen to him.

Paul is held in high esteem by his Western admirers. The highest accolade came from William M. Ramsay (1851–1939), an archaeologist and New Testament scholar, who set the tone for this towering admiration: "He is the most powerful, the most tremendous, the most creative and epoch-making fact in the life of mankind. Human history culminates with him, and takes a new start from him."[1] Paul's great achievement in the eyes of Euro-American scholars is that he turned Christianity, which was essentially a West Asian religion, into a Western one. The Christian faith, which originated in West Asia, moved with Paul through Asia Minor to Greece and Rome and, in course of time, to the rest of Europe and America.

In Western hermeneutics, there are conflicting pictures regarding Paul's ability as a theologian and his legacy to Western theology. On the one hand, he is seen as an honorary European who possessed the logic of a European mind. For instance, when comparing John and Paul, John Robertson (1782–1868), minister of Glasgow Cathedral, pointed out that the two men differed widely in the way they thought and articulated theological matters. The issues that were prominent in John's writings, such as the Incarnation, the relation between the Father and the Son, and the mysteries of the Divine Being, were the invention of the "speculative" thinking of the Oriental churches, whereas Paul's theological interests, such as election, grace, and faith, were the product of a "logical mind of the West." Furthermore, it was Paul who provided the materials for the great battles of Western theology. Robertson's conclusion is that Paul "in a way is the representative" of the West and that the "theology of Western Europe is chiefly derived from the epistles of Paul."[2] W. M. Ramsay held similar views. When comparing Paul and John, he wrote that "to us in the West it is sometimes necessary to read Paul in order to understand John; often Paul comes nearer to our way of thought than John."[3] Paul has the image of a serious theologian who transformed a village faith full of stories and parables into an urban faith, one that was philosophically sophisticated. In Matthew Arnold's (1822–1888) words, it was Paul who turned the "religion of the heart into theories of the head about election and justification."[4] Arnold blamed the Puritans and the nonconformists for reading Paul's "Eastern language" literally and extracting theological tenets that emphasized feelings and sentiments. Even when Paul expressed himself emotionally or "oriently," as Arnold put it, Arnold defended the apostle by saying that the "fault is not with him if he is misunderstood, but with the prosaic and unintelligent Western readers who have not enough tact for style to comprehend his mode of expression."[5]

Along with the idea of a systematic thinker, Paul is also hailed as a European hero who transformed the "primitive Judaic Church into the church of the Roman world" and far beyond it. This was attributed to his "extraordinary versatility and adaptability."[6] He was also applauded for rescuing Judaism from its burdensome laws.

On the other hand, in some Western circles, Paul is seen not as a serious and revered Western theological thinker but as an Oriental with intuitive religious feelings. He is seen as, at best, a synthesizer who borrowed from Jewish apocalyptic thinking and applied this to Jesus. His famous doctrine of justification was an amalgam of many things. Basically, it was a "popular-picture world." It was "one note, which, along with many others—redemption, adoption, etc.—is harmonized in the one chord that testifies to salvation."[7] The image of Paul as a "cosmopolitan Greek of the Roman empire" also came under scrutiny. W. Wrede argued that we should not assume that Paul came under the influence of Greek culture and that even if he did, it would have been an indirect influence. Wrede wrote that there was a definite atmosphere in houses in the Jewish quarter of great cities that "denied admittance to the Hellenism which breathed around them."[8] Wrede even questioned whether theology was the right word to use for the writings of Paul. His style of thinking was "fragmentary,"[9] and his leading thoughts were full of "contradictions."[10] All those rich Pauline phrases such as "power of Christ," "riches of Christ," "blessing of Christ," and "fullness of Christ" in Adolf Deissmann's estimation were not "dogmatical but poetical"[11] expressions of religious experience. Deissmann accused Western scholars of uprooting Paul from his "antique Oriental world" and transplanting him "into the modern Occidental world."[12] Deissmann claimed that Paul did not coin these sophisticated phrases for the benefit of the universities of the nineteenth or twentieth century. They came out of Paul's practical understanding of religion. Phrased in more practical terms, Christ meant more to Paul "than Christology, God more than the doctrine of God."[13] Paul did not work out a "complicated dogmatic system" to show how salvation was brought about by the grace of God but expressed it like an Oriental storyteller in the "fullness of similes."[14]

This Paul was an Eastern mystic with religious inclinations rather than an "ethical theorist."[15] He was essentially more a "man of prayer, a witness, a confessor and a prophet, than a learned exegete and close thinking scholastic."[16] His mission was, as Deissmann put it, "the mission of an artisan, not the mission of a scholar."[17] His main contribution, according to Deissmann, was that he made the Gospel intelligible to so many because he expressed it in popular colloquial language. Paul would not have found open access to the Hellenized world had he not "spoken to Hellenized men in the Hellenistic popular language."[18] A similar view was taken by Wrede, who claimed that Paul's letters were not "literary productions" but "purely personal utterances, intended for small circles."[19] Basically, his letters were "popular in tone."[20]

In this view, Paul's world was the world of the wisdom of Oriental rabbis and visionary speculators. His zeal, his fanaticism, and his ambition to outshine his contemporaries were deemed to be Oriental characteristics. His principal ideas, on guilt, remorse, death, and a remote and vengeful God, were seen as further Oriental traits. Suzanne Marchand has drawn attention to the fierce battles in nineteenth-century Germany over the influences, background, origins, and meaning of Paul's world, which had come to be seen less as Greek or Christian than as Gnostic, "mystical," "syncretic," or, in short, "Oriental."[21] The idea here was to contrast "the syncretic, Oriental intellectual Paul" with "the plain-spoken, universal ethicist Jesus."[22]

Besides this contradictory image, there is also a notion that Paul was an active proponent of Roman and Western civilization. He played an energetic role in what Ramsay called "romanizing an oriental land."[23] Ramsay claimed that "Paul's career cannot be properly understood, unless his Roman point of view and his imperial statesmanship is fully taken into account."[24] In his several works on Paul, Ramsay reconfigured Paul as an advocate of Roman civilization and a campaigner for the Christian mission battling against barbarians and lesser races. In Galatia, Paul was seen as challenging his audience to choose between the progress of Rome and the backwardness of the Orient. The Galatians were trapped in a classic predicament—either they continued with their benumbing and degrading Oriental superstition, with its priesthood and temples, or they chose the new life of progress, freedom, and intellectual advancement provided by Rome and Western civilization. In this march toward progress, Ramsay reminded his readers that "the influence of the new religion of Christ" offered by Paul was, "necessarily and inevitably, on the side of Graeco-Roman education and order, and that it proved far more powerful than either Greek or Roman government."[25] In other words, Paul was a "Western warrior" (in Brigitte Kahl's phrase) who concurrently championed the cause of both Western civilization and Christianity.[26] Just like the Roman empire, which was able to subjugate weaker nations, Paul was able to overcome the inferior religions of Asia and the morally decadent Jews of the Diaspora with his new religion of Christ.

Paul's place in Asian biblical hermeneutics is also an ambiguous one. His attitude toward Asia does not help. There was a reluctance on his part to engage with Asia. The great Oriental cities were hostile to Paul, so much so that he himself said, "concerning our affliction which befell in Asia, that we were weighed down exceedingly, beyond our power, insomuch that we despaired even of life" (2 Cor. 1:8). There were two opportunities of an Asian engagement, both missed. In 48 CE he was in Antioch in Pisidia, and had he turned westward, he would have reached the Lycus Valley and Ephesus. Instead he turned east, which took him to the Lycaonian towns. The second was the occasion when he was whisked away (presumably by the Holy Spirit) to the southern Greek towns of Macedonia and Achia, so that Asia had to wait.

What this chapter aims to do is to explore the ambiguous place accorded to Paul in Asian Christian thinking. It tracks the various ways in which Paul has been used, abused, embraced, and rejected by Asian Christian interpreters, missionaries, and orientalists. The chapter hopes to show how he was perceived both as a lackey of colonialism and as a companion in the struggle of Asian Christians against dogmatic forms of Christianity introduced by missionaries. The chapter also brings to the fore the troubled relationship of Asian women with Paul. The chapter has two additional features: It revisits Paul's complex relationship with the Roman empire, and it offers a critique of his Athenian speech, which has been seen as a model for interfaith relations.

Colonialists and Their Paul

In the colonial context, Paul was seen as an astute missionary strategist whose ideas were valid for modern-day missionary activities. The person who single-handedly advocated this idea was Roland Allen (1868–1947), an Anglican missionary who worked briefly in China. The title of his book, *Missionary Methods: St. Paul's or Ours?*, published at the height of colonialism, encapsulates the book's basic message. Allen's main thesis was that the missionary methods of Paul were not something that belonged to a bygone era but rather were applicable to missionary endeavors in a colonial context. Allen, in the preface to the second edition of the book, stated that the study of Paul's missionary methods and principles had convinced him that they had solutions to "most of our present day difficulties" and he believed that missionaries had "still much to learn from [Paul's] example."[27] Toward the end of the work, Allen poignantly wrote that "at any rate this much is certain, that the Apostle's methods succeeded exactly where ours have failed."[28] In the words of Bernard Lucas, a Congregational missionary who worked in India, Paul's "broad-minded tolerance and large-hearted sympathy are great object-lessons for the Indian missionary."[29]

Paul was invoked during the colonial period in a number of ways to service the missionary task. What he said in connection with the various heresies and philosophical systems of the Greeks and Romans of his time were now transferred and applied to the various sacred texts the missionaries confronted every day in Asia. Max Müller urged the missionaries to follow the advice of Paul to the Thessalonian Christians—"Prove all things; hold fast that which is good" (1 Thess. 5:21)—before they came to any conclusions about the religious practices of Indians. In the Thessalonian context, Paul counseled his readers not to make assumptions in advance and not to despise all the manifestations of the spiritual gifts and words of prophets prevalent among the believers, but he did not provide his readers with criteria to judge them. Paul's suggestion, made to solve an internal problem among the believers, was employed by Müller to urge missionaries not to prejudge the various religious texts they encountered, but to study the Koran of the Mohammedans, the Zend Avesta of the Parsees, the Vedas of the Brahmins, the Tripitaka of the Buddhists, the Sutras of the Jains, the Ch'un-ts'ew of the Confucians, and the Tao Te Ching of the Taoists. The technical term Paul used, "prove/test," came from the banking world of the Near East,[30] where an observant money changer discriminated between which currency was valid and which was a forgery. The implication was that the missionaries should be like astute money changers and test and verify various Indian religious practices and sacred writings before discarding them. In practical terms, it meant that in the open market of various religious ideas, one should scrutinize the genuine and the fake before rightly rejecting any.

Paul as Colonial and Postcolonial Practical Guide

Paul and his epistles were presented by some missionary commentators as offering sound advice to the newly converted. Some of the problems and difficulties that confronted Christians in India were seen as similar to those Paul dealt with in his epistles. In the Indian Church Commentaries, a series produced during the colonial period, easy parallels are drawn between the complications and troubles found in the churches described in the Pauline epistles and in the current churches in India. These commentaries made a case for Paul and his epistles offering a practical guide to the newly converted. As one commentator suggested, there may have been other epistles "of greater use in the explanation of Christianity to heathens," but as far as addressing the day-to-day practical questions of the newly converted,

Paul's writings took a "leading place among the writings of the New Testament."[31] What distinguished Paul was that he addressed both the age-old concerns of non-Christian Indians and the contemporary questions faced by the Indian converts. Paul in his letters was seen as wrestling with issues that had long preoccupied India, such as "the significance of suffering, the relation between the spiritual and the material, between God and men, and the place and character of asceticism."[32] At the same time, Paul addressed some of the questions that the new adherents faced, such as regarding interreligious marriage, sharing food offered to other gods, excommunication, litigation, the position of women, and dealing with them in a Christian manner. Whereas Paul's letters were seen as offering solutions to "daily difficulties and problems,"[33] by contrast the Hindu scriptures were dismissed as "philosophical disquisitions on the meaning of life," containing "ritual directions" and "hymns which wrestle with the mystery of external nature," which had "little relation to the ordinary life."[34]

Enlisting Paul's writings to solve problems was a practice that continued in some commentaries written in independent India. One such series was included in the "Christian Students' Library." In his commentary on Romans, W. B. Harris provides guidelines for how to deal with the threatening emergence of renascent Hinduism and Islamic fundamentalism in post- Independence India. He advises his readers to take note not only of ancient Hinduism but also of the new Hinduism that had been reinvigorated by Swami Vivekandana, activated by Gandhi, and given a scholarly boost by Radhakrishnan. "This modern Hinduism," Harris points out, "is the main driving force behind the vigorous life of independent India, with its five-year plans, its concern for social service, its efforts for the peace of the world, its Sarvodaya movement aimed at establishment of a 'classless, casteless, and conflictless society.'"[35] Harris finds a "radical unsatis-factoriness" in this new-look Hinduism because it desperately recy-cles worn-out ideas from the teaching of the old Vedanta—including a god who is impersonal, truth that is unknowable, and salvation that is individualistic. More specifically, the newly interpreted Hinduism lacks a "sense of sin."[36] In order to preach the Christian message of forgiveness and salvation, Harris proposes that the idea of sin has to be introduced to Hindus for the sake of their salvation. He informs his readers that Paul's message that all have sinned and are in need of salvation, a message "contained in *Romans,* has to be proclaimed to the Hindu."[37] What Harris tries to do is to inculcate a sense of sin and guilt among people whose spiritual aspirations are not determined by such Christian concepts.

As regards Islam, Harris concedes that the letter to the Romans offers some common starting points that are familiar to a Muslim, such as submission (Rom. 10:2), the idea of slaves of God (6:22), and predestination and election (8:16). But there are significant theological schema at "the heart of *Romans*" that need to be interpreted to Muslims—for example, the sinful status of human beings and the need for a redeemer, the unity and the sovereignty of God, and the work of the Holy Spirit.[38] Not only Paul's message but Paul himself was presented as an "exemplar of his teaching." T. Walker, who worked among the "low caste" Nadars as a missionary of the Church Missionary Society in Tirunelveli, South India, made use of the ex-ample of Paul to simultaneously boost the confidence of members of the low castes and denigrate the high castes. To achieve this, Walker situated Paul within the Indian caste system and presented him as a subverter of the system from within. In his commentary on Philip-pians, Walker writes: "to use Indian language, [Paul] was born and bred in the very highest caste, and in one of the noblest gotras of that caste."[39] To strengthen his case further, Walker comments that Paul was a scion not only of the lordly caste of Israel but also of one of the most notable subsections of that caste—the tribe of Benjamin. Walker goes on to write that Paul, who "held by birth and education, a position of influence and social superiority,"[40] gave up his old "pride and pedigree" and became a bond slave of the Lord. As a result, he abandoned everything he had once held dear in his caste, including scrupulous observation of his caste customs: "But what things were gain to me, those I counted loss for Christ" (Phil. 3:7). Anyone who is familiar with the Indian caste system will know that there are two deeply buried subtexts that Walker would like to convey—one for the high caste and another for the low caste. The indirect message to the high caste, especially to Brahmins, was that there was no point in holding on to the age-old ceremonial purities and caste privileges, but that, like Paul, they should give all this up and embrace the new faith. The challenge Walker posed to his readers was this: "Are we, in India, as ready as was the Apostle Paul to write loss over all that we used to prize as birth-status and caste advantages? Why cling to the titles and customs of caste, when Christ presents Himself to us as our 'all in all'?"[41] At the same time, Walker assured the lowly placed Nadars that "humble-minded believers are the real aristocracy in God's sight, and the proud and high-minded have a low place in His regard."[42] In spite of all Paul's privileges and advantages, he was a person who practiced what he preached—a caste warrior who rebelled against his caste and the system it spawned. Walker's message was unambiguous— Indians should follow the example of Paul and abandon caste pride and self-importance.

During the colonial period, some missionaries portrayed Paul as an ideal imperial hero, a loyal, nonpolitical citizen of the empire, one to be emulated. Bernard Lucas, one of those who was instrumental in founding the United Theological College in Bangalore, encouraged both missionaries and Indians to look up to Paul and learn his lessons. He cast Paul as a person who gave birth to a Christian imperialism. In his view, Paul as a Roman citizen was "deeply sensitive to the Roman imperial ideal." Christianity presented a "grander and wider scope for the development to that ideal" than the political systems of the day offered, and Paul dedicated his life to the "realization of Christian imperialism to which his genius gave birth."[43] Paul's missionary propaganda was influenced by the Roman imperial vision, and as such he "never came into conflict with it." Lucas's Paul was a highly depoliticized person because the "higher politics of the kingdom of heaven" absorbed his energy. It was not his political commitments but his Christian imperialism that clashed sharply with the religious exclusivism of Judaism, and his defense of Christianity had "untold value to the church." Lucas reminded his follow missionaries that there was "an imperial ideal working itself out in India in the twentieth century, to which the English missionary needed to be as sensitive as the Roman Citizen was to the Roman ideal."[44] Lucas ended his book *The Empire of Christ* with these soaring words: "The bondage of Western dogma may be as injurious to the Eastern Church, as the bondage of Judaism was seen to be to the Gentile Church of the Apostle's day. The breaking of caste may be regarded as of as much importance as abstinence from meats offered to idols. In dealing with the nations which make up the Indian Empire today, we need the Apostle's consummate statesmanship, his large-hearted sympathy, and his wide tolerance, for we are heirs with him of the same imperial ideal."[45]

Another missionary, Walter Kelly Firminger, who worked in Calcutta, made the case for Paul as a person who worked along the lines of Roman imperial policy, and he urged his compatriots "to exploit, in Christ's behalf, the benefits of all that Rome stood for as a civilizing agency."[46]

THE COLONIZED AND THEIR PAUL

While some missionaries and colonialists enlisted Paul for their cause, the colonized had other ideas about him. J. C. Kumarappa, an Indian Christian who joined Gandhi's freedom movement, found Paul unhelpful, especially in India's struggle against the British. For Kumarappa, Paul was a person who was steeped in Western tradition and "whose acquaintance with the Aristotelian doctrine of subordination of the individual to the state" could not carry much weight in colonial India. Paul's reasoning in Romans 13—"For there is no power but of God: the powers that be are ordained of God"— Kumarappa dismissed as "weak." He posed the question, "if this sweeping statement were to be accepted without any qualification should we not be 'kicking against the pricks' by waging war on Hitler and Mussolini? Who wields greater power than these dictators?"[47] Paul was a man led to see the Roman authorities as ordained by God. Writing at a time of civil disobedience in India, Kumarappa found Paul falling into line with the religious or political powers of the day, whereas Jesus's life was "a continuous fight against usurpation and unreasoning authoritarian rule."[48] Kumarappa was suspicious of Paul's assertion of Roman citizenship. Paul's appeal to Caesar was a ploy to avoid being tried by the Jewish authorities (Acts 25:11). Although Paul rebelled against these authorities, in Kumarappa's eyes he remained a religious conservative because he continued to obey the Jewish ritual practices of his day—for example, circumcising Timothy.

Kumarappa claimed to see a number of similar characteristics in both Paul and Indian Christians as he perceived them. Both were proud to be part of the empire, were thoroughly denationalized in their manners and customs, and were brought up in "a tradition of loyalty to a foreign empire."[49] He also warned Indians to be careful about distinguishing between Paul's private opinion and what Paul pronounced as the commandment of God. The demarcation between these two positions was blurred, and one had to guard against giving precedence to "the commandment of men" over "a divine one."[50] Kumarappa attributed the origins of the missionary movement to Paul, "the child of imperial Rome and not to Jesus the Nazarene."[51] It was the literal reading of Paul that persuaded missionaries to reach out to far-flung nations, whereas Jesus's command was to go the "lost sheep of the house of Israel." Kumarappa often paraphrased biblical verses, as he did of Jesus sending off the disciples: "Go not to the distant parts of the world to those professing other religion, but go rather to your own neighbours and teach them the right path."[52] The message to the missionaries was clear—take care of your own "natives" and do not interfere with the lost souls of faraway lands.

Direct Experience, Not External Verification

For early converts, Paul acted as an important ally in their confrontations with missionaries. For these newly converted Asian Christians who were suffocating under various Western doctrinal and denominational impositions and who preferred to opt for the path of direct experience of the risen Christ as sufficient for their faith, Paul offered an attractive alternative route. When missionaries persisted with the idea of mediating the knowledge of God through scriptures, sacraments, or institutionalized forms of Western Christianity, the Pauline notion of direct, personal knowledge and experience of God without any intervening intermediaries proved to be attractive to these Asian Christians. For such strong individual Asian Christians, Paul provided both legitimation of their work and ministry and, more pertinently, independence from mission agencies. The Japanese convert Kanzō Uchimura (1861–1930) found Paul's example of the spiritual experience of the risen Christ more essential to his faith than adherence to any formalized structure of Christianity, and this was seen as more appealing in the Japanese context. Uchimura reckoned that such an idea of Christianity as less formal and as essentially spiritual fitted in with the "Japanese or rather samurai frame of mind." As supportive evidence, Uchimura summoned the words of Paul: "But God hath revealed them unto us by his Spirit: for the Spirit searcheth all things, yea, the deep things of God. For what man knoweth the things of a man, save the spirit of man which is in him? even so the things of God knoweth no man, but the Spirit of God. Now we have received, not the spirit of the world, but the spirit which is of God; that we might know the things that are freely given to us of God" (1 Cor. 2:10–12). For Uchimura, all forms of Christianity, whether ritual, doctrinal, or denominational, were "positive hindrances," including that of the historical Jesus, whom Paul himself found of no great theological value. Uchimura was convinced that God was "known through the spirit and by the spirit, without forms, without rites, without dogmas, without instituted churches." For Uchimura, Paul was a "visionary" and a "lawless destructive man" because he seemed to have "disregarded forms!"[53]

Similarly, charismatic individuals such as Kawai Shinsui (1867–1962), the founder of Christ Heart Church in Japan, utilized the Pauline experience of direct encounter with the risen Christ to break with the mission churches and, in doing so, endeavored to provide a strong indigenous leadership. True, Paul was not one of the twelve and part of the original band of disciples, but what made him special according to Kawai was Paul's direct experience of God. Kawai, who initially regarded the institutionalized churches as "terrestrial paradises," discovered, after reading the life story of Paul, how Paul's "close communion with God" was more critical to the apostle's life and ministry than any allegiance to denominational control. Kawai, who had a series of revelatory experiences on various mountains including Mount Yatsugate, Mount Komagatake, and especially Mount Fuji, during one of which he claimed to hear the voice of God, wrote in his spiritual autobiography: "As Jehovah appeared to Moses in thunder in Mt. Sinai, and as Christ called Paul in lightning in the neighbourhood of Damascus, God renewed all things in me through sacred mount Fuji."[54] For Kawai Shinsui, the core of the Christian faith was found in Paul's letter to the Galatians, where he talked about the importance of the unmediated revelation of God. Kawai saw a similar dynamic being played out between Paul's link with the Jerusalem church and Kawai's own church vis-à-vis himself and the Western mission churches. More pertinently, the spiritual Christ whom Kawai encountered was not the Christ of Peter, James, John, and Paul, as conveyed by the West, and restricted to Semitic ideas, but a multicultural Christ who embodied the minds of the Buddha and Confucius.

At a time when missionaries emphasized that Indian Christians should "accept the faith from the Church and verify it in experience."[55] Paul provided an alternative model. Pandippedi Chenchiah (1886–1959) challenged the dominant ecclesiastical notion that "Jesus rules through the church, contacts through the sacraments." For Chenchiah, the sacraments, the church, and the Bible were all "secondary" or "indirect" instruments, and, more crucially, through these channels the "direct knowledge" of Jesus was not possible. Chenchiah taunted the missionaries with two questions. One was, "if God speaks to us today, why hear his words through a book written about 20 centuries ago?"[56] The other was, "if [Jesus] appeared to St. Paul, why not to you and me? Why do churches and books intervene and bring Him to us like water from a distant fountain?"[57] In Chenchia's attempt to free himself from the clutches of the church and its teaching, Paul's assertion of an unmediated relationship between the faithful and the divine provided Chenchiah with a convenient clue to challenging the missionaries in three ways. First, Paul did not rely on or receive his faith from the Jerusalem church, and there was no record of his beliefs and experience being authenticated by the apostles at Jerusalem: "Far from doing so, he traces his salvation to direct contact with the historic Jesus appearing to him. He traces his gospel not to the Church but to the vision. He goes further, and says he received even the description of the institution of the Lord's Supper from Jesus."[58] Second, the Pauline statement that Jesus as a historical person is no longer with us was a sure signal that "the direct contact with the risen Lord is possible and we do not travel back to the days of his flesh to contact him."[59] Third, there is Paul's assertion of the mystical union of the body and the risen Christ. His claim that through faith one shares in the crucifixion and resurrection of Christ, that the old body is no more, and that the living Christ is present in a believer further reinforces the idea that one need not subject one's beliefs and experience to the church's scrutiny. Chenchiah was even willing to disregard the very apostle who provided him with the example to resist the church's authority. If Paul's theology proved to be a hindrance, Chenchiah teased, "why should a Hindu understand complicated Pauline theology to follow Jesus?"[60]

What in effect Uchimura, Kawai, and Chenchiah did was to challenge the dominant Protestant view that God's revelation came through the prophets, Jesus, and the apostles and that this route of revelation was completed with the canonization of the Scriptures. These three interpreters made it clear that revelation is an ongoing process and God continues to reveal deeper truths to those who are open to listen, hear, and act.

The Apostle as a Samurai

In the Japanese context, where the samurai or warrior-class ethic dominates, Paul has been seen as a genuine samurai who embodied the Bushido values. In Uchimura's view, Paul as a "disciple of Jesus Christ was a true Samurai, the very embodiment of Bushido." Uchimura saw parallels between Paul and the Japanese samurai. Both were loyal to their master, both hated money, and both viewed commercialism with suspicion. More important, both preferred death to dishonor: "for it were better for me to die, than that any man should make my glorying void" (1 Cor. 9:15). Uchimura claimed that because he was "independent, money-hating, [and] loyal, . . . Paul was a type of the old Samurai, not to be found among modern Christians, both in America and Europe, and alas also in Samurai's Japan."[61] Uchimura felt that, though Bushido was the "finest product of Japan" as an ethical system, on its own it would not save Japan. Rather, "Christianity grafted on Bushido will be the finest product of the world," and this hybridized version of Christianity had the capacity not only to save Japan but also the world: "It will save, not only Japan, but the whole world. Now that Christianity is dying in Europe, and America by its materialism cannot revive it, God is calling upon Japan to contribute its best to His service. . . . For twenty centuries God has been perfecting Bushido with this very moment in view. Christianity grafted upon Bushido will yet save the world."[62] It should be noted, however, that the high-culture image of a samurai may not have great appeal to those Japanese Burakumins who are relegated to the margins of society.

Paul as Cultural Ally

Paul provides easy ammunition for those who wanted to oppose indigenous religious customs. One of these customs that the missionaries opposed was Chinese ancestral worship. Missionaries found that this ancient habit was based on filial pietism and that the Chinese were inadvertently offering food to idols rather than worshiping the true God. For missionaries, the act was essentially idolatry. Khiok-Khng Yeo, a Chinese, reread Paul's handling of idol meat in 1 Corinthians 8 with a view to providing some hermeneutical support for Chinese Christians who wanted to hold on to both their Chinese and their Christian identities. Yeo's contention was that using imperatives as divinely ordained was not going to bring the Chinese people closer to the Christian God. Using the rhetorical method, he found, first, that Paul did not prohibit a total ban on idol-meat eating. Such a prohibition would contradict the nature of the gospel Paul preached. Second, Yeo argued that any prohibition should be informed by proper knowledge of the custom or rite practiced. The Corinthian passage clearly shows that Paul was familiar with the arguments of the idol-meat eaters. Third, Paul showed pastoral sensitivity to both the strong and the weak. He urged the "strong" to be less overbearing and the "weak" to be more eloquent. Finally, Paul was more concerned with the interpretative process than with providing a decisive answer. Yeo concluded that Paul's theology and rhetoric suggest that all faith communities can enter into dialogue where "the uniqueness of each is differentiated, affirmed, and esteemed, while the commonalities of all are shared, identified, and celebrated."[63]

Paul and Asian Women

What Gordon Zerbe, the Canadian biblical scholar who worked in the Philippines, said about Filipino women could well have been said about other Asian women theologians—they have politely avoided Paul.[64] Like their male counterparts, Asian women seem to have been drawn to Jesus and to the Gospel writers rather than to Paul. Their major monographic works concentrate on the Gospels. While Yamaguchi focuses on Martha and Mary in John's Gospel, Kinukawa and Seong See Kim[65] identify leadership roles afforded to women in Mark's Gospel and demonstrate how this kind of alternative discipleship has the potential to empower contemporary Christian women.

Generally, the work on Paul by Asian women centers around the patriarchal nature of Paul's thinking, or deals with the liberatory or oppressive messages present in Paul's letters. The tendency in these works is to simultaneously rehabilitate and disparage Paul. The argument goes like this: Paul by nature is not antifemale. He moved with a number of women, showing especially his coworkers and women missionaries respect, trust, admiration, and affection. He even treated them as equals. However, he was not entirely free from the cultural world he inhabited and at times he betrayed patriarchal tendencies. This is explained away as influenced by his rabbinical training or by the compromises that Christian communities had to make living among citizens of the Roman world. Although the Korean feminist biblical scholar Hyunju Bae typifies such an approach, her writings are slightly different from the others in three respects.[66]

First, she tries to identify the historical Paul, which no other Asian interpreters have ever attempted; second, she provides the rationale for the hard-line thinking of the Deutero-Paulinists; and third, she works from a larger hermeneutical base that goes beyond the canonical texts and includes the Acts of Paul and Thecla. She distinguishes between a historical and a canonical Paul and finds the historical Paul an ambivalent figure. He had a radical streak that made him take an anti-Roman stance. He honored and respected women and offered them a critical role in the Pauline churches. But Bae finds Paul's anti-imperial posture and his egalitarian attitude toward women not radical enough. She laments that his message was limiting as well as liberating. The historical Paul is full of "ambiguities and ambivalences," but there is a vastly different historical Paul who had a courteous and companionable relationship with women colleagues. This discrepancy was later exploited differently by the heirs of Paul. The Pastoral epistles and the Acts of Paul and Thecla came up with diametrically opposed solutions to the ambiguities in Paul's thinking. The writers of the pastorals toed the line of conservatism and distanced themselves from Paul's teaching on women's right to pray and prophesy, whereas the Acts of Paul and Thecla incorporated such radical elements as Paul's encouragement for women to take up celibacy, his amiable friendship with women, and his opposition to gender restriction, which no longer had purchase in the new life offered by Christ.

To her credit, Bae does not sanitize Paul of his troubling views on women but declares that she continues to be inspired by his liberatory vision, while also posing critical considerations: "However, we also need to acknowledge that although the historical Paul was not a male chauvinist who would reject any meaningful relationship with women, his symbolic universe and discourse were not free from deep-seated androcentrism, contradictions, and ambivalence towards women and the feminine gender. Paul's ambivalence creates the ambivalence of Asian feminist Christian readers of his letters."[67]

One of her conclusions—that Christian churches have unashamedly drawn authority from Paul to marginalize and stigmatize women—would likely gain almost unanimous approval from fellow feminists: "Under the name of Paul, women's lives are still restricted and adversely affected in many Christian denominations of Asia."[68]

One interpreter who found Paul's teaching on women not good enough and rejected it outright was not an Asian female theologian but an Asian male. This was Kumarappa, who questioned the applicability of Paul's directives, which were constrained by Paul's cultural background and theological upbringing. Kumarappa attributed Paul's regressive attitude toward women to his early training as an orthodox Pharisee, which would have prevented him from questioning women's subservience, the roots of which lay in the curse of God on Eve. It was the Jewish influence in his early life that prompted Paul to instruct women that they should cover their heads. Kumarappa argued that Paul's instruction on women was given 2,000 years before to "peculiarly situated congregations"[69] and that he does not have the final say.

Multifaith Muddle at Mars Hill

Those who are engaged in interfaith dialogue appeal to Paul's speech on Mars Hill as a model for dealing with people of other faiths. His speech, in Lucas's estimation, made him a "missionary to pure gentiles."[70] Adolf Deissmann called it "a manifesto of worldwide importance in the history of religions and of religion."[71] Max Müller equated this speech to that of Krishna in the Bhagavad Gita, thus implicitly elevating Paul's address to a divine status: "It always struck me as a wonderful guess at the Divine, when in the Bhagavadgita the Supreme Spirit is made to say: 'Even those who worship idols, worship me.' St. Paul's 'Unknown God' springs from the same source."[72] According to Walter Kelly Firminger, a contributor to the Indian Church Commentaries, the great achievement of Paul's speech was that it did not present any doctrines that seemed strange or revolutionary to his hearers, instead expressing what they "long felt to be the desire of their own hearts."[73]

Paul was credited with proclaiming boldly "what ye therefore worship in ignorance I set forth unto you." What was this mysterious theological truth that was unknown to his hearers and which Paul was supposed to have declared? The various interpreters have their own particular conjectures. The following is a random selection.

For K. M. Banerjea, one of the nineteenth-century pioneers of Indian Christian theology, the Athenian speech was proof that Christ fulfilled vicariously a mediatory office anticipated by the ancient Indian Rishis. The offering of sacrifice for redemption of sin was a primordial practice and a primitive revelation given by God to all humankind. It was an institution ordained by God to represent the future sacrifice of Christ. What the apostle Paul said to the Athenians of old might "be predicated of our primitive rishis." The Rishis, too, longed for "intercourse with the unseen Being," but "they knew not how to obtain that communion with the Father." In their ignorance, the Rishis continued this mysterious practice of offering of sacrifice for redemption without understanding its "true import." Banerjea claimed that the "true doctrine of vicarious sacrifices," as expounded in the teaching of Christ, had since come to the descendants and successors of the ancient Rishis.[74] Firminger, too, took it as a fulfillment of the expectations of the Vedic poets. What the Vedic hymns sought after as the unreachable, formless, colorless, and absolute transcendence of God was now being revealed as the God "whom you seek is near you."[75]

Raymond Panikkar, promoter of interfaith theology at Vatican II, regarded the speech not as a "zealous strategy" of the apostle but as an "unveiling of the true face of God." Moreover, Paul was proclaiming not another God but the mystery of the hidden God in the form of the Christ in whom we live and move. Panikkar urged the churches to follow in the footsteps of Paul so that they "may speak not only of the unknown God of the Greeks but also of the hidden Christ of Hinduism. Hidden and unknown, indeed!"[76] The task of the Christian mission was to unveil the concealed God in Hinduism and tell Hindus of the God who had been mysteriously leading them to truth. Hindus should be told that Christ, whom "Christianity recognizes and worships," is "already there in Hinduism," but this "Christ has not unveiled his whole face, has not yet completed his mission there. He still has to grow up and to be recognized."[77] As a humble *bhāsyakāra* or commentator, Panikkar saw his ultimate exegetical aim as to point out that *"that from which this world comes forth and to which it returns and by which it is sustained, that 'that' is Christ."*[78] A passage from Isaiah that Panikkar used as an epigraph to one of his chapters further confirms his idea of the hidden presence of God in other cultures and nations: "I was ready to be sought by those who did not ask for me; I was ready to be found by those who did not seek me. I said, 'Here am I, here am I,' to a nation that did not call on my name."

Robin Boyd, a post-Independence missionary who was responsible for introducing Indian Christian theology to a wider audience, suggested that in order to understand the Athenian speech, especially about the revealing of the unknown god, one has to see it in the context of the old cosmic covenant. Paul's statement had to be read in conjunction with God's first covenant with Adam and Noah, that is, with the human race. Hinduism was part of this cosmic covenant, which points toward a future "fuller covenant, *new* covenant in Christ."[79] Boyd did not provide any evidence of how the ancient Vedic Hinduism became part of this cosmic event.

The Mars Hill image of Paul as a supporter of those who were yearning for God is not easily sustainable, especially when one compares some of his actions reported in the Book of Acts. There are two incidents in his life that show that he was not always supportive of unearthing hidden gods in other peoples' religion. These two events go against the popular notion that Luke's Paul is more tolerant than the strident Paul one comes across in his letters. Both events happened at Ephesus. In the first instance, instead of a one-line inscription "to the unknown God," Paul found a whole heap of books. Preaching with power and with the aid of the Holy Spirit, he was able to win over a number of Jews and pagans who were well versed with the religious contents of these books. The result was that the newly converted brought their scrolls and burned them. The value of the burned books was about 50,000 drachmas. We might not know the entire contents of these destroyed scrolls, but newly discovered papyri written three centuries after Paul's time show what ancient magical literature was like. Deissmann, who studied these texts, was of the view that, apart from containing the usual magical hocus-pocus, the texts possessed by these citizens of Ephesus indicated that they were, "though heathen, not altogether unprepared for Bible things."[80] If Deissmann is right, these books might contain allusions to traces of Christian teachings. But it appears that Paul did not show any enthusiasm for unraveling the hidden message, as he tried to do in his speech at Athens, as though he found such books a threat to his theological agenda.

The other incident at Ephesus resulted in riots. This was Paul's first head-to-head encounter with "pagan" religion. It was not such a polite engagement with another religion as at Athens. Paul's message was stated very emphatically here—any human attempt to reach God is an offense to God. There is no roundabout way of unveiling the hidden identity of an unknown god, but a direct clash with the popular great goddess Diana. Unlike at Athens, where Paul queried only the religious ignorance of the hearers, here he challenged both the religion and the economy of the people. This direct open clash resulted in a considerable number of people turning away from the worship of gods (Acts 19:6), which is in contrast to the cynicism and suspicion shown by the Athenian crowd soon after Paul's polite speech (Acts 17:32–34).

Paul's speech is generally regarded as delivering a theological body blow to three of Asia's religious tendencies—natural revelation, mystical philosophies, and image worship. His speech exhibits a number of standard colonial practices. One is that the master knows better than the subjugated people, and it is the master who can redeem the "others" from their ignorance and bring them into the center of civilization—in this case, the Pauline version of Christianity. The speech essentially colonizes the "other." Paul's multireligious openness presupposes a common commitment to Christ, but this Christological exclusivism refuses to recognize that there are other ways to God's salvation.

The second colonial practice exhibited in Paul's speech at Mars Hill is a classic case of the appropriative nature of colonialism, where authority is achieved not by confrontation but by an incorporation and absorption that recognize the autonomous characteristics of the other. The eventual aim of colonial discourse is not to establish distance and hostility between the colonizer and the colonized but to make the colonized sympathetic to the colonial mission by establishing common ground or, as a missionary put it, "some little oasis of truth, reason, or good feeling in the hearer's mind," thereby "turning a sinner from the errors of his ways."[81] What Paul was trying to do in the speech was to establish a spiritual and familial bond between himself and his audience. By identifying the basic values of the Gospel, which were concealed in the cultural and religious world of his listeners, Paul was making them feel that they were morally refined and enhanced by virtue of their participation in a vision of the Christian Gospel.

Third, Paul in this speech not only appropriated native theological resources to colonial ends but also absolved the natives of their theological ignorance. Under the pretext of speaking on behalf of his audience, Paul was able to establish the unmistakable superiority of his newfound faith. What this speech does is to awaken the Athenians to their own religious ignorance and amazingly transforms them from being the baffling "other" into recognizable and, above all, model Christians.

The powerful agenda that pervades the Mars Hill speech is the idea of one God, and linked to this is the idea of the unity of the human race. This is classically expressed in this speech (Acts 17:26). When such a notion is read along with Paul's egalitarian vision imagined in the famous passage in Galatians, it effectively removes any possible liberatory content in various cultures, religions, and societies. The traditional and popular image of Paul is as a designer of multicultural, multireligious communities. What he envisaged was not equality but identicalness or, as Daniel Boyarin put it, "coercive sameness."[82] This was the result of Paul's passionate desire that humanity be one under one God—a "universalism" that was born of the union of Hebraic monotheism and a Hellenistic desire for unity. This "among other things produced an ideal of a universal human essence, beyond difference and hierarchy."[83] In Boyarin's words, "For Paul, the only possibility for human equality involved human sameness. Difference was the threat."[84] Difference must be erased for the sake of harmony and order. Paul's apparent tolerance "deprives difference of the right to be different, dissolving all others into a single essence in which matters of cultural practice are irrelevant and only faith in Christ is significant."[85] Paul's colonial intentions are unambiguous in this statement: "One Lord, one faith, one baptism, One God and Father of all, who is above all, and through all, and in you all" (Eph. 4:5–6). Such a hard-line approach rules out any pluralism or diversity. Paul's emphasis on Christ serves to nullify and discredit other voices.

Paul's Writings: Compliance or Counterimperial Gospel?

Paul's attitude to the empire was a complicated one. His own writings present a conflicting picture. On surveying the material, one can see four images of Paul emerging—a pro-empire enthusiast, an anti-imperial hero, and both a victim and a perpetrator of colonial hegemony. Since the literature on these various positions is vast and complicated, I will give a representative sample of each.

Some biblical interpreters project Paul as a person who operated contentedly and even enthusiastically within the Roman imperial order. Richard J. Cassidy is of the view that Paul "advocated an approach of full compliance with the demands of the Roman rulers."[86]

For instance, Paul's positive attitude toward the Roman authorities in Romans 13 could be attributed to the Roman system of travel, communication, taxation, and law and order, which were beneficial to Paul's task as an itinerant missionary. As Cassidy puts it, Paul was "equally at home with the other aspects of Roman rule: Rome's economic and social, as well as its political innovations."[87] True, he encountered imprisonments and countless beatings from local Roman authorities, but such hardships, in Cassidy's reckoning, were the work of a few rogue elements rather than officially mandated by the Roman authorities. Paul as a radical critic of the empire, in Cassidy's view, is found not in his own writings but especially in the second half of Luke's account of Paul in Acts. In Luke's version of Paul's life, we see him as a person traveling in various Roman provinces, such as Judea, Syria, Galatia, Asia Minor, and Macedonia, and encountering the political authorities there. Even in such confrontations, Cassidy points out that Paul was cooperative, so that he was able to explain himself when he was approached by the Roman officials. Luke's portrayal of Paul's brushes with imperial officialdom does not make him "anti-Roman." What it does do is make him a "de facto disturber of the Roman peace."[88]

The second set of scholars project Paul as a virtual opponent of Roman rule. Some of the essayists in *Paul and Empire* exemplify this position.[89] Paul's anti-imperialist stance is seen in his use of the imperial discourse to subvert the very system that spawned it. His use of words such as *sotéria* (salvation) and *parousia* (used to describe the triumphant entry of emperors into cities), which had echoes of imperial ideology, were appropriated and used in direct contrast to the Roman uses. A staunch anti-imperial Paul is configured as challenging the Roman claim and offering to provide salvation, justice, peace, security, and the Good News. Another disturbing aspect of Paul's actions was the establishment of citizens' assemblies—*ekklésiai.* Paul found assemblies in various Roman cities; these later became markers for various institutionalized Christian denominations. He was credited with "building an international alternative society (the 'assembly') based in local egalitarian communities ('assemblies')."[90] These were virtually a replacement within the Roman imperial order. They were not cultic communities but "political assembly of the people 'in Christ' in pointed juxtaposition and in 'competition' with the official city assembly."[91]

The third group of interpreters, moving beyond the entrenched binary positions mentioned above, envision a more ambiguous figure and characterize Paul both as a resister and as an endorser of the colonial supremacy. Their contention is that in dealing with the empire, Paul's writings demonstrate substantial strain and inconsistency. On the one hand, Pauline texts imply that Paul was co-opted into the imperial schemes and applauded its appeal and advantages. On the other hand, there are signs in his writings that demonstrate that he was far more critical of the imperial project than often given credit for. Some of the contributors to the volume *The Colonized Apostle* typify this stance.[92] Gordon Zerbe's words expertly sum up this position: "In contexts where Paul's authorial voice is venerated, it will be natural to highlight Paul's anti-imperial perspective ... in contexts where readers are open to placing Paul in broader dialogue with other voices in the Christian canon and in the emerging Christian assemblies (including those that were silenced), it will be appropriate to highlight how Paul both challenges and reinscribes imperial and subordinationist schemes."[93]

The three above-mentioned positions may not be mutually exclusive. My inclination is to side with the first one and place Paul as an immigrant who was co-opted by the imperial system. As I have already dealt with this elsewhere in the rest of the section, I would like to draw attention to the theological imperialism of Paul, which has not been given much attention.

There are a number of signs of colonial tendencies in Paul's writings. First, Paul played an important part in naturalizing Western culture in Asia minor.[94] He was a great asset in strengthening the hold of the empire. More than the physical occupation, it is the cultural control—for example, through the introduction of the language of the invader—that gives power to empires. Paul proved to be a key ally in this regard. The Roman empire succeeded in imposing one of its languages, Greek—"the chief agent in Graeco-Roman culture"[95]—in central districts of Asia, and the Christian church was very effective in abetting the imperial policy. Paul wrote all his letters in Greek, and there was no attempt to translate the Christian message into the indigenous languages of Laconia or Phrygia. In producing his letters in Greek, he was an ally in spreading the official language. The newly converted Christians were forced to hear about the Gospel in the language of the colonizer. As Ramsay put it, Pauline Christianity "did far more thoroughly what the emperors tried to do."[96]

Second, Paul's writings are replete with the classic colonial standard of Western civility—obedience, humility, submission, patience, sexual continence, and discouraging of self-assertiveness. The Indian Church Commentaries produced during the colonial Raj endlessly repeat these values as worthy of practice. There were nine volumes produced.[97] For instance, T. Walker in his commentary on Philippians warns of the "dangers which arise from human pride and self-assertiveness."[98] All these encouragements to polite behavior and good manners enabled the colonizer to control and sustain the empire.

Third, Paul's scheme of salvation is couched in the standard colonial practice of absorbing the "other." Under the guise of offering
salvation, he tries to incorporate the Gentiles into the Abrahamic
family. The salvation Paul promised depended on the Gentiles becoming the Children of Abraham. The Gentiles are redeemed from
their own religious allegiances and absorbed and brought within the
context of Semitic theological and moral value. More to the point,
the Gentiles were offered redemption via the Jewish heritage, which
acts as their only hope. The Gentiles could be part of the covenant; a
privilege offered to the Jews was enlarged to include all humanity provided that they become integrated into Abraham's family. In other
words, salvation for the Gentiles was offered not on their own terms
but articulated through the identity of descendents of Abraham,
through their history and memory.

Fourth, colonial control in Paul is seen in his use of the image
of the body of Christ: "You are Christ's body and each of you a
limb or organ of it" (1 Cor. 12:27). In this statement, at the surface
level it looks as if Paul was encouraging interdependence and the
need for each other. A closer reading of the passage will reveal that
the initial shared reliance on one another is replaced with a hierar-
chical order. Paul arranges a pecking order that puts the apostles
first, followed by the prophets, teachers, and miracle workers and
ending with charismatic speakers. It is a carefully arranged order.
Paul's own status and calling as an apostle comes first, and charismatic speaking is placed last. Paul, who affirmed a variety of gifts
and acknowledged the contribution of various persons, now com-
plicates the issue by posing a series of questions: Are all apostles?
Are all prophets? Are all teachers? Are all workers of miracles?
Have all the gifts of healing? Do all speak with tongues? Do all
interpret? (1 Cor. 12:29–30 KJV). Inexplicably, Paul drops the image

of the body and the idea of mutual dependence and suddenly announces that he knows what is the proper order: "But strive for the greater gifts. And I will show you a still more excellent way" (1 Cor. 12:31 NRSV). In the next chapter, in his now well-known passage on love, Paul makes it clear that love is the highest gift of all and that it is love that controls, regulates, and restrains any charismatic challenge.

Finally, Paul's colonial outlook is evident in the famous household code, where relations between husbands and wives, parents and children, and masters and slaves are exploited to establish a benign structure of hierarchy and a gentler form of control. In the name of maintaining family and social harmony, a chain of command is established. At the outset, the relations between husband and wife give the impression of familial affection. However, a careful analysis will reveal that the dominance of husband over wife is established as a pious duty: "Wives be subject to your husbands; that is your Christian duty." The preeminent position of the husband is sanctified as a Christian obligation. Similarly, parental power is given very strong approval: "Children obey your parents in everything." The parents' authority is presented as exercising prudence: "Fathers, do not exasperate your children; instead, bring them up in the training and instruction of the Lord." Slaves fare badly. Unreasonable emphasis is laid on the slaves, who are asked to give "entire obedience to the earthly master." Paul does not question the institution of slavery as such. The exploitation of the slave is facilitated by ascribing to their submission a higher function. The slaves are told that, whatever they are doing, they are "doing it for the Lord and not for men." Instead of offering the slaves freedom, they are brought under the further control of a new master, Christ, who is more exacting than their previous, earthly masters. All

Paul's impressive Christological declarations of release and reconciliation of slaves end in a newer form of slavery where the slaves themselves embraced their own condition. Paul's vision may give the impression that it disturbs the absolute rule and exploitation that Roman male-headed families hold over the dependents, that the domestic peace that Paul preached may be seen as affectionate and to offer a fair deal to family members, that his apparently egalitarian and progressive pronouncements may seem to run counter to the exploitative nature of families under imperial rule, but Paul's language of mutuality and reciprocity fails to challenge the structures that sustain these inequalities and oppression. Rather, it perpetuates them.

Paul's message is mainly about maintaining the status quo. His Gospel call, as Deissmann pointed out many years ago, "never implied the social uprooting of anybody." What it did on the contrary was to ennoble the "feeling of solidarity among the humbly situated."[99] Ultimately, Paul's hierarchy-less, raceless, genderless society presupposes a common commitment to Christ and absorption into Christ's spiritual body. There are two sayings of Paul that need addressing. One is from Philippians, where he says "that at the name of Jesus every knee should bow, in heaven and on earth and under the earth" (2:10 New International Version); the other is from Romans: "every knee shall bow to me, and every tongue shall confess to God" (14:11 KJV). However much you try, these two sentences do not improve on rereading. Those who fail to conform and confess are excluded and are "on the way to destruction" (1 Cor. 1:18). Paul's idea of commitment and absorption into common culture means "ultimately (as it has meant in the history of European cultural imperialism) merging all people into the dominant culture."[100]

To bring this section to a close, let me draw attention to a hostile, pro-imperial image of Paul that goes back to the days of the early church. Paul was portrayed as a "villainous Jew with a passion for dominion."[101] Such an image appears in the Judeo-Christian documents incorporated within *The Establishment of Proofs for the Prophethood of Our Master Mohammed (Tathbit Dala'il Nubuwwat Sayyidina Mahammad)*— a tenth-century text written in Arabic by 'Abd al-Jabbar of the Mu'tazilah school of Islamic thinking, which was renowned for its metaphorical interpretation of the Koran. Within this document there are sixty folios dealing with Christianity. Shlomo Pines, who studied the documents, believes that the tradition of negatively portraying Paul might go back to the first century or the first half of the second century and might have been written down in the fifth century. For our purposes, what is interesting about these quite independent and little-known Jewish Christian texts is that they contain verbal attacks directed toward Paul for his compromising theological attitude and practices. He is seen as a person who lusted for worldly dominion, unashamedly aped Roman customs, and, more significantly, was responsible for the separation of Christianity from Judaism. He was accused of denying the authority of the laws of Moses, restricting circumcision to Jews only, and permitting pork eating on the ground that nothing that enters from outside defiles the body. In keeping with the Roman practice, Paul prohibited polygamy and divorce, thus currying favor with the influential Roman women. In short, these documents provide no evidence of Paul opposing a single Roman practice or custom, whereas there is clear proof of him describing the Torah as wholly evil and denying the religious teachings of Christ. In effect, what these documents demonstrate is that as a result of Paul's activities, "Christians became Romanized *(tarawwamū)* and the Romans were not converted to Christianity."[102]

Conclusion

Paul has not always had a favorable image. C. S. Lewis once commented that everything people "disliked in Christianity was therefore ascribed to Paul."[103] Even in the early church, as the author of the second epistle of Peter complained, there were some things in Paul's letters that were hard to understand (2 Pet. 3:16). In the Asian theological landscape, Paul is not always a sought-after figure. Ernest Renan might have exaggerated when he said that, after 300 years, Paul's reigning influence in the West was coming to an end.[104] As far as Asia is concerned, his reign has not even started. The one aspect of Paul that has attracted Asian interpreters has been his insistence on experiencing God without any external interventions. Apart from this, Asian interpreters have spent little energy on Paul, and he has not been popular in Asian theological reflection. The early Indian interpreters, such as Rammohun Roy, focused mainly on the Synoptic Gospels during the colonial days. Kumarappa, a rare Indian Christian who joined Gandhi in India's independence struggle, dismissed Paul as irrelevant. A. J. Appasamy, theologian and South Indian bishop, found special significance in the spiritual message of the fourth Gospel. Addressing the students of St Paul's School in Calcutta, Sir Narayan Chandavarkar ignored Paul and asked the students to emulate his daily habit of reading the epistle of James before dawn, as a way of focusing their thoughts on the Lord.[105] Korean Minjung theologians, in their struggle against political oppression, largely drew from the Jesus tradition. A recent collection on the use of the Bible in China does not have a single article on Paul. One of the essays, which surveys New Testament studies in China from 1976 to 2006, while listing various interpretative outputs on Jesus and John, does not mention any significant work on Paul by Chinese scholars.[106] Paul became alive in Asia for a brief period at the time when the "Theology of Struggle," a Filipino version of liberation theology, emerged in that country in the 1970s, as a response to the dictatorial rule of Ferdinand Marcos. Gordon Zerbe's excellent article shows how "echoes of Paul" were found in this theology of struggle. Zerbe's selected study of the Filipino theologians shows how these interpreters, whose concern was praxis, "favour a contemporizing, analogical hermeneutic as opposed to an exegetical and historical one."[107]

In spite of seeing Paul as an archetypical Western intellectual, John Robertson, the nineteenth-century Scottish theologian cited earlier in the chapter, was not advocating that the Pauline form of theology, which was so influential in the post-Reformation Western churches, be imparted to the colonies. For those who were in the business of Christianizing India, Paul's message was not to transfer to the Eastern world a Western pattern. That would be like expecting the "oak of Britain" to "flourish in a climate fitted for the Palm."[108]

Just as in the case of Jesus, it is not easy to recover the real, historical Paul. In the early part of the twentieth century, Deissmann aspired to rescue the "Germanized, dogmatized, modernized, stilted Paul" and "the paper Paul of our western libraries" by sifting through the maze of Paulinism buried in the New Testament.[109] As he discovered, the task is not easy and is made the more difficult by the type of documents that are available to us. The words of Paul recorded in the New Testament, especially those reported by Luke, are not the authentic words of the real Paul. They were heavily edited to suit the Christian agenda and are an apologetic of the early church. Most of these writings were redacted after his death to boost the image of the apostle. Biblical interpreters have seen in Paul what they have wanted to see. In a sense, the different appropriations of Paul described here may be seen as a living commentary on Paul's own words found in the Corinthian correspondence where he declares his intention to be all things to all people (1 Cor. 9:19–22 NRSV). The real Paul will remain a mystery, and perhaps the most appropriate way to end is to state what Paul himself said in a different context—we know in part.

6   Exegesis in Eastern Climes

This chapter brings together some of the distinctive and recent features of the appropriation of the Bible in Asia. It will highlight the following: employment of the Bible in a multireligious context; the recent surfacing of minority voices, such as the Dalits, Burakumin, women, and indigenous people; and the two recent entrants on the scene—postcolonialism and Asian diasporic interpretation. In addressing these, I shall bring out issues at the center of interpretation, the personalities who shaped the debate, historical moments that informed the discourse, and the methods and theories that fashioned reading practices.

The Multireligious Context

One of the critical questions that Asian Christians face is how to respond to the presence of many scriptural traditions in Asia. The oldest response and one that continues to have purchase among Asian churches is the comparative method. It has its origins in the colonial period and it persists even today. Comparative study focuses mainly on similarities and differences between Christian and other textual traditions. Its main purpose is to draw attention to the religious deficiencies of other sacred texts and to claim superiority for the Christian faith. The comparison undertaken has largely to do with doctrinal and conceptual matters and is carried on at the redacted level of the texts rather than by scrutinizing them closely. This is mainly because those engaged in such study have not been professionally trained as biblical scholars. The method here is to compare Christian tenets, such as the Incarnation, the resurrection, and the apocalypse, with Hindu notions of avatar, rebirth, or *kaliyuga* (the age of darkness—the last age [*yuga*] in the Hindu cycle of four ages). This comparative study works on a binary understanding that perceives the East as spiritual, mystical, and intuitive and the West as material, intellectual, and rational. Another feature of such a comparative method is to essentialize the religions of Asia. They are seen as static and homogenized, thus flattening out the inner contradictions that are intrinsic to these traditions. The comparative method works on the assumption that Christian texts contain the sole truth and that this truth should illuminate and purify the defects in the scriptural texts of other people. This method has been to a large extent aggressive and Christian-centric. Recently, scholars in Asia dissatisfied with the comparative approach, which does not do justice to the theological integrity, cultural legacy, and social location of these religious texts, have come up with a number of other reading strategies.

One is the "symbiotic" reading suggested by Aloysius Pieris, which came out of Pieris's long and innovative involvement with Buddhist-Christian dialogue in Sri Lanka. What he proposes is "a living encounter of the texts," which results in articulating "implicit meanings which these texts would not reveal unless they are mutually exposed to each other's illuminating disclosures."[1] This symbiotic approach is "conducive to reciprocal spiritual nourishment among the members of multi-religious communities."[2] He explains the method thus: "a seminal teaching in the Scriptures of one religion, sown and buried in the texts, when exposed to the warm light that comes from the teachings of another religion's Sacred Writ, sprouts forth and grows into a fruitful source of new insights. In this symbiotic approach, no room is left for diluting or distorting the basic teachings of either religion; and no effort made to indulge in easy equations or odious comparisons."[3]

The exegetical principles envisaged in symbiotic reading are not exclusively Christian. Pieris reminds us that these resonate with the hermeneutical practices of the Sarvastivada school of Buddhism and the exegetical works of Buddhagosa. To illustrate this method, Pieris analyzes the way poverty has been portrayed in the Gospel tradition and in the Buddha's teaching on the Fourfold Noble Truths. He notes that there are two kinds of poverty mentioned in two Gospel passages in Matthew and Luke. Matthew speaks of the spiritually poor—or the voluntarily detached, as Pieris defines them (Matt. 5:3)—and Luke describes the poor as the dispossessed (Luke 6:20). The spiritually poor are the renouncers of Mammon-Worship, whereas the dispossessed are the victims of Mammon-Worship. Both the detached and the dispossessed are integral to the liberation proposed in the Gospels and are chosen as partners to usher in the Reign of God. Pieris observes that there is a similar idea in the use in the Pali Tripitaka of *appicchata* (the detached ones) and *daliddiya* (the broken or the downtrodden ones). While acknowledging that the biblical teaching does not correspond with the two forms of poverty as envisaged in the Buddhist text, Pieris concedes that there are remarkable similarities between them. In dealing with the social evil of greed, the Tripitaka offers emancipation from private possessions and the elimination of abject poverty. Just as in the case of the Gospels, the Buddhist text teaches that Nirvana is intrinsically linked to the eradication of poverty and personal greed. Pieris points out that the Christian and the Buddhist texts agree that economic poverty in itself is not a highly meritorious state but that the morality the poor exhibit and the ethical life they strive for are far more important. The natural characteristic of such greedlessness is sharing and generosity. In Pieris's view, the Buddhist Sanga and the Christian church are called to be "contrast societies," promoting less acquisitive communities. Pieris assures those who see such an interpretation as "so Christian as to be unbuddhistic" that it is a "thoroughly Buddhist exegesis of the Pali Scriptures, originating in a biblical reading of it."[4]

The second new approach is cross-textual reading, as advocated by Archie Lee. He, too, is challenged by the rich textual tradition of the continent. His contention is that Asian Christian readers do not approach Christian texts with a blank mind. They bring a number of religious, social, and secular textual traditions to their reading. To address this phenomenon, Lee places side by side Chinese classical writings (Text A) and the Hebrew scriptures (Text B) with a view not only to eliciting a better understanding of the two texts but, more important, to addressing the religio-cultural identity of Asians who have been converted to what he calls a non-Asian religion such as Christianity. Archie Lee admits that the Chinese classics and Christian sacred texts have the potential to be both liberating and enslaving. The task, then, is to read both texts to expand our horizons. For Lee, this cross-textual exercise is not merely a meeting of ideas or enhancement of texts but is also about the transformation of the whole of life and a process of self-discovery for the readers or, as he puts it, borrowing from Richard Wentz, about "enriched-transformed existence."[5] A cross-textual reading of the flood narratives in the

Hebrew and Chinese traditions is among the many examples worked out by Lee. In this, Lee reads cross-textually the biblical narrative with those of the flood myths of the Naxi, an ethnic minority in China. He focuses on the mythic themes in the structure of flood stories and the conception of the relationship between the divine and the humans in the religious world of the flood narratives and the Naxi myth. In this cross-textual reading, Lee demonstrates how the non-Christian Chinese receive and appropriate the biblical flood story and how Christians, in turn, receive and appropriate the Chinese flood myths. There are similarities in the stories. The flood is sent by God to destroy the creation. Escape is provided in both narratives. In one case, it is the ark and, in the other, the leather drum. Sacrifice is offered as thanksgiving. In both stories, the flood stands as the dividing line between the first and the second creation. Where the narratives differ dramatically is when it comes to the dividing line between the human and the divine. In the biblical story, the punishment is for overstepping the boundary between the divine and the human. In contrast, in the Chinese myth, the aspiration to become divine is not only endorsed but encouraged. A non-Christian Chinese reader, with an eye to the parallel text from the Naxi flood myth, will not read Genesis 6:1–4 as a punishment for human sins but as the regeneration of humanity in the divinity-human intermarriage.

The third new approach is the contrapuntal method of reading advocated by postcolonial interpreters. Contrapuntal reading places next to each other the mainstream and the marginal—Christian and non-Christian, secular and sacred, textual and oral—and looks for connections, disagreements, and inconsistencies between them, not with a view to imposing artificial amicable alliances but to achieving a counterpoint of voices that maintains rather than irons out tensions. Such a method is an attempt to go beyond the earlier discredited comparative hermeneutics used by both colonialists and nationalists. The former enlisted it to pass judgment on other peoples' stories and the latter to dismiss Western knowledge as tainted and to project the indigenous heritage as ideal and noble. By way of illustration, and drawing on the work of George Soares-Prabhu,[6] we may take as an example a reading of the missionary commands found in Matthew 28:19 and Mahavagga 1:10–11:1. Both of these texts belong to narrative contexts and emphasize the importance of the missionary task for their respective communities. In Matthew, the missionary command is given by the resurrected Jesus as a culmination of his life and work, whereas the Buddha's commission is narrated as one of the incidents in Buddha's earthly life and as such is comparable to the commission found in Matthew 10. Buddha's exhortation to preach was not accorded any special importance. Both commissions express identical interests. For both, the authority of the mission is predicated on the sender. In one case, it is the Buddha's authority and, in the other, the authority of Jesus; for both, mission involves teaching, communication of religious doctrines, and praxis; and both conclude with an assurance of the presence of the sender: "Lo, I am always with you."

While there are duplications in the two texts, they also show remarkable differences. In Matthew, the mission to preach derives its strength singularly from Jesus: "All authority in heaven and earth has been given to me." In the Buddhist commission, in contrast, the authorization gains credibility because of the liberation attained both by the Buddha himself ("I am delivered from all fetters human and divine") and by his disciples ("You, also O Bhikkus, are delivered from all fetters divine and human"). Phrased differently, the Buddhist mission rests as much on the Enlightenment of the Buddha as on his Bhikkhus. Both masters want their disciples to teach. In the

Buddha's case, he wants his followers to preach the dhamma—a perfect and pure life of holiness. Matthew's Jesus invites his hearers to be "perfect as the heavenly father is perfect" (Matt. 5:48). For both, the purpose of mission is the liberation of humankind, but they express this differently. The Buddhist text is quite explicit. The monks are sent out "for the profit of many, for the happiness of many, and out of compassion for the world." The purpose of the Buddhist mission is the welfare of all, which includes not only humankind but the created order as well. Such a concern and affection is missing in the Matthaean command. The first Gospel is silent about the welfare of the "nations" to which the disciples are sent out. Matthew's text is not about being of service to the people but about winning adherents, about numerical and institutional expansion. The nations are perceived as objects of mission. They have to be baptized and converted. Both the Buddhist and the Christian commissions recognize and are mindful of the universal nature of their mission. Matthew makes it clear that the mission is to "all nations." The Buddhist commission goes a step further. It distinguished not between nations but between gods and humans and is more sensitive to the unity of humankind than to national differences.

Finally, the idea of the establishment of Buddhism in a given geographical area, with such implications as winning souls and establishing communities, is absent from the Buddhist command. Unlike in Christianity, there are no instructions or rites from the Buddha for establishing *sasana* (the teaching of the Buddha) in a country. Buddhism is about personal realization of the truth. Once a person is awakened to the truth, Buddhist ideals are established in that person. The Buddhist history records the disciples of the Buddha going back to their countries and making numerous converts, and the Buddha himself was invited to these countries, but there is no mention of an establishment or institutionalization of Buddhism. The notion of establishing Buddhism came later, with the conversion of Asoka. It was he who adopted Buddhism as a state religion and sent out missionaries with a view to converting nations. The Christian text is about conversion, whereas the Buddhist text is about enlightenment. In Christianity it is the person of Jesus who saves, whereas in Buddhism the identical redemptive function is performed by the teaching of the Buddha.

These three approaches—symbiotic, cross-textual, and contrapuntal—call for closer scrutiny. For want of space, let me offer a brief assessment of them. What these approaches do is to go beyond the impasse created by the old comparative method. The underlying features of all three methods include maintaining the theological, cultural, and historical integrity of the texts and permitting them to speak on their own terms.

There are subtle differences between these methods. Pieris's symbiotic method is largely confined to religious texts, whereas the other two methods are more open and deal with both religious and secular texts. For the symbiotic and cross-textual approaches, texts are settled and secure, but for contrapuntal reading, texts are not final or finished products but sketchy and on the move. While Pieris's and Lee's reading practices aim to arrive at a rounded and in some sense complete meaning, contrapuntal reading strives to acknowledge and uplift the clashing and contradictory voices enshrined in the narratives. What is clear in all three cases is that each text acquires its religious worth through its relationship to the other and obtains its meaning through its connection to another text. The multitextual and multireligious Asian context further makes it patently clear that knowing one textual tradition alone is not enough. In the current context, characterized by a variety of texts, concentration on a single text may not facilitate either its appreciation or that of other texts.

Marginal Readings

MINJUNG: READINGS OF THE CONSCIENTIZED MASSES

One of the provocative and challenging theologies to emerge in the 1980s in Asia was Korean Minjung theology (*Min* meaning people and *jung* meaning conscientized masses). This theology was a specific response to the oppressive political situation prevalent in Korea at that time and the rapid industrialization that disadvantaged the poor. The starting point for this theology was the Minjung, who were culturally rich but oppressed politically, exploited economically, alienated socially, and denied education. They were the custodians of the indigenous culture and historical heritage of the people. This theology emerged as a way of giving a voice to the Minjung. There were a number of attempts to read the Bible in the light of the concerns of the Minjung, and along with Korean cultural resources, the Bible provided an important source. Although Minjung theology has evolved over the years, the early work done on the Bible remains innovative. The following are two illustrations.

The first was Ahn Byung Mu's rereading of the *ochlos* in Mark.[7] Using the traditional historical-critical method, Ahn Byung-Mu rereads Mark's Gospel from a Minjung perspective. His contention is that mainstream biblical scholarship has paid little attention to the socioeconomic milieu in which Jesus undertook his work and has also failed to identify the social background of the crowds associated with Jesus. In his study of *ochlos* (the crowd) in Mark, Ahn has demonstrated that Mark deliberately avoided using *laos*, a favorite term in Luke, which meant religious people, the people of God. Instead, he chose *ochlos*, indicating a group who were abandoned and marginalized—the sinners, the tax collectors, and the sick. In other words, *ochlos* were the alienated, dispossessed, and powerless, or simply the Min-jung. Jesus accepted this group unconditionally. *Ochlos*, for Ahn, is not a fixed identity but a fluid one that is defined in a relational way. In this sense, one cannot understand Jesus without the *ochlos* and vice versa. Jesus's messiahship was exercised in his identification with the suffering of the Minjung.

The second example comes from Cyrus Moon. Unlike most Ko-rean interpreters, Moon does not see easy parallels between twentieth-century Korea and first-century Palestine. His exegesis is much more nuanced. He starts with the premise that the contemporary Korean situation and the historical situations of biblical times are not simi-lar. His contention is that the liberation theology espoused by Moses in the Exodus cannot be simply applied to the current Korean Min-jung. One big difference between the two situations is that modern Korea is not under the occupation of a foreign ruler as was the case of the Israelites. True, Korea was under Japanese occupation, but that was decades ago. The present oppressors are the Korean people them-selves, the so-called ruling class. Acknowledging this difference, Cyrus Moon nevertheless concedes that there is some sort of resemblance between Micah's time (eighth century BCE) and the twentieth cen-tury because the Korean Minjung are exploited and have little con-trol over their destiny. In looking at Micah, Moon argues that Mi-cah's division of the people of his nation into two categories—"my people" and "this people"—provides a clue to the current situation. In Micah's usage, "My people" were "the have nots, the victims of social injustice," oppressed and exploited by "this people," not foreigners but the ruling class who were the part of the same society. It was "this people" who "had taken houses and land from the poor by physical force and coercion."[8] In Moon's view, there is a telling distinction be-tween the liberatory message of the Exodus and the prophetic message of Micah. The former is about freedom from oppressive foreign powers, whereas the latter is about the judgment of the dominant class, which oppresses its own people. Micah, as a commoner, identified himself with the oppressed and championed their cause and suffered for them, prefiguring the suffering of Christ for the oppressed. Moon's inference is that in all the liberatory acts of God in Korea, one can see the suffering of Christ.

BURAKUMINS: THE THORN IN THE JAPANESE CROWN

The Burakumins are a part of Japanese society whose presence challenges the monolithic picture of Japan. They are the most ostracized of people, and there are three million of them. They are not part of the Japanese success story. Their discrimination is not based on race but determined largely by the type of "mean and filthy" work they do. They are the outcasts who were assigned by the dominant Japanese society to deal with dead bodies, butchering, and tanning. Their discrimination is based on Shinto and Buddhist ideas of pollution and purity. *Buraku* means "special village" and *min* means "people." *Burakumin* thus means people from specially designated villages. The origin of the Burakumin remains a mystery, but the formalization of their status can be traced to the Edo period (1603–1867). It was during this time that, under strict military rule, Japanese society was stratified. At the top were the samurai—the warriors—followed by farmers, artisans, craftspeople, traders, and shopkeepers. The Edo rulers realized that in order to sustain this hierarchy they needed an underclass that would allow the commercial class to think that they were not the lowest of the low. So the Burakumin class was created and placed on the bottom rung of society. In the early days, they were associated with leather work, shoe making, and dealing with dead bod-

ies. In parallel with the Indian untouchables, Burakumins were sometimes called *eta,* meaning dirty, or at worst they were called *hinin,*
which meant nonpeople. As the years went by, most people forgot
why the Burakumins were originally considered inferior, so the areas
they lived in rather than their occupation became their descriptor.

The Christians among the Burakumins, who face discrimination
both in society and in the church, have found resources in the biblical
tradition to recover their self-identity and self-worth. Tero Kuribayashi,
who himself is a Buraku, has repurposed the biblical symbol of the
crown of thorns. The choice was symbolic and deliberate. The crown of
thorns was chosen with a view to contrasting it with the Japanese imperial crown of chrysanthemum. For Kuribayashi it has a double
significance—humiliation and triumph. Traditionally, Jesus's crown of
thorns, in Kuriyabashi's view, signified "mockery, humiliation and
dishonour," but "Paul, however, saw in Jesus' crown of thorns the exal-
tation that was the ultimate outcome of his humiliation."[9] Kuribayashi
writes: "But for Paul as well as for the people of the early church, Jesus'
crown, together with the cross, was a symbol of victory."[10] A symbol
that was seen as the supreme example of endurance, devotion, and piety
was thus turned into a symbol of God's solidarity with the rejected and
despised of the world. Jesus's historical cause for the poor and the oppressed has become a symbol that both points to the pain of the marginalized and reveals the hope of their final victory. Another Japanese,
Hisao Kayama, has pointed out that the story of Cornelius, with its
potential overtones of pollution and purity, is a story with which a Japanese Burakumin could easily identify. His plea is that just as Peter was
"transformed through the vision and encounter with Cornelius,"[11] so
Japanese society, which is bedeviled with the purity–impurity divide,
should be transformed by its encounter with the Burakumin.

INDIGENOUS PEOPLE: RECLAIMING THE LAND

Those people once known as "tribals," "aborigines," or "primitive people" now fall under the umbrella term of "indigenous peoples." These are mainly peripheral people who, as the United Nations Working Group on Indigenous People put it, "today live more in conformity with their particular social, economic and cultural customs and traditions than with the institutions of the country of which they now form part." Asia has the highest number of indigenous people, and a large majority of them live in China and India.

Christians among the indigenous people find that the dominant biblical interpretation fails to address their concerns, which are more ecological than theological. Wati Longchar, an indigene of Northeast India, contends that both missionaries and mainstream biblical scholarship overlook the main concerns of indigenous peoples. Missionaries, in his view, introduced anthropocentric reading, which emphasized the revelation of God through the written word and through the person of Jesus, thus undermining the divine revelation through the natural created order. Conversely, mainstream Asian scholars spend most of their energies relating the biblical texts to the religious texts of Hindus, Buddhists, and Sikhs in order to clarify and build communal harmony but pay little attention to the realities of the indigenous peoples. Longchar thinks that both missionaries and mainstream Asian interpreters have had a condescending attitude toward indigenous people's earth-centered religion, culture, and ethics. The missionaries were dismissive of the religious fervor of the indigenous as "devilish," whereas mainstream Asian scholars were disrespectful toward their spirituality as "not philosophically deep enough to interpret the Bible."[12] The interpretative process of the indigenous people is totally different. What disrupts the lives of the indigenous people is alienation from "mother earth . . . in which their personhood, spirituality, and identity are inseparably rooted."[13] The sense of injustice indigenous people experienced arose from economic poverty, unemployment, or disease, and these were all as a result of being alienated from the land. The starting point for reading the Bible, therefore, is the land, which is "the point of reference and key to understanding human self-hood, God and spirit."[14] The harmony in and within this space is the first act toward liberation. When justice is done to the land and harmony is achieved, the well-being of creatures and the created order are established. Longchar remarks that such a harmonious existence is envisioned by the Psalmist (96:11–12). For all marginalized people, the ultimate aim of hermeneutics is to gain dignity, recover their rights, and reestablish their identity.

Nirmal Minz is another indigene who analyzes the biblical accounts of the covenant to understand the tribal situation in India. Using the history and the experience of Chotanagpur tribals, Minz investigates four biblical accounts of Abrahamic, Noahic, Mosaic, and Davidic covenants. Minz points out that the Abrahamic covenant (Gen. 12:1–4) has certain merits with which the tribals can easily identify. Like the patriarchal family, the tribals, too, were a migratory people, who moved from the Indus Valley to the present homelands, thus exhibiting a spirit of "adjustment and adoption." Minz notes that although the tribals lack a comparable figure such as Abraham, there are many features in the life of the patriarch that resonate with the tribal reality. But the Abrahamic covenant has an inherent message that is awkward for the tribals. The Abrahamic covenant makes a distinction between people and land, and, more worryingly for the tribals, places a strong emphasis on the people over the land. Such a prominence accorded to people, in Minz's view, is alien to the tribal way of thinking. Minz finds the Mosaic covenant (Exod. 19:1–24) problematic. It signals two reversed experiences of the Indian tribals. His reading of this covenant goes against the traditional understanding of the narrative. To begin with, the Indian tribals were under captivity not in a foreign land but in their own homelands under different pharaohs at various times in their history. The local "pharaoh" varied from the Brahmanical Nagbansi kings who, in order to maintain law and order, introduced the zamindari system, which neutralized the power of the tribal chiefs. The Muslim invaders replaced folk cultural activities such as communal singing and dancing with individual performers; the British colonialists among other things introduced a concept alien to the tribals—personal ownership and the right to buy and sell lands. The biblical Exodus proved to be a turning point in the history of the Israelites—a disparate collection of nonpeople were made into a cohesive group of people. The Indian tribal experience has been the opposite—a people who had common identity and purpose were forced to become a nonpeople and lose their identity. The Exodus, for Indian tribals, is leaving their promised land (homelands) and searching for a "second-rate shelter." Minz, in desperation, poses the question: "when will the pharaohs let these people go and rediscover their homeland and become again the people worthy of their name in Mother India?"[15] The Davidic covenant (2 Sam. 7:1–17), in Minz's view, was instrumental in establishing a king and a new kind of aggressive politics in Israel. It was used as a pretext for God's sanction and had a devastating effect on the indigenous people. This was comparable to the introduction of a king over the tribals by the "Brahmanic craft of myth-creation."

In the final analysis, for Minz none of these covenants—Abrahamic, Mosaic, or Davidic—have anything positive to say to the tribals. The exception is the Noahic covenant (Gen. 9:8–19), which he regards as a universal one, but more to his purpose it included both people and the created order in nature. Such an inclusive understanding, in Minz's view, falls well within the tribal concept of the harmonious and interconnected relationship that exists between humanity, nature, and spirit. Minz contends that a proper harmony of people and the created order is essential and that any severance of this relationship results in a double tragedy—the dehumanization of people and the pollution of the environment. However, this universal covenant with Noah has to be read in conjunction with Isaiah's image of the suffering servant, lest it reinforce the idea of tribal superiority. The old ethnocentrism and triumphalism ought to be replaced with the "servant politics" of self-offering and formation of a universal brotherhood and sisterhood in Jesus (Col. 3:10–11). The underlying hermeneutical question that runs through Minz's exegetical quest is, what kind of a God sides with the powerful and the strong and leaves the poor and helpless in the lurch?

DALITS: READING THEMSELVES OUT OF THE STIGMA

One of the new words to enter the public discourse is *Dalit.* This is the self-designated term chosen by those Indians who were once known as "outcastes," "untouchables," "depressed classes," or "harijans." The Dalits, nearly 15 percent of the Indian population, find themselves placed at the bottom of what is known as the caste system. Their marginalization was due to the fact that they were seen by traditional Hindu society as ritually impure, the inherited stigma continuing to reinforce their inferior status. The Dalits have rejected the earlier labels, which they found paternalistic and insulting, especially Gandhi's label, harijans. They chose for themselves the term *Dalit*—a term first used by Jhotirao Phule to describe their actual reality. There is uncertainty about the etymological origins of the word. Some trace it to the

Sanskritic root, which aptly describes both the abject state of the Dalits and also the potential to blossom into wholeness. The adjective *Dalita* means split, broken, destroyed, crushed, trampled on, but the noun *dala* means something unfolding into fullness. There are others who trace the contemporary usage to the Marathi word *dala*, which means "of the soil" or "of the earth," "that which is rooted in the soil." Whatever the root meaning, the term has been appropriated to describe both the stigmatized status of the Dalits and also their latent capacity to blossom.

The Indian church is unfortunately not exempt from the pervading influence of the caste system. The Dalits have employed profitably a number of biblical images and characters mirroring their plight and degradation. The chief among the biblical images is the image of the suffering servant—the figure of Jesus as the one "wounded for our transgressions." For the Dalits, Jesus as a suffering leader resonates with the Dalit state of servitude and suffering. The other image is the Psalmist's reference to a "worm not human," which is indicative of their depressed state. Another image is that of the biblical shepherd. James Massey points out that the image of a shepherd offers contradictory signals. On the one hand, shepherds in the Bible were described as "abhorrent" (Gen. 46:34); shepherds—like the Dalits— were employees without any contract (Gen. 31:41) and were always on the move because any permanent "habitations of shepherds" was seen as disastrous a threat to those in cities. On the other hand, the Bible records the profession of the shepherd as one of the oldest, going back to Abel, Adam's son. Most of the patriarchs are identified as shepherds. Among the Israelite kings, King David, from whom Jesus was descended, was a shepherd. An image used in the Bible for God is that of a shepherd. With these paradoxical views, Massey revisits Luke's account of the angels announcing the birth of the Messiah

(2:8–20) and extracts two hermeneutical insights. First, it was to the shepherds that the message of salvation was first announced, and second, it was in a manger, "a place of their level," that the savior was born. Thus, the shepherds—the excluded—become the "first favoured group/community."[16]

Recently, Maria Arul Raja has engaged in an intertextual study of biblical texts and the Dalit world and their experience with a view not only to empowering the Dalits but also that they may recapture their respectability. In his study, Arul Raja juxtaposes two murdered warrior-heroes—Jesus and the south Indian Mathurai Veeran. Both defied the unjust norms of the ruling elite: casteism, in the case of Mathurai Veeran, and authoritarianism and ritualism, in the case of Jesus. Both died as wounded heroes and were later elevated to a divine status by their respective communities as an act of reparation for injustices done to them. "By venerating [Mathurai Veeran's] memory as a protector God," writes Maria Arul Raja, "the Dalit community seeks to retrieve their original identity as brave warriors with a sense of discerning for themselves what is right and what is wrong."[17] Arul Raja's contention is that the defeat and death of the murdered heroes was now transformed into a "weapon of the weak" and used as a springboard to "evolve new ethical alternatives."

Surekha Nelavala provides a Dalit woman's perspective in her engagement with Mark's account of the Syrophoenician woman (Mark 7:24–31). She challenges the text "to respond to the particular oppressions suffered by Dalits and particularly Dalit woman within the casteistic context."[18] She juxtaposes her own autobiographical narrative with Mark's account of the Syrophoenician woman and detects exceptional parallels between the two. In both cases, the women were outside the mainstream, a Dalit in one case and a Gentile in the other. Both were polite in their approach and have an open encounter with a male figure. Initially, both met with rejection and humiliation. Where the Syrophoenician woman differed from Nelavala's own experience was that, in the end, the biblical character was not only smart and persistent enough to get what she was after but also in the process was instrumental in rectifying the mistaken attitude of Jesus. Navala's reading is refreshingly different in one respect. Unlike in other feminist readings, she does not overemphasize the witticism and the verbal victory of the woman over Jesus. While acknowledging the liberating potential the Syrophoenician woman's story has for women, what is so striking about her, for Navala, is that she is able to change some of the inherent biases of Jesus. The implication of the encounter is that "without the oppressor's readiness to change, the voice of the oppressed is in vain."[19] Phrased differently, a complete liberation ultimately depends on the oppressed and the oppressor working in tandem. A similar hermeneutical insight was expressed by Gnanavaram. In his exegesis of the Good Samaritan parable, Gnanavaram sees the Samaritan—the marginalized Dalit figure—and victimized traveler as one in their struggle to achieve liberation. One without the other makes the liberation look shallow.[20]

ASIAN WOMEN, BIBLICAL WOMEN

Asian women from various contexts have used their experience, cultural insights, and indigenous religious texts to open up the biblical texts, while others have used critically and profitably historical-critical methods in their engagement with the biblical texts. Satoko Yamaguchi has drawn on critical feminist theories to rehabilitate two biblical characters—Martha and Mary—whose roles have been obscured and downplayed in the fourth Gospel. In spite of the fact that their stories were locked into a "kyriarchal," a master-centered paradigm, Yamaguchi offers a revised reading of them as not wealthy but humble women who "made the best" of Jesus by expressing "their solidarity with their beloved teacher and friend."[21] Both biblical characters emerge as models of active discipleship and possibly as potential prophets. Yamaguchi's hermeneutical aim is to retell the stories in a way that can assist in reenvisioning Christian identities.

In the work of Hisako Hinukawa, the culture of honor and shame, which is found in both Japan and Palestine, with its distinctive characteristic of group solidarity and dyadic personality, provides a new perspective to read Mark's Gospel.[22] Some women interpreters incorporate religious and cultural stories of their ancestors to reformulate and reconstitute their identity. One such attempt is made by the Vietnamese American Mai-Anh-Le Tran, to interweave stories from two different cultural worlds—Jewish and Vietnamese. She juxtaposes three female characters: two from the Hebrew scriptures, Lot's wife and Ruth; and one from a Vietnamese folk tradition, a young wife called Tho Thi. Two are turned into pillars—one of salt (Lot's wife) and the other of stone (Tho Thi). Ruth was made into a "pillar of redemption" for her loyalty and self-sacrifice. Tran challenges the way these three female characters have been textualized and their actions interpreted as a patronizing celebration of their "gentle and gracious womanhood." Tran sees them as han-ridden women and full of defiance. In her view, these stories "demand a different understanding of divine and human justice."[23]

Minority hermeneutics thrives on victimhood. The examples here are no exception. The discourse is replete with phrases like "doubly oppressed" and "triply oppressed." While these labels rightly reflect injury and stigma, the danger is that these descriptors may stiffen into a creed and hinder progress. Minority hermeneutics has been successful in exposing the tyrannical features of the powerful, but it has yet to analyze the oppression that goes on within its own fold.

Those who belong to the margins of society often invent a reactionary identity that is idealized or rooted in the mythological past. Marginal hermeneutics is essentially about empowering. When Dalits, Burakumins, Asian women, and tribals read the Bible, their aim is not only to seek historical insights in the texts but to find liberatory resources that will both confront and challenge the oppressive forces and at the same time empower them to regain their dignity.

New Developments

POSTCOLONIAL READINGS

Like many "isms," postcolonialism pursues a particular grievance—the impact of European colonialism. The mention of postcolonialism raises the specter of empire, conquest, slavery, racism, sexism, and orientalism, and it is seen as being implicitly critical. Postcolonialism, at its simplest, can be seen in two ways. One is historical, marking the dismantling of the empire and its attendant instruments of power; and the other is an intellectual project that searches for "alternative sources, alternative readings, alternative presentation of evidence."[24] In the latter sense, it pays much attention to the intricate relations between the native and invader societies and cultures, wrestles with questions of identity and representation, and invests much in theories of indigenousness and diaspora. In this sense, essentially postcolonialism identifies the dominant power, exposes it, and engages critically with it.

Empires and colonization—that is, the control of another people by power and force—have existed in all historical periods. Current postcolonial study began its career by investigating the modern colonization, which started with the European conquest of overseas countries in the sixteenth century and culminated in the nineteenth. This subjugation was unique in its scope, scale, and style, and its cultural and political reverberations are still with us. Later, the same scrutiny was extended to other empires and other forms of colonization. Postcolonial theory, like any critical category, has evolved over the years. The initial, primary phase was of textual analysis dense with new theoretical categories. This gave way to conceptual and disciplinary challenges posed by globalization, environmentalism, religious fundamentalism, and terrorism. The current phase confronts the contemporary neo-imperial practices of market economy and humanitarian intervention—the new form of the "white man's burden" assumed on behalf of humanity. A new class of politicians, bureaucrats, corporate entrepreneurs, disaster experts, and others takes upon itself the task of civilizing and developing the uncivilized and underdeveloped. A noticeable example is that of Western trauma experts parachuting into disaster areas, following events such as the 2004 Indian Ocean tsunami and the 2010 Haiti earthquake. In the name of humanistic intervention, Western solutions are applied to health and psychological problems that could have been solved by indigenous resources.[25] Postcolonialism has opened up a metropolitan canon dominated by English, French, and Spanish texts to include literature produced, among others, in Swahili, Hindi, Chinese, and Tamil. It has now come to embrace a larger set of conceptual and ideological positions and interests. It has also moved from the earlier hostile Occident-Orient binary division to cross-cultural contact and dialogue between the once colonized and the colonizer.

The nature of colonialism has also changed. External colonialism has been replaced by an internal type. Initially imperialism was an overseas venture and a European mercantile project procuring luxury goods for the aristocracy from foreign lands, later becoming a nationalist project where the economic benefits began to reach the working class. Now colonialism has turned inward, and the postindependence nationalist governments wage war against their own civilians, grabbing lands, minerals, and other indigenous resources in the name of developing them.

Like many critical theories, postcolonialism reached biblical studies late in the 1990s.[26] The academic climate of the time played a critical role. Postcolonial biblical criticism was an inevitable progression from the then prevailing interpretative practices that went under the name of contextual, vernacular, or liberation hermeneutics. While these interpretative approaches were rightly preoccupied with questions of economic exploitation and victimhood, postcolonialism was able to add another increasingly problematic issue—the cultural implications of living in diverse religious and racial communities in a globalized society. This was also the time when the biblical "Orient" was rediscovered by those biblical scholars, especially in America, who were trying to apply social scientific and anthropological approaches to biblical texts. In their attempt to wrestle with and give a form to the biblical Orient, these scholars unwittingly regurgitated the old orientalist stereotypes, thus forcing those from the Orient to investigate both the Orient itself and the orientalist practices of these biblical scholars.

Postcolonial biblical criticism has several textual functions. First, it pays attention to the presence of the empires of the biblical world. The ancient Israelites were under the control of the Egyptian empire. The Judean scribes, priests, and prophets who shaped the Pentateuch and prophetic books of the Hebrew scriptures were confronted with Persian and Assyrian empires. The books of the New Testament emerged during the Roman empire. In studying the Bible, a postcolonial critic interrogates the texts with a series of questions. For example: How are these imperial powers portrayed? Do the biblical authors support or challenge them? Where does their allegiance lie—with the subjugated people or with the dominating power? Second, it asks how, in their examination of biblical texts, biblical commentators interpret these empires. Do they support or oppose them? How do they represent the "other"? What kind of Oriental images appear in their work? Do they unwittingly reorientalize the Orient? Third, it examines the role played by the Bible in colonial expansion and its veneration and degradation in the colonies.

Fourth, postcolonial criticism engages in a work of retrieval. This involves bringing to the fore forgotten, sidelined, and often maligned biblical figures and text; reclaiming the resistant literature of the "natives" themselves as they talk back to the master by using the very texts provided by them; and recovering the hermeneutical work of a few missionaries and orientalists who, though invariably compromised with the ideals of empire, were at the same time ambivalent about its usefulness. Fifth, it pays scholarly attention to Bible translation projects and their positive and negative contributions to indigenous languages. Finally, it address issues that have arisen in the aftermath of colonialism—migration, multiculturalism, nationhood, and diaspora.

There are a number of examples of Asian postcolonial readings. One such reading was undertaken by Philip Chia at the time when Hong Kong was about to enter the postcolonial era. He was drawn to postcolonial criticism not because it was "a new toy of the literary approach" or that it was replacing earlier categories such as "third world theology" or "Asian theology" but because it was for him a "matter of life experience."[27] In his reading of the Book of Daniel, Chia finds resonances with the experiences of the Hong Kong people. The well-known fourfold strategy of the colonizer recorded in the book—segregation, language, education, and naming—was all replicated in colonial Hong Kong. The common practice of the colonizer was to select and separate the colonized elite, transform them through the introduction of a new language, reeducate them, and, as a final act of domination, provide them with new names. Just as Daniel and his friends were renamed with Chaldean names, so were the many Chinese who changed their names under British rule and education. "One of the agonizing features in the search for identity of the colonized," Chia writes, "is the naming of oneself as the subject/object of/by the colonizer."[28] Such an act simultaneously affirms and dishonors the colonized. Daniel was not an acquiescent victim. His political critique and act of resistance became evident when he refused to accept food from the royal table. This was not only a dissident gesture but also a "challenge to the colonizer's claim of life controlling power."[29] In Chia's view, "the experience of Daniel is too much of a common experience of the colonized, say for those who experienced the British colonial rule, and subsequent neocolonial rule."[30]

The other example is Seong See Kim's rereading of four Markan women from a Korean postcolonial feminist perspective. She examines the stories of the poor widow, the anointing woman, the women at the cross and the burial, and the women at the empty tomb. Making use of postcolonial concepts, such as the "third space" and "hybrid subject," and viewing these biblical women through the prism of Taoism and Buddhism, she shows how "these women become subversive and threatening in (post)colonial situations and can function as examples of empowerment for contemporary women and men who are struggling in the postcolonial world."[31]

Uriah Y. Kim is a Korean American advocate of Asian American postcolonial hermeneutics. He rereads the history of Josiah under the Assyrian kingdom from his own experience living as an Asian American in America.[32] Kim's contention is that the Deuteronomistic history has been written from the perspective of Western national, imperial, and colonial interests, and he sees his task as recovering the forgotten or overwritten inscription and to reconstruct an ethnic and political identity for Asian Americans. Just as Asian Americans were located in a political and ideological landscape that was not of their own making, Josiah and his people were placed under the imperial forces of the Assyrian empire. In spite of living under conditions that were not of their choosing, the Josiah court produced the Deuteronomistic history both as an attempt to construct their own history independent of Assyria and to retrieve their own historical inscriptions and customs. Taking a cue from the court historians of Josiah, Kim urges his fellow Asian Americans to write their own history and remember their own stories. But he is quick to caution that these stories and histories should not essentialize or homogenize the diverse Asian American community in America.[33]

Postcolonialism, like any other theoretical category, has its share of faults and weaknesses: among them, privileging Western colonialism as a marker for defining history and culture, which ignores and does injustice to indigenous cultures that thrived even before the advent of modern colonialism; the exclusive focus on writings in English, thus overlooking vernacular, resistant literature; the failure to reach the grassroots level. Nevertheless, postcolonialism is a useful tool. It makes scholars vigilant about how they conceive and dispense knowledge. It questions the unipolar world that places the West at the center. More important, learning from the past experiences of colonialism, it provides insights and warnings when the contemporary world is faced with new versions of colonialism in the form of globalization, a market economy, and invasion of other countries in the name of liberal interventionism.

ASIAN DIASPORIC READERS

Another new arrival on the scene is the diasporic interpretation facilitated by movements of people—a sign of the modern world. The presence of a sizable number of Chinese, Japanese, Korean, Indian, Filipino, and Vietnamese in the West and in particular in North America has given birth to what is now known as Asian American biblical hermeneutics. Those who are engaged in such an enterprise are a mixture of second- or third-generation Asian Americans and newly arrived professional migrants located largely in Western academies. As an identity marker, the designation "Asian American" functions as a blanket term reflecting the variety of Asia's nationalities, religions, and languages, but at the same time it blocks out the inherent differences within these communities. Asian American biblical hermeneutics emerged in the late 1990s in the form of edited works that demonstrate both the variety and range of their hermeneutical work. Like most hermeneutical movements, Asian American hermeneutics is not a homogeneous entity. It incorporates a wide variety of ethnic experiences and records numerous views on the Bible. This varies from a wholesale adoption of biblical tenets to complicating and at times rejecting the Bible in favor of other life-enhancing sources, such as the praxis of Jesus advocated by Leng Leroy Lim or—by several interpreters—ancestral wisdom.[34] As a recognizable and distinct corpus, Asian American hermeneutics is relatively new. It is too early to evaluate this emerging work, though, in a short period, and taking advantage of the interpreters' diasporic status, the work has come up with refreshing readings of biblical characters buried deep in the narratives and has unearthed biblical events that were otherwise overlooked by the mainstream.

Surveying the literature, it is evident that Asian American hermeneutics is passing through a series of phases. An earlier, integrative
phase has now given way to one of pointed questions both about
biblical texts and about the interpreters' own self-identity. In an attempt to project themselves as an amiable and accommodative immigrant community in an often hostile foreign land, the earlier generation of Asian Americans sought out biblical figures such as Ruth
as ideal inspirational foreigners. Sometimes the risky actions of Esther were recalled as a warning to be vigilant in a foreign country.
Esther, living in an alien land as part of a subjugated and marginalized community, succeeds in concealing her Jewish identity but re-
claims it when the very existence of her people comes under threat.
Her story is employed as a reminder that Asian Americans might
prosper and present themselves as a pliable community denying their
Asianness, but when subtle discriminatory decrees threaten the community, they should, like Esther, be prepared to take "risky actions
that break decorum."[35]

Sometimes figures once enlisted as powerful role models are inter-
rogated for their continued usefulness. One such heroine was Jael,
hailed as a woman warrior. Ten years after announcing her initial
enthusiasm, Yale Gee poses a series of sharp questions about the role
of Jael: How does Jael's ethnicity influence her status as a woman
warrior? As an ethnic figure, whose ideological interest was she serving? Was she the fifth columnist working for the invading Israelites?
What happened to her ethnicity in the subsequent narration of her
story?[36] Sometimes historical parallels are sought between the Asian
American experience in America and that of the biblical communities.
One such parallel is the first book of Peter's community in Asia Minor
and the nineteenth-century Protestant Chinese community in San
Francisco. Both communities were resident aliens who found that

embracing a new religion increased their marginalization and discrimination rather than bringing any relief. The Chinese were further marginalized because of their distinctive physical features, their dress codes, and hairstyles. Faced with hostility from both Christian churches and their own communities, these Chinese Christians formed a mutual self-help society, *Zhengdaohui,* which was based on Christian discipleship rather than on traditional Chinese family ties and village connections. This achievement of solidarity and communal identity was, in Russell Moy's view, the fulfillment of the Petrine vision. Moy further claims that such a race- and religion-related marginalization will be of help in understanding the plight of the sojourners in 1 Peter. Moy also points out that what was fascinating about the nineteenth-century Protestant Chinese was that in their study of the Bible they never saw any resemblances between their plight and that of the sojourners described in 1 Peter.[37]

One of the issues addressed by Asian American hermeneutics is a question that hardly comes up in any other hermeneutics—that of intercultural adoption. The sizable number of Asian American adoptees leads Mary Foskett, herself an adoptee, to examine two biblical narratives, Exodus 2:1–22 and Romans 8 and 9, as a way of exploring the issues. In this Exodus narrative, Moses eventually realizes that he is not an Egyptian but an Israelite. Foskett notes that as the narrative stands at the redacted level, the story of the adoption of the Hebrew-born Egyptian Moses is submerged in the overarching story of God's triumph and the liberation of the Israelites. In her view, the narrative glosses over any constructive assessment of Moses's formative years, and furthermore it accords as much textual space to the killing of the Egyptian as to the verification of Moses's self-identity and portrays him as the leader of his people. In doing so, the text "reinforces the notion that intercultural adoption signifies, at worst, a betrayal of one's own origins, and at best, a dislocation that can only be corrected by a return to one's 'true identity.'"[38] In contrast to the images of adoption in Exodus 2, Foskett finds the spiritual adoption envisaged by Paul in Romans 8 and 9 offering more rounded images that do not erase race or ethnicity. In Paul's adoptive vision, believers are being instituted into an adoptive relationship with God based on the exemplary adoptive bond that exists between Christ and God, where origins are not lost but a newly found identity is forged. What is crucial to Paul is "not what believers have been, but what they have become and are becoming."[39]

What Asian American biblical hermeneutics has done is to move the focus from the narrative to the identity of the interpreter. Every writer begins by declaring his or her racial, ethnic, and social location. These hyphenated identities have become a rich resource for illuminating the texts. Much of their exegetical work has benefited from liberationist, feminist, and postcolonial insights. Their theoretical vision is framed and enabled by the writings of Edward Said, Rey Chow, and Amy Ling, to name a few. Asian American biblical scholars constantly face the radicalized landscape of American orientalism and nationalism. Mainstream America already has a fixed idea of what an Asian is, and the temptation is to play to that scripted role. As a minority community, Asian Americans also have the experience of being dehumanized by white racist America. The internment of ethnic Japanese in North America during World War II and the series of anti-Chinese and Filipino immigration laws are examples of this American nationalism. What is clear in such circumstance is that integration is not attractive. At the same time, it is too easy to feign and seek security in a fake Asianness.

Asian American interpreters are engaged in a constant negotiation and translation between the homes they have left behind and the new home they are trying to settle in. In this negotiation, as several of the interpreters have noticed, they face the embarrassment of double rejection—being rejected by the host country as not being Asian enough and scorned by the cultures they left behind as being too Western and co-optive. Much worse is the reception within their own study programs, where Asian American religious studies are "simply ignored or, worse, vilified."[40] There are signs in their writings that Asian Americans would like to move beyond the traditional preoccupations with ethnic identity and would like to be part of the American Christian story. This largely depends on the kind of politics that prevails in America and the kind of spiritual and social fabric it can offer. The question is what can America possibly offer spiritually to these diasporic scholars who come from countries such as China, India, Japan, and Korea, which were the veritable birthplace of every imaginable religious tenet of humankind.

Concluding Observations

Asian biblical scholars have been active in addressing a number of hermeneutical issues that affect them. Issues related to plurality of texts, identity, and agency have been given scholarly attention.

The visibility of Asian biblical scholars in the international scene in recent years has been remarkable. But their contribution is limited to the hermeneutical issues confined to narrow Asian or Asian American concerns. Asian biblical interpreters have yet to make their mark in the Jesus Seminar, the study of the Gnostic Gospels, and biblical archaeology. They can raise issues and bring new perspectives that have not hitherto been registered by those who work in these fields.

For instance, the involvement of Asian interpreters would help to challenge the scholars of the Jesus Seminar, who, in their study of Jesus, are so obsessed with the Judaic or Hellenistic heritage that they overlook or ignore the potential influence of Eastern religions—a point I made in Chapter 1. This would also assist in correcting the dominant image of an Asian interpreter as one who is good only at handling identity or contextual issues.

Asian biblical hermeneutics has come a long way since the days of scholars who worked with a predatory tendency—claiming every-thing that is good in other scriptures and adding them to the Bible. Not so long ago, J. N. H. Wijngaards, a missionary who had a long experience of working in India, was able to claim condescendingly that "'Whatever is true, noble, right, pure, lovely and honourable" (Phil. 4:8) in the non-Christian scriptures should be attributed to the "one God and one Mediator between God and men, *the* Man Christ Jesus, who gave Himself a ransom for all" (1 Tim. 2:5–6).[41] Now there is a recognition, at least among the Asian scholars who work in aca-demic settings, of the need to accord an equal dignity to different textual traditions. More than that, the task is seen as teasing out tex-tual contradictions, omissions, and silences and offering an explana-tion for such elisions and differences.

Asian biblical interpretation has become an overcrowded site with many marginal voices, and rightly so. What the marginal hermeneuts such as Dalits, Burakumins, tribals, and women have done is not only to stir the minority to study their history, myths, and traditions but also to enable them to follow their own logic and argument wherever it takes them. Such an exercise permitted them to focus on the given ethnic, sexual, regional, or geographical identities. This chapter has provided examples of the attractive way the people on the margins have appropriated the biblical narratives. However fascinating these examples may be, such a hermeneutics has its own quota of flaws and faults. To begin with, the voices of self-identity can be subjective, dictatorial, self-righteous, and give the impression that they know what they want. In other words, marginal hermeneutics thrives on fueling ideas of victimhood and superiority. It has made the feelings and sense of victimhood the center of everything. Now it has become nothing more than one's own caste, one's own tribe, and one's own clan. Hermeneutics has become an indulgence to express individuality and group feelings. What these yearnings have done is to commodify feelings and aspirations. This means marginal hermeneutics has no grand ideas to work with nor big visions to dream. The end result is that marginal hermeneutics reinforces a sectarian and ghetto mentality that it claims to undermine and subvert.

When one goes through Asian biblical hermeneutics, one cannot help but notice that a homiletical agenda is sometimes explicitly or implicitly running through some of these interpretations. Even some of those who opt for postcolonial reading see their task as rescuing the Bible for the church. Asian biblical interpreters work under the notion that the texts can be somehow salvaged if they are interpreted through ethnic, marginal, or postcolonial concerns or read in conjunction with folk, Buddhist, or Taoist texts, so that meanings can be minted for the contemporary society. Aligned to this is the notion that if we manage to place the texts largely in their supposed contexts and read through the invented or imaginary marginal status, somehow we can arrive at the rightful meaning. There exists a reluctance to admit to the contradictory and ambiguous nature of biblical texts. The text that offers release and freedom can also enchain and restrict. There is no critique of the Bible itself. Asian biblical interpreters are tightly tethered to the Bible, and they need to be un-shackled from it. So far they have used the Bible profitably to liber-ate themselves; now they need to liberate themselves from the Bible in order to find meaning and solace beyond its brutal and offending tendencies.

7 Between the Lines of Asian Fiction

The Christian Bible, as David Norman wrote, is accorded a "unique place not just in religious consciousness but in linguistic and literary consciousness" of the West.[1] As a foundational text of Western civilization, the Christian Bible has provided rich resources for its language, literature, art, and film. Apart from being treated as a literature in itself, the Christian Bible has been an inspiring source for Western culture. The Book of Books has begotten many books. Freed from their ecclesial and pietistic environment, biblical stories have been retold and modified to meet a variety of needs and occasions. These fictional avatars of the Christian Bible amuse and annoy in equal measure those who love the Bible. Sometimes these rewritten stories are quite devotional and true to the biblical models; at other times they abuse the text, assail and mock its morality, and cause offense to both religious authorities and pious devotees. Christianity as an institutional religion may be on the decline in the allegedly secular West, but the Bible continues to generate meaning, stimulate, and supply raw materials for questions that affect the Western attitude to love, life, death, war, and reconciliation.

The influence of the Christian Bible on Western culture, especially on its literature, has been widely acknowledged and celebrated. The scenario in Asia is slightly different. A cursory glance at Asian literature will reveal that there is a paucity of explicit citations of biblical material. This lack of interest should not be seen as a sign of indifference or resentment toward the Christian Bible. The Christian Bible is not the sole supplier of creative or imaginative content in Asia. More pertinently, the Christian Bible's impact on Asian literature is not that deep or penetrative. There are other resources that lend artistic and literary support and capture the imagination of Asian authors and artists, such as the stories of the Ramayana; the Mahabharata; the Jataka Tales of the Buddhists; the folktales of Chinese, Koreans, and Thais; and the myths of tribals. Asians are soaked in these stories, which influence and affect their creative thought processes.

This chapter will draw attention to the sporadic examples of how the Christian Bible found itself in the Asian literary landscape. In doing so, it will highlight some of the ways the Bible has functioned both as a divine word of God and as an artifact with numinous qualities; it will draw attention to the way Asian authors have used the Bible both for a critique of and as a collaborator with institutionalized churches, Christian fundamentalism, and Western imperialism. It will narrate how biblical personalities and passages figure explicitly or implicitly in these novels and how these writers often present them from a totally new angle. It will also bring to light instances where the Bible has been marginalized or even rejected. The chapter will end with a few hermeneutical observations.

Rigid Institution, Flexible Words

Sarah Joseph's novel *Othappu* is unusual among Asian novels in that it is packed with direct and indirect biblical citations. *Othappu*, literally meaning outrage or scandal, explores feminine spirituality, family, sexuality, personal piety, and the ineffectiveness of institutionalized Christian churches in a South Indian Christian society that is self-conscious about its Christian piety. More than anything else, *Othappu* is about a woman's yearning for a true understanding of spirituality and her own sexuality. The novel unfolds at many levels, but its enduring value lies in its trenchant critique of class and caste and particularly the role of the church in perpetuating such divisions. It gives a glimpse not only of the psychological and theological pressures of living in a Christian religious institution but also of how individuals face up to them.

The novel is about two women characters—a Roman Catholic nun, Sister Margalitha, and a born-again Protestant charismatic, Rebekka. These are two different personalities, but what is common to them is that they clash headlong with the patriarchal institutions of church, family, and law. Sister Margalitha renounces her current life twice, on both occasions in search of God. The first time she gives up the comfort of the materialistic world to enter a religious order. The second time she leaves the cloistered life in order to find God in a secular world, when, freed from rituals and regulations, she rediscovers her faith and God in the service of the poor. Rebekka, a mother of two, proclaims herself "the Lord's chosen one" and "selected by God." The sign of this special status was her receiving the Holy Spirit, a privilege that had passed by priests and nuns. The author's message to the church hierarchy is clear: God elects not institutions but individuals. Now as "the handmaid of God," Rebekka assumes presumptuously the powers that had been the exclusive privilege of the priest of the established church—laying on of hands with prayer. She, too, follows a spiritual path further from the institutionalized church and is not afraid to raise her voice against private and public power. Unlike Margalitha, Rebekka is not interested in bringing material benefits to the poor. Her way of serving God is to bring spiritual blessing by praying with the poor. When Margalitha asks her how she transforms prayer into service, Rebekka replies, "People receive peace when I pray. That is all I know."[2]

Sarah Joseph's *Othappu* is littered with biblical quotations and allusions. The characters in *Othappu* effortlessly use biblical texts in their everyday language. Sometimes they quote verbatim from biblical verses, and at other times they allude or paraphrase. When Karikkan, a feckless priest, is about to take his priestly charge, his mother reminds him of his responsibility toward the vulnerable. Her words are a paraphrase of what is commonly known among biblical interpreters as the Nazareth Manifesto: "Help the poor. Do not forsake the homeless. Stand with those who struggle and suffer."[3] When Margalitha renounces her convent life, she is torn between two options—whether to lead a secure life by finding employment or to live the life of an itinerant. The first choice would bring a comfortable life, house, and new clothes. The second would result in eking out a miserable existence not knowing where the next meal was coming from. Her inclination is take the risk and live as a free spirit. She decides to live by the biblical injunction. The path she opts for resonates with the words of Jesus to the disciples: "travel light. Do not take a staff, bag, bread, money or sandals for the journey. Other than what one was wearing, not even a second set of clothes. It is to the poor, the marginalized, and those who are excluded from the privileged enclave of knowledge that one is to go. Wherever you reach, stay there till you have to leave the place, eating and drinking whatever they offer."[4] She even adds her own list of injunctions, which are not found in the original saying of Jesus: "Not to stay anchored anywhere: no native place, home, clan, religion, language, or culture.[5]

In *Othappu*, the Bible becomes an easy instrument for critiquing the institutionalized church. When Karikkan, the spineless priest, gets his Episcopal Letter of Appointment—the letter from his bishop—he is horrified to find that it contains words like "authority" and "administer." All along he has understood his vocation as service and pastoral. Now his cherished calling is reduced to holding onto power and maintaining institutional interest. He wonders whether as a church administrator he can set the people free. The verse that is alluded to here is Luke 4:18, which speaks of the liberation the Gospel brings to the poor and the vulnerable.[6] Margalitha shows her displeasure at church ceremonies and celebrations not only by paraphrasing the word of the prophet Amos but also by contextualizing them to suit the Indian situation: "I hate your feast days. I take no delight in your pious gatherings. I will not look at your holy sacrifices. Nor hear the sound of your veenas" [stringed musical instrument used in South India]. I abhor your music. Why then these churches, bishops' palaces, prestige, wealth, institutions?"[7] Sometimes the original biblical verse is alluded to in order to evoke sarcasm. Margalitha's decision to join the convent is received with mockery by her father, who uses words of Jesus to both ridicule her decision and to take a shot at the Catholic Church: "What did you go out into the wilderness to see? A reed swayed by the wind? If not, what did you go out to see? A man dressed in fine clothes? No, those who wear fine clothes are in king's palaces. Life in a king's palace: is that what my daughter wants?"[8]

There are segments in the novel that parallel events in the New Testament. Thus, *Othappu* echoes the nativity scenes described in the Gospel. On hearing that Margalitha is pregnant, Rebekka visits her, and this is likened to Mary's visitation to her cousin Elizabeth. On her visit, Rebekka uses words that resonate with the Gospel text: "The Lord is with you. Rejoice and sing praises to unto the Lord" (Luke 1: 30, 39–45). There are parallels between Mary giving birth to Jesus and Margalitha giving birth to her child. Like the biblical Joseph, Karikkan does not want to acknowledge that he is the father. The indecision of Karikkan resembles the initial hesitation of the biblical Joseph. At this point in the story, the author quotes the Matthaean verse: "Mary was pledged to be married to Joseph, but before they came together, she was found to be with child through the Holy Spirit. Because Joseph, her husband, was a righteous man and did not want to expose her to public disgrace, he had in mind to divorce her quietly" (Matt. 1:18–19). Whereas in the biblical story Joseph accepts both the child and the mother, Karikkan, who lacks moral courage, refuses to take responsibility and leaves Margalitha with words that resemble those of Jesus: "My time has come." Just as with the visit of the Magi in the biblical story, three nuns from Margalitha's convent carry gifts for the newborn. Unlike the gifts that befitted the offices of Jesus as king (gold), lord (frankincense), and redeemer (myrrh), the erstwhile convent sisters of Margalitha shower the newborn with gifts that are of practical value—a baby frock, a towel, and a large piece of cloth with folds, pleats, and frills.

One of the biblical books that gets a prominent mention in the novel is Ecclesiastes, which functions as both a liberatory and oppressive text. When Margalitha leaves her religious order and is faced with an unknown and turbulent future, she reads Ecclesiastes continually for seven days. What makes her read this book from the

Hebrew scripture is unclear. She might be attracted by the book's questioning of those who affirm absolute faith in ownership, status, achievement, and even wisdom itself. Or she might be drawn to the message of the book—that everything is futile, transient, and devoid of any substance. Whatever the case, after finishing reading, she goes on to write a letter to Karikkan. The theme of the letter is taken from St. John's Gospel—the wind blows where it pleases (John 3:8). The content of the letter is not revealed. There may be symbolism in the choice of the verse from John. This verse comes immediately after Jesus's conversation with a Jewish establishment figure, Nicodemus, telling him that an old external water ritual is being replaced with an internal spiritual revival. Translated into Margalitha's life situation, it indicates that she is now on the verge of moving from a ritual- and regulation-ridden church to a freer, more spontaneous, and secular ministry characterized by service.

The same book, Ecclesiastes, is summoned by Chandy-Doctor, a strong-willed Pentecostalist, in this instance as a weapon for haranguing his opponents. Chandy-Doctor is an unscrupulous character who doubles both as a medical doctor and as a faith healer. When Rebekka audaciously tries to expose his corrupt dealings at one of his prayer meetings, he uses the sledgehammer words from Ecclesiastes to put her in her place: "I find more bitter than death the woman, whose heart *is* snares and nets, *and* her hands *as* bands: who so pleaseth God shall escape from her; but the sinner shall be taken by her" (Eccles. 7:27; emphasis in original).

The novel demythologizes supernatural elements in the Bible. A clear case in point is the biblical miracle of the feeding of the 5,000. This is seen not as a paranormal event where loaves were amazingly multiplied but as an occasion to share everything among all those who are present. After a Eucharist that consists not of the regular wine and wafers but of indigenous substitutes, water and boiled tapioca, Manikyan, the Dalit whose aspiration to become a priest was thwarted by the caste-ridden church, thus exhorts his congregation mainly of poor laborers and Dalits: "take and eat this." After his exhortation, the poor share the food that they have brought with them. These are the people who have been kept outside by the mainstream churches for not belonging to the right caste. Manikyan explains to them that there is nothing miraculous about Jesus feeding 5,000 people with five loaves and two fishes. He goes on to tell them: "right before you, there is a hungry multitude. You have only five loaves and two fishes, but there are more than five thousand famished people.... You must share it five thousand times. Each share may be tiny to the point of insignificance. Even so, if insofar as you divide and distribute what you have equally, every one is sure to get a share. It may not fill the stomach but it will fill the heart."[9] The miraculous aspect of the event is the redistribution of the resources within the community. As Manikyan tells the assembled congregants, this was Jesus's way of "distributing a nation's wealth."[10]

The novel encourages the discernment of God through the natural order and through mundane things in life. God's self-disclosure is experienced not through historical events or through liturgical or cultic remembrance of past events but through cosmic revelation. The text subverts the traditional way of experiencing God through sacred history. Margalitha comprehends the inexplicable nature of God through the realm of nature and through mundane and ordinary events of life. For Margalitha God speaks through "the fall of a dewdrop to the ground, the flap of a butterfly's wings, the drop of a leaf, the flowering of a tree." For her the words of God come through "wind, rain, thunder, waterfalls, and earthquakes."[11] Phrased differently, God's word permeates the environment and the social order.

In *Othappu,* the Bible is not always celebrated for its liberationist potential. At times, it is unhesitatingly rejected. The Paryans, the Pulayans, and the Dalits, who experience the persistence of caste stigma in the church, liberate themselves by burning the Bible. Even after their conversion, these marginalized people feel frustrated at the church's reluctance to change the system, and so they resort to extreme measures by setting fire to the very book that promised their emancipation.

The characters in the novel use biblical verses in their everyday conversation, but they do not interpret the Bible literally. For them, the meaning is not rigid but flexible to meet new demands. When Karikkan tries to emphasize the social elements of the Gospel, his elder clergy berate him for finding meaning in the words of the Gospel writers that they themselves would not have thought about. Karikkan's riposte is that the word of God is not a stagnant pool: "It is an onward flowing river of life. We have built a thousand check dams to stall it. No, it must flow. We must let it flow on. To the future. To all sorts of places. Then there will be changes."[12]

The novel provides rare glimpses of Malayali Christian society, but is, in effect, a powerful indictment of the hypocrisy that plagues Christianity in many parts of the subcontinent.

World, Town, Texts

In Gish Jen's novel *World and Town,* an Asian encounters the Bible in a Western context. In this case, biblical texts act as a conduit by which a person is convicted, absolved, redeemed, and then plucked out of a familiar cultural context and placed in an alien one. In essence, the Bible becomes a provider of chapter and verse for a type of American fundamentalist Christianity promoted by evangelical churches in the United States.

World and Town is about a fictional small town in America, which is challenged by globalization, immigration, religious fundamentalism, global warming, and the impact of the aftermath of 9/11. As if these were not enough, this rural town is further challenged by the arrival of corporate power in the form of a cell phone tower and a Walmart-type supermarket. Gish Jen is a Chinese American novelist, and her *World and Town* is full of colorful characters. For our purpose, the important characters are two lesser ones, Sophy Chung and Ginny Everett. Sophy is a fifteen-year-old Cambodian refugee who lives with her parents, who are trying to adjust in America after their traumatic experience of facing the Khmer Rouge back at home and roughing it in refugee camps in America. Ginny is a born-again Christian who lives with her Eastern Orthodox husband and has become a religious fanatic with an urge that comes with many newly converted to "set the world back right."[13] In her hands, the Bible becomes a daily guide. For Ginny, the Bible has the power to transform the sinful Sophy into a "child of God." Ginny represents a strong literal Biblicism common among evangelical Christians. As the novel pans out, it becomes clear that Sophy becomes a white woman's burden as Ginny sees that it is her responsibility to rescue Sophy both from her dysfunctional family and from her Buddhist tradition.

As Sophy struggles to make sense of her father's superstitions and violence and her mother's ritual-heavy Buddhism, she is drawn to the evangelical Christianity of her local church. Sophy finds refuge in the Heritage Bible Church, a fundamentalist church in the northern New England town of Riverlake. She is particularly attracted by the rewards offered here and now on earth by the biblical faith. This is in contrast to her mother's passive Buddhism, which promises merits in the next birth. In order to achieve this good karma, her mother has to engage in endless good deeds. In reading the Bible, Sophy discovers, from the Letter to the Ephesians, that no amount of humane and philanthropic work will help, as her Buddhist mother believes, and that people are saved by faith and faith alone. She learns that salvation is a gift and is not something that you earn through good works. The novel expresses Sophy's new scriptural discovery and her guilt thus: "She wanted to be reborn into the right life, her real life. Her old life was just so wrong."[14]

Sophy comes under Ginny's influence, and her conversion to Christianity follows the typical pattern of a white woman dictating and manipulating a second-generation immigrant teenager. Rather than helping her to mediate between her religious and ethnic narratives and biblical ideals, Ginny unleashes the whole gamut of evangelical piety. The way Ginny allures Sophy resembles the familiar evangelical hermeneutical strategy known as the "Roman Road." This strategy involves pronouncing everyone a sinner, making people ashamed of their past, and instilling the need for forgiveness through the death of Jesus Christ. All these are supported with choice verses from the Letter to the Romans. Ginny tells Sophy that all are born to reflect the glory of God, but all have a sinful nature. She employs the memorable words of Paul that evangelical Christians often use: "For all have sinned, and come short of the glory of God" (Rom. 3:23). To avail of this grace, Sophy has to be born again. To gain this forgiveness, Sophy is made to confess her sins publicly in front of the church members. Although Sophy hesitates and is embarrassed to go before the altar, Ginny bolsters her confidence by reminding her of biblical sinners such as David and assures her that she is not alone but is walking with God. To strengthen Sophy's resolve, Ginny quotes a verse from Isaiah: "Fear not; for thou shalt not be ashamed: neither be thou confounded; for thou shalt forget the shame of thy youth" (54:4). She also reminds Sophy of what God told Jeremiah, that there would be a new covenant with the people of Israel and he would remember their sins no more. And just as God forgot the sins of Israel, Ginny tells Sophy that God will "forget yours too, child."[15] What the biblical prophecy foretold of a nation is now applied to the fate of an individual.

Once Sophy has been received into this narrow form of Christianity, she is forced into a neat evangelical assessment that divides the world into "us" and "them," "saved" and "damned," "sacred" and "profane." The drastic consequence of such a contrastive dual thinking is that Sophy is urged by her pastor and Ginny to leave her home, family, and her religious and cultural practices and integrate into a narrow type of white evangelical Christianity represented by the Heritage Bible Church. Such a separation, she is told, has a biblical warrant: "Verily I say unto you, There is no man that hath left house, or parents, or brethren, or wife, or children, for the kingdom of God's sake, who shall not receive manifold more in this present time, and in the world to come life everlasting" (Luke 18:29–30). What was used by Jesus in a context where the rich were asked to relinquish all their wealth and relationships for the sake of the kingdom is directly applied to the hapless Sophy, who is asked give up the only connections and possessions she has in the alien American environment—her family and her trailer home.

Sophy's life is further made difficult by Ginny, who wants Sophy's family to be reported if they oppose her newfound life. In support of such a drastic action, Ginny paraphrases the alleged saying of Matthew: "If the member refuses to listen to them, tell it to the church;

and if the offender refuses to listen even to the church, let such a one be to you as a Gentile and a tax-collector" (Matt. 18:17). At one stroke Ginny not only brings division within the family but by identifying Sophy's parents as Gentiles and tax collectors they are also made objects of mission. In Matthew's Gospel, the Gentiles and tax collectors are targets of conversion, and the implication here is that people such as Sophy's parents should be eventually won over, too. Sophy's loyalty to her family comes under severe strain when her new church tells her to cut herself off from her delinquent brother, whom she loves very much. Again another biblical verse is produced to support such an action: "And if thine eye offend thee, pluck it out, and cast it from thee: it is better for thee to enter into life with one eye, rather than having two eyes to be cast into hell fire" (Matt. 18:9). All this is presented as God's grand plan for Sophy. In order to reinforce the idea, Ginny cites the verse from Ephesians that God has "predestined us unto the adoption of children by Jesus Christ to himself, according to the good pleasure of his will" (Eph. 1:5). To compensate for the loss of her family, God's plan is to give Sophy a "new family"[16] in the form of the Bible Heritage Church and its members. The idea of predestination is so drilled into her head that Sophy even believes that the destruction of the Twin Towers on 9/11 is part of God's plan.

Sophy's understanding of the Bible is not as rigid as Ginny's. Sophy does not passively accept everything Ginny tells her about the Bible. She does not see herself as one of the sinners described in the Bible. The image she chooses for herself is that of Esther, who made it in a foreign land. The choice of the biblical Esther is revealing. Just like the Esther of old, Sophy suppresses her ethnic identity to become part of American evangelical Christianity and rediscovers her cultural roots when that community goes against her family.

Sophy draws on her Buddhist faith, which provides her with cultural equivalents to enable her to make sense of difficult and strange biblical concepts. The Gospel that is regarded as universal and easily digestible needs indigenous resources to unravel its mystery. For her, grace is a "kind of like good karma."[17] Similarly, on reading Paul's ruling in Ephesians about women subjecting themselves to their husbands, she amusingly observes that Paul is seeing "eye to eye with Confucius."[18] For her, Paul's views on women resonate with the Confucian ideal of social relationships. Unlike evangelical Christians, Sophy does not uphold the Bible as the literal and inerrant word of God. She has doubts about some of the biblical claims, especially Mark's verse about faith moving mountains.

While other ethnic groups in the United States have organized themselves into countercultural groups, fusing creatively Korean, Chinese, and Japanese ethnicities and biblical norms, Ginny and her Bible Heritage Church offer no choice—only the white American middle-class version of biblical faith.

The novel provides a counterbalance in the form of Hatti who finally finds a way to harmonize her own rationalism with what she considers others' "nutty superstitions." She says that what we need is "vision with a small v. Something more Inuit-like—more oriented toward the living. Something more Confucian." As this humane novel shows, nothing is gained by giving up one's most cherished beliefs, but humanity is strengthened by giving equal dignity to the ways communities have come to appreciate life's ultimate purpose. More specifically, a better world and a better town are built only by active compassion and solidarity.

Terrorizing Texts, Resistant Readings

In José Rizal's novel *Touch Me Not* the Bible is seen as both an offending text and a useful resource to challenge the institutional church. *Touch Me Not* is set during the Spanish occupation of the Philippines. It was first published in 1887 and is probably one of the earlier literary examples of resistance writing against European colonialism. The novel's title is part of the saying attributed to the risen Christ to Mary Magdalene: "Touch me not, for I am not yet ascended to my Father" (John 20:17). There is no clue in the novel as to the meaning of the saying except that the novel touches on some of the worst examples of imperialism and church corruption, missing from earlier Asian artistic expression. The novel is seen as having played a crucial role in the demise of Spanish rule in the Philippines. It continues to be popular in the Philippines. This may be due to the fact that the book not only accurately reflects the time in which it was written but also resonates with events in the contemporary Philippines.

Rizal's novel is a critique of both the Spanish government and the Roman Catholic Church. The guilty characters in the novel are mainly Catholic priests. The depiction of the Catholic friars who controlled the country must have created quite a stir and scandal at the time. These priests are portrayed as materialistic, selfish, ill-mannered, egotistical, and evil, and they are shown committing the very sins that the converted local Filipinos were warned against. It is perhaps, then, no surprise that Rizal ran into trouble with the colonizers and the clergy. He was first exiled to Mindanao and was later arrested for "inciting rebellion," this based largely on his writings. He was executed in Manila in 1896 at the age of thirty-five.

In *Touch Me Not*, the Catholic Church is seen as teaching rituals and superstitions instead of preaching the gospel of Jesus. The church comes across as an opponent of one of the chief features of the Enlightenment—the supremacy of reason, which challenged the authority of God's word.

The Bible, in Rizal's novel, is seen not as a book full of love, justice, and compassion but as a book of terror, torture, and torment for those who deviate from the path of God. This comes out clearly in a sermon Father Damaso, a manipulating priest, preached to his Filipino congregation, and which made most of them yawn. Speaking in a language that is totally unfamiliar to him—Taglog—Father Damaso selects a biblical passage that comes from the Apocrypha, the second book of Esdras: "I looked at my world and there it lay spoilt, and at my earth and it was in danger from men's wicked plans" (9:20 Revised English Bible). The passage goes on to speak about the punishment meted out to those who despise God's ways. The whole sermon portrays the Filipino converts as sinners and heretics for not showing respect for the ministers of God. For such disrespect, they are condemned as being worse than the Protestants and the local Chinese. Father Damaso finds the solution for such disobedience in the dire words of Jesus, though this has no bearing on the Filipino context: "If thy right arm offends thee, cut it off, and throw it into the fire." Father Damaso, in his eagerness to convey God's wrath, freely mixes the eighth and ninth verses from Matthew 18. In purposely choosing these verses, he is directly implying that any harm done to the Catholic priests will be rewarded with grave punishment. Those who are familiar with the Matthaean context will know that these harsh punishments—cutting off hand or foot and plucking out the eye—are reserved for anyone causing harm to the "little ones."

The "little ones" in Matthew are the vulnerable who need protection. Here, the all-powerful Roman Catholic priests are in a roundabout way suggested as the helpless "little ones," and the inference is that any local Filipinos who are bent on harming the priests or the Catholic Church will have to face cruel consequences.

The employment of the Bible is not one-sided and confined to the Roman Catholic priests only. The local Filipinos, too, use it as a way of critiquing some of the corrupt and twisted teachings of the Roman Catholic Church. The person who does this is one of the minor characters of the novel, Don Anastasio or Tasio, the town philosopher or the mad man. He has a curious mind, and his fellow citizens consider him as both clever and crazy. He spends most of his time alone reading books and uses his textual knowledge to oppose the doctrinal teaching of the clergy and the corrupt colonial administration.

One such doctrinal instruction that comes under severe scrutiny is the Roman Catholic teaching on purgatory. Tasio tells the deputy mayor and his wife that the teaching was first designed by Zoroastrians. It was Zarathustra who introduced the idea that the living can redeem the sins of the deceased by reciting verses from the Avesta and by doing good works. It was later that the Zoroastrian priests exploited this practice to their advantage by establishing the idea of purchasing one's salvation. Souls could be saved from torment with payments of money to absolve the sins of cheating, lying, and failing to keep one's word. Using his study of the scriptures, Tasio makes it clear that the idea of purgatory was "neither in the Bible or in the Gospels." He goes on to say that neither "Moses nor Jesus makes the slightest mention of it and the one cited passage in the Maccabees is insufficient."[19] Drawing on his study of Church history, Tasio tries to convince the deputy mayor and his wife that purgatory was not a biblical precept but formalized by the church authorities much later.

He reminds them that it was the Council of Trent under Pius IV in 1563 that issued the decree permitting prayers, alms, and good works as effective ways, other than the Eucharist, of saving souls.

The other Roman Catholic doctrine that comes under examination is the idea that salvation is exclusively reserved for Catholics. Contrary to the Catholic teaching, which has a restrictive understanding of salvation for humankind, Tasio says that God's salvation belongs to all. In questioning the churches' teaching that only Catholics will be saved and that even among them only 5 percent will be redeemed, Tasio says that on this issue he is on the side of the biblical Job. To illustrate what he has in mind, Tasio quotes an enigmatic saying: "Then let thistles grow instead of wheat. And weeds instead of barley" (Job 31:40). On reading this long monologue, one discovers that Job, among other things, explores the question of the parenthood of God and wonders how all are children of the same God and how God makes sure that both the righteous and the unrighteous are rewarded.[20]

The picture of the biblical god that emerges in Rizal's novel is a complicated one. The institutionalized church portrays God as one who demands absolute loyalty and as a vengeful God who defends the righteous and abandons the sinners to their fate, whereas the Filipino reading tries to recover an inclusive God who cares for human beings.

The Prophet Elijah as an Indian Idol

One of the biblical figures who is most visible in Asian novels is the prophet Elijah. He regularly appears in the novels of Esther David. David's novels are about the Bene Israel (Children of Israel) community of

India. She herself is a Bene Israel Jew. By way of brief introduction about this community, the Bene Israel is one of the three major Jewish communities in India, the other two being the Cochin Jews of southern India and the Bagdhadi Jews. Bene Israel Jews believe that they are the descendents of the tribe of Zebulum and claim that they were the original and the earliest Jewish settlers in India. Their accidental arrival was marked by dramatic events. The legend has it that those Jews trying to escape the persecution of Antiochus Epiphanes (c. 215–164 BCE) came as far as India and that their ship was wrecked on the Konkan coast on the western coastline of India. Having lost many of their books in the Arabian Sea, they preserved their tradition by retaining orally major prayers such as the declaration of faith, Shema Yisroel ("Hear o Israel, the Lord our God is one"), and the prayer to Eliyahu Hannibi or the prophet Elijah. This community easily incorporated a number of Indian customs and rituals in order to survive in India, including not only substituting coconut milk for dairy products to meet the Jewish dietary rules but also singing *kirtans* (devotional responsory chanting) about Moses, the Exodus, and the parting of the Red Sea set to the tune of popular Marathi kirtans about the birth of Krishna.[21] Such singing was undertaken while making the unleavened bread for the Passover.

Esther David's novels are about love, longing, guilt, dishonor, the success of the Bene Israel community, and their struggle to preserve their Jewish heritage in a land that throbs with a multiplicity of religions. Her novels tell the everyday story of Bene Israel, their immigration to Israel, the families who have been left behind in India, and their synagogues and homes, which have been abandoned and are in ruins. The narration is about how the characters constantly negotiate the fraught relationship between the ancient land and survival in a new society, which, if not antagonistic, is indifferent.

I do not have the space here to fully evaluate Esther David's novels and her enormous contribution to literature. For our purpose, I will pay attention to the important figure of the prophet Elijah, who appears frequently in most of her works. The Bene Israel believe that the prophet Elijah visited India twice. In the first instance, he was supposed to have revived those ancestors who had drowned in the sea when they were escaping from persecution. In the second instance, before his ascension to heaven, Elijah flew to India, leaving behind the marks of his horse's hooves and the chariot's wheels in a rock near Sagav, a hill station in Maharashrata, Western India. The rock is known as Eliyahu Hannabi cha Tapa. This has become a place of veneration and pilgrimage not only for the Bene Israel community but also for other faith communities. The popular belief is that the prophet Elijah did not die but is supposed to be wandering the earth, and the symbolic evidence of that is that he finds himself in the plot lines of Esther David's novels. The Prophet Elijah that emerges from Esther David's novels differs from the Elijah found in the Bible in a number of ways.

First, the prophet Elijah is not an ardent advocate of monotheism, for which he was famous in the Hebrew scriptures. Ironically, he becomes part of the multitude of Indian gods and goddess. During the reign of King Ahab, the prophet Elijah fought to preserve monotheistic ideals and shunned any influence of foreign and Gentile gods. In David's novels, the prophet Elijah becomes part of the Indian collection of deities—so much so that Rachel, the eponymous heroine in the *Book of Rachel* often says, "This is the land of the Prophet Elijah."[22] He even has a *bindi*—a red mark on his forehead, which symbolizes the third eye of the Lord Shiva. Abigayail, a character in *The Book of Esther*, whispers to Bathsheba that the prophet Elijah is "their Ganesha." As the narrative puts it, "in the land of idols, the relic was the image which helped the Bene Israel relate to their prophet."[23] More-over, he is not intolerant, as he is presented in the Hebrew Bible. In the Shalom India Housing Society, the prophet appreciates Ha-dasah, a writer of Jewish stories who cooks a non-kosher meal for the Passover and invites all communities to her sedar table. What annoys the prophet is not that Hadasah fails to observe the dietary restrictions but that the bindi that she is wearing is bigger than his.

Second, the prophet Elijah is turned into the very Baal he so much detested. In Esther David's narration, he is not the prophet who taunted King Ahab and the Israelites for worshiping false gods such as Baal. Now, in a foreign country, he assumes the characteristic of the object of his scorn. *Baal* is an etymologically enigmatic word that has many meanings. As a god of fertility, he is basically a pro-vider of life. He was ardently worshiped because prosperity and peoples' well-being were dependent on him. Elijah now takes on the role of the Indian god Ganesha. Like Ganesha, the prophet becomes provider and solver of everyday problems. In David's novels, Bene Is-rael families often call on Elijah to intervene in their lives and help them with the mundane daily problems they face. These personal favors vary from sorting out their love lives to making sure their chil-dren do well in school, saving families from harm, and uniting an estranged mother and daughter. Often the prophet answers their prayers, but at times he seems to have gone deaf. For example, the in-numerable pleas for a Jewish wife of Ben Hur, one of the residents of the Shalom Indian Housing Society, are apparently not granted. Sometimes the prophet takes some time, a year in the case of Jacob,[24] to come up with a solution. Often, though, his resolutions are those his devotees prayed for or expected.

Third, the prophet Elijah as encountered in Esther David's novels is not the one starved of food and fed frugally by the widow of

Zarephath but one who is overfed, enjoying sumptuous food and drink provided by the Bene Israel community. Plates of flaked rice and fruit are offered to him.[25] Ceremonially prepared malida, a platter consisting of dates, bananas, grapes, oranges, and sweet limes, is presented in thanksgiving for a secret wish granted.[26] His thirst is also well catered for. Most households have a special glass for the prophet and leave a goblet of sherbet or a glass of wine for him, and they leave the door open for him, just as Hindu homes leave the door open for the goddess Laxmi to enter.[27]

Fourth, the prophet Elijah is not stern and serious as often perceived in biblical portrayals. In Esther David's novels, the prophet emerges as a figure of fun. He suffers from long travel, jet lag, indigestion, and a hangover following the innumerable drinks he had during Passover. The four cherubs have a hard time looking after him.[28] To help him over his hangover, the cherubs rub his brow with tiger balm (an Indian pain reliever famous in Indian households) and make him numerous cups of black coffee; if this does not work, they give him aspirin dissolved in soda and milk. Although forbidden by Jewish law from worshiping idols or graven images, the Bene Israel community, finding themselves living in a country surrounded by the images of a multitude of deities, have created the cult of Elijah in order to help preserve Judaism. Pictures of Elijah hang in Bene Israel homes, despite Judaism's proscription, and his portraits adorn the households of Esther David's novels. A laminated calendar of Elijah hangs in Rachel's house.[29] The characters in David's novels often keep a chair for the prophet, to whom they bow, asking for health and happiness for the family.[30] Just like Hindus, Indian Jews offer coconuts at the shrine of their prophet Elijah.[31] Candles are often lit, in another Indian ritual appropriated by the Indian Jews.

At the time of Jesus, the prophet Elijah was held up as a fine exemplar of the Jewish prophets. This is illustrated by the question the disciples asked Jesus: Why do the scribes say that Elijah has to come first? In Esther David's novels, Elijah becomes Immanuel—God with us. His continued presence is felt by many characters. Rachel thinks that it is Elijah who is sitting next to her in the catamaran on her way back to Danda, the place where she lived. Another character, Satish Chinoy, says that he had a "strange but mystical encounter, a divine one" with the prophet and was shaken by the experience.[32] What emerges in Esther David's novels is a figure of the prophet Elijah who is charitable, comical, and compassionate, not fanatical and uncompromising as the Hebrew scripture portrays him.

Pilate as the Savior's Savior

Paul Zacharia, a novelist from Kerala in India, in his novella *What News, Pilate?* retells the trial of Jesus from the perspective of Pilate. The novella, as the author acknowledges, is based on Matthew 27–28, Mark 15–16, Luke 23–24, and John 18–20, though Zacharia employs hardly any direct biblical quotations. Jesus's appearance before Pilate is told mainly through letters written by Pilate and his secretary Ruth. Pilate writes to Antonius, his onetime boozing and fornicating partner whom he had last seen twenty-five years before when they were chased out of a Roman brothel by a stern madam for demanding Arab eunuchs after growing tired of Turkish beauties and Macedonian boys. Now Antonius runs a refuge for prostitutes, and Pilate is a Roman governor.

To Pilate, Jesus comes across as incoherent and politically disorganized. In Pilate's perception, Jesus was essentially a "truthful fellow who had fallen into a trap of his own making."[33] He is generally regarded as a man living in his own dream, without "any political authority or the military backing or the magical powers necessary to achieve" his goals.[34] Pilate writes to Antonius: "The way I understood it, he was neither a rebel nor a liar but an innocent man in search of a dream, and even in the thick of danger, he was in the grip of that dream."[35] In Pilate's view, it was Jesus's own folly that led to his death. As Pilate cannily observes, Jesus "can't be a saviour one minute and need saving himself the next."[36] Pilate looked on Jesus with a mixture of awe, pity, and envy, as the Galilean was adored by beautiful Jewesses. Unknown to Pilate, his wife also was a secret admirer of Jesus.

The overwhelming picture of Pilate is that he was voraciously bisexual but lousy in bed, as those who participated in his sexual escapades—Mariam, Anna, Rahel—testify. At the trial, he is not a detached and dispassionate judge. Pilate ogles the Jewish women who have gathered. But much worse, he feels sexually attracted to Yeshu. As Jesus stands in front of him charged with rebellion against the Roman empire, Pilate has the urge "to hold him to [his] chest like a kitten or a puppy, to fondle him and take care of him" or to "hold him in [his] palm like a nestling and stroke him."[37] It is through the fanciful musing of Pilate's secretary, Ruth, that we come to know more of Pilate's limitations and Yeshu's mesmerizing qualities. She teasingly ruminates on the contrasting powers of Yeshu and Pilate: "How can we ever make you understand that the joy Yeshu gave us was not what you think? . . . It was our hearts that he kissed like the breeze on a rose. It was our souls he entered, breaking through our allurements."[38] Pilate might look a harmless ravisher, but as Ruth sarcastically comments, "the simpleton within you carries out evil work too, with equal dispassion."[39]

In Zacharia's novella, Pilate is a complicated figure. The novel is not at all about his debauchery or about a calculating bureaucrat who wants to be remembered in history. There is a contemplative streak to him: "Tell me, is there anything a Roman governor might not do? And do my desires have limits? I love wine, women, food, soft beds, fast horses and the company of birds and animals. What can I do? History has cast all this bait my way. I nibble at each in turn and wait. The day will come when I swallow the bait and history's fishing rod casts me ashore. *Dhum!* Some thrashing about and it will all be over. History will no longer have any use for me."[40] What saves this flawed character is his love for birds and animals. He collects books and love poems. He is not the weak and indecisive figure who wants to appease the baying Jewish crowds as depicted in the Gospels, but as a man, he shows some modicum of moral scruples. He feels genuinely sorry about handing Jesus over to his opponents. Pilate tells his friend that he has sent so many people to death and has not felt a thing about it. As a ruler, sentencing was one of his duties. But he saw that Yeshu's case was different. "I felt a little distressed," he confesses to Antonius. He was genuinely trying to "rescue that young man Yeshu from those Jews."[41] Pilate shows an indisputable admiration for Jesus. Pilate writes to Antonius that Yeshu was the first person in his life that he had tried to save. In Paul Zacharia's novella, Pilate, the philanderer and pen pusher, tries to become the savior's savior.

Mischievous Priests, Mean Texts

In the Japanese writer Endo's novella *Yellow Man,* the Bible is seen as an incendiary book that induces people to act violently. The disgraced French Roman Catholic priest Durand, who took a Japanese wife, was pelted with stones by the very same students whom he had taught the catechism and the Bible. They "stoned him with stones," thus "literally executing the commands of the Bible."[42] The biblical phrase to which Endo alludes here comes from the book of Deuteronomy, which sanctions such violent acts (Deut. 22:23–24). Fallen from grace, Father Durand does not find the Bible offering any consolation to people like himself. All that the Bible has to offer, in his view, is punishment. In a state of despair and shame, Father Durand recalls the severe and outspoken verses in Matthew that offer drastic action to disciples who commit wrongdoings: "And if thy hand offend thee cut it off; it is better for thee to enter into life maimed, than having two hands to go into hell, into the fire that never shall be quenched." In the experience of Father Durand, the Bible has no message for Judases like himself who have lost their vocation. The fallen priest wonders why there is no saying in the Bible such as "Judas, I offer my hand to you, too. There is no sin in my book for which you will not be forgiven. My love is infinite." Disappointingly, all that the Bible records, according to Father Durand, are these terrible words: "Good were it for that man if he had never been born."[43] Those familiar with the Bible will immediately recognize the words of Jesus uttered to Judas at the Passover meal (Matt. 26:24). In *Yellow Man*, the Bible comes across as a book that communicates God's displeasure and judgment. In other words, the Bible does not offer redemption to people like Father Durand who have committed mistakes. The Bible is seen as a mean and merciless book.

The Bible as Word and as Object

In Yiyun Li's story "Son," the Bible is used as a book that possesses some power other than its normal textual impact. It is portrayed as a book with, besides its textual content, mystical and magical powers that have the potential to transform the lives of people. Its contents are rarely revealed. It is not only the textual but also the nontextual dimensions that offer meaning, connection, and vitality.

Han, the son in Li's story, is a thirty-five-year-old, single software engineer who returns to China after living in America for ten years. As a naturalized American, he has a new passport, but he also has an old Chinese worry—how to avoid the matrimonial proposals his mother will have lined up for him. For he is gay. But a surprise is awaiting him. Instead of choosing from an array of girls provided by his mother, she wants him to make a different choice—to join the Christian faith. As a way of enticing him, the mother, who remains nameless, presents him not with an album full of pictures of girls but with a specially ordered gold crucifix on a gold chain. The woman who has all along been obedient to the Communist Party and to her husband has now found a new purpose in life. The duteous Chinese mother has now become a Christian. To become a Christian is probably the only conscious decision she has made in her life. The God of the Bible has taken the place once reverentially reserved for Marx.

The newly converted mother wants her son to become a Christian like her. She urges Han that he "can always start with reading the Bible."[44] She tells him how people who did not believe her at first later saw their lives being changed as a result of reading the Bible. But the reader never comes to know which biblical passages inspired this Chinese or her fellow converts or what biblical insights prompted this transformation. This was the same woman who had earlier burned the Bible presented to Han by one of his friends. Han had been given this "precious gift" by a teenage boy. They were in love without realizing it. At that time, the publication of the Bible in China was closely supervised, and it was not easily available in bookshops. Han admired the trouble his friend had taken to find him a copy of the Bible for his thirteenth birthday. He kept it as a souvenir of his first love and took it with him wherever he went. Unknown to his mother, both boys spent a lot of time reading the Bible after school and finding "a heaven in the book while their classmates were competing to join the Communist Youth League."[45] Both were enamoured of the stories, and the "bigness of the book made their worries tiny and transient." While their classmates found fault with them for not being political, both laughed it off, knowing that the Bible allowed them to "live in a different, bigger world."[46] One day Han's father discovered the Bible and his mother promptly burned it, pouring the ashes into the toilet bowl. She not only subjected the sacred text to physical desecration but also ended Han's relationship both with his friend and with the Bible.

After her husband's death, Han's mother exchanges one loyalty for another. Marx, "her old god," has been exchanged for the God of the Bible. Now in the new capitalist China, it is the Bible that attracts her devotion and loyalty. But the son thinks that she and others like her were duped by the state. The church she attends is the church approved by the Communist Party and not the clandestine underground house churches persecuted by the state. He asks his mother whether she knows that the "state-licensed Churches recognize [the] Communist Party as their only leader." And he fervently hopes that some day she "will come up with the old conclusion that God and Marx are the same."[47] The Communist god has gone and she now has a new god in the form of the Bible to please her. For her son, this was all a trick by the Communist Party.

In the end, Han has to reveal his sexual orientation to his mother. She is not surprised. She tells him she suspected it all along, which is why she did not bother with any matchmaking. With his bitter experience in America with right-wing Christians, Han knows that he would be damned in China just as the counter-revolutionaries were condemned by the Marxists. In spite of her idiosyncratic manners, his mother understands him better than he was willing to allow. When self-pityingly he says that he will be damned, his mother tells him he is wrong: "God loves you for who you are, not what others expect you to be. God sees everything and understands everything."[48] Han is well aware of what the Bible has to say about homosexuality. He was reminded routinely in US shopping malls by people with hand-written signs condemning homosexuals. The cynic in him thinks that her new biblical "god is like the Chinese parent, never running out of excuses to love a son."[49]

In her effort to make Han a Christian, the mother does not use any biblical text. The Bible-reading mother does not quote from the Bible. She uses a saying from Confucius to remind her son that it is "never too late to know the truth. If one gets to know the truth in the morning, he can die in the evening without regret." In return, the son employs another Confucian saying: "When one reaches fifty, he is no longer deceived by the world."[50] In the crucial moment of the story, the Bible is relegated to the margin.

In essence, the Bible provides an alternative world for both the mother and her Chinese converts and for Han and his friend when they show an interest in the Bible. For the mother, the Bible offers freedom from the Marxist faith, and for Han and his friend, it helps them escape from their classmates competing to join the Communist Youth League.

For the mother, the Bible is both the divine word of God and a numinous artifact. She wants her son to read the Bible, but at the same time, as a physical object it acts as a potent force and a reminder of the providential presence of the divine. For her and other Chinese converts, the wonder of God is experienced not only through the meaning of the written word but also through the mere materiality of the Bible. The Bible, as the written word of God and an objective entity, represents the presence of and closeness to God.

In Yiyun Li's story, it is the Bible itself as a magical object rather than the use of any particular chapter or verse that offers meaning. The practical benefits of reading the Bible are described in vague terms. All that the reader is told is that the Bible presents Han and his unnamed friend with a substitute world and a new paradise, which are more seductive than the tedious earthly kingdom preached by the Communist Party. The power of the book entirely absorbed them. Yiyun Li's characters are not enslaved to the text. It is not the textual but the nontextual dimension that offers meaning, connection, and vitality. The mother and son's relationship to the text is not defined entirely by the Christian text but by the textual resources available in Chinese culture.

Bad News according to the Bible

The Bible provides the background for religious tensions in Rishi Reddy's short story "Lord Krishna." This story is about second-generation Indians and more specifically about Telugu Hindus in the United States. Set in Wichita, Kansas, controversy is caused by re-marks made in a class by the evangelically minded history teacher, Gabriel Hoffman, who is also a minster at the local church. Hoffman has a very strong conservative theological streak and has been sup-porting missionaries in Cameroon. The students in his class know his theological interests, and they also know that his teaching can be disrupted if they ask questions about religion. In earlier classes the students had heard him say how Jesus would have handled the Iran hostage crisis. A guest minister, who addresses the Friday morning school service, delivers a sermon about the devil. The students take this as a chance to distract Hoffman. Prompted by students who are uninterested in what Hoffman is teaching, he begins to speak about Satan. He starts insisting that it is important for "the spiritual life and the salvation of their souls" to know about Satan. He goes on to write several New Testament references to Satan on the board. But the reader never comes to know what these verses are, except for one that Hoffman bellows to the class: "Get thee behind me Satan." He provides the context in which this was uttered by Jesus. He tells the class that Satan exists even today, and the "Bible refers to him as a real entity."[51] Wanting to make Satan real and vivid, Hoffman does not repeat biblical portrayals of him but contemporizes Satan as a real adversary. His chilling presence is felt in everyday activities: "He makes you yell at your parents, or causes your brother to crash his car. He's at work when a drunk man beats his wife, or when a healthy person hears voices, or when a five-year old boy, like that poor child on the west side, jumps off a balcony to his death."[52] The implication is that the existence of Satan is real, and his presence leads human beings to hazardous situations. Hoffman's portrayals of Satan echoes the words of the first epistle of Peter, where Satan is described as a treacherous person, a roaring lion, who roams all over the earth "seeking whom he may devour" (5:8).

The Bible in Rishi Reddy's short story comes out not as a book of good news but as one that provides warnings and cautions people to be alert and vigilant. The Bible gives the impression that the presence of Satan is palpable and that he is waiting to allure people. Because the Bible validates his existence, Satan has become a constant threat to those who are less watchful. Such a description of Satan causes tension and stress for pupils such as Krishna, the Hindu boy, who sees

Satan as a trickster who can dupe impressionable people. When a five-year-old boy from Krishna's neighborhood falls from a balcony, it is believed that he was conned by Satan. When Krishna thinks about it, he "felt the hair on his neck rise."

As in the case of Yiyun Li's story, the biblical verses are mentioned only indirectly, but the biblical idea of Satan causes terror and tension in the classroom. The menacing presence of the Bible is evidently clear to the reader. In presenting only the darker side of the Bible, kinder and softer images of the Bible—loving one's neighbor, turning the other cheek—largely go unmentioned.

Comments, Observations

Most of the authors referred to here, except for Yiyun Li, Esther David, and Rishi Reddy, are Asians who are also Christians. These novels tease at some of the guiding principles of Christian faith and snipe at the church's bigotry and its heartless bureaucracy. The characters in these novels find organized religion both odious and unproductive. We hardly see them sermonizing. At times, to use the phrase of Simon Coleman, the Bible is "hyper-materialized" in their works, while at other times its appearance is suggestive and slight.

For these authors, the usefulness of biblical texts lies at their redacted or literal level, so there is an easy identification with biblical sayings, characters, and situations. These authors are keen to latch onto texts that make sense to their imaginary characters or fit in with the plot. They focus on texts that appeal immediately to their story line. In doing so, the counternarratives enshrined in the biblical texts get ignored or overlooked. Father Durand, in Endo's novel, complains that there is no word of consolation for people like him but fails to note that the same Passion narrative has words of forgiveness for all, even Judas, betrayer of Jesus. Similarly, Matthew 18:8, about amputating hand or foot or removing eyes, which sounds gruesome, appears in two novels, giving the impression that the Gospel is about causing physical pain and divisions among families. The other side of the Gospel—the Gospel as love, mercy, and forgiveness—hardly gets a mention. Finding echoes of one's own theological positions strips away complex nuances and a variety of positions within the biblical texts. The serious consequence of such an analogous identification is that it prevents competing narratives and ambivalences embedded in the Bible from shining through.

Viewed as a coherent and single text, the Bible in these novels makes connections and relationships with characters' own lives easy, but at the same time it can disconnect and make spiritual alliance difficult. Shlomo, the visiting historian from Israel, sends Esther, in David's *Book of Esther*, a couple of Bibles. Her response on receiving these reveals the effect they have on her: "I was deeply touched and the children experienced a sense of bonding with their religion, as they caressed the leather-bound Bible. It seemed to root us to something which had always been vague and distant."[53] In Esther's case, the Bible leads her to reacquaint herself with the religion of which she had only a dim and indistinct understanding. It also acts as a reminder of a lost tradition, history, and culture. But conversely, the same Bible generates alienation and distance. Chiba, a Japanese Christian who is unsure of his faith, writes to his former priest: "I simply didn't have the stomach to digest this white man—this Christ with blond hair and blond beard, as shown in your illustrated Bible."[54]

In these novels, the relationship to the Bible is defined as much by its materiality as by its spiritual content. In contrast to its actual content, the Bible as a physical object is meaningful. It is more than an object of sheets of paper and ink. It is regarded as a numinous book, signifying nearness of God and God's protection. Beyond the practical benefits of reading, the Bible is revered. Sometimes the Bible is caressed, as often by Sophy. At other times the Bible is placed prominently in the sitting room of the house. But not all characters hold the Bible in awe. Being unused and unread, it is allowed to gather dust. In Rachel's house, the holy books collect "layers of dust."[55] In Amy Tan's novel *The Joy Luck Club,* its usefulness lies in propping up the broken leg of the kitchen table.[56] The Dalits in *Othappu* abandon the Bible for being irrelevant to their cause. In Chan Koonchung's futuristic novel *The Fat Years,* the foreign imported Bibles are rejected as the Christian church benefits from the economic success of China.[57]

To the authors we have looked at, the Bible, one of the effective instruments of colonialism, has limited purchase in Asia. It will always be seen as a book from the outside and the religion it preaches as foreign. The skeptical narrator in Shusaku Endo's short story "Mothers" captures the mood aptly: "The words of the priests, and the stories in the Bible . . . they all seemed like intangible happening from a past that had nothing to do with us."[58] The Asian attitude to the Christian Bible can be summed up in the words of Sophy, the Cambodian immigrant to the United States. As a communicative artifact, she found it "hard and weird," and it "sounded so strange with all the *thous* and *shalts* and *saiths* and *begats.*"[59] But what she liked most was that as a physically produced instrument, the Bible was "soft, and nice to hold," and, more important, "you could kind of bend it in your hand." This is exactly what these Asian authors have been doing with their Bibles—bending it to suit their authorial needs.

Conclusion

The Asian biblical interpretations discussed in this volume make clear that the highly cherished Protestant principle of scripture alone has little purchase in Asia. The reformers' claim that the Bible is sufficient and the sole truth is untenable in a continent that teems with textual traditions. What is more, such a claim is misleading. Asian interpretation has shown that when an Asian Christian reads the Bible, he or she does not read it alone but alongside something else. It has always been the Bible plus the Bhagavad Gita or the Dhammapada or the Analects. Read in Asia, the Christian Bible needs to be illuminated by other textual traditions in order to gain credibility and relevance.

In the former colonies, the Christian Bible has a contaminated image that is not entirely due to its association with modern colonialism. The fault lies to some extent in the Bible itself because of the innate colonial impulses enshrined in some of its narratives. It has also been contaminated by the colonial mindset through which these narratives have sometimes been expounded by Western interpreters. Nevertheless, Asian interpreters, from the time when modern colonialism first introduced the Bible, have refused to accept the Bible or its interpretation as these were presented to them. In the hands of the Asian biblical interpreters assembled here, its sacredness, universality, and canonical status have all been vigorously questioned. Put another way, the status of the Christian Bible as an unsurpassed spiritual source has been under constant investigation and scrutiny.

Asia never had a Christian Asoka who was able to provide state patronage. The successful spread of Buddhism both east- and westward was largely due to the emperor Asoka's missionary efforts. Oriental Christianity did not have such indigenous support, and it hardly penetrated the Asian cultures, as the Orthodox, Catholic, and Protestant churches did the West. Bible reading and biblical interpretation are undertaken in a continent where Gospel and church are not in charge and, more pertinently, where Asian societies and cultures do not depend on Christian values for their good governance or development. The Christian Bible plays only a marginal role in Asia. Unlike in the West, where it is a preeminent cultural authority, in Asia the Bible is one of many textual authorities. The task, then, is not to clamor for its unique authority or to call for it to be made the foundational document but to help Asia move toward a postscriptural society liberated from the monopolistic claim of any particular sacred scripture. The task becomes urgent at a time when religious fundamentalists of all religions resort to their respective scriptures to justify their hatred and violence against others.

One critical question has been hardly addressed by Asian biblical interpreters or for the matter by Asian theologians—namely, biblical monotheism. The monotheism of the Bible is a problem in a continent that brims with gods and goddesses. Most Asian Christians either previously belonged to one of the polytheistic faiths that flourish in Asia or live among those communities whose worldview is polytheistic. People today are complex and multifaceted, drawing from a large pool of religious, cultural, and ideological alternatives in order to forge and determine their identities. Moreover, for many there is no longer a fixed center holding everything together. In such a scenario, can one go on affirming monotheistic ideals that stand for a single perspective and reality? Monotheism suppresses diversity and ignores the possibility of many centers. The biblical understanding of Yahweh as a single god to be worshipped was a late entrant in the history of Israel. To use the colorful phrase of Karen Armstrong, Yahweh had been a "member of the Divine Assembly of 'holy ones,'"[1] and the Israelites continued to worship a multitude of holy beings until the time of the destruction of the temple by Nebuchadnezzar in 586 BCE. Asian interpreters need to revisit this critical issue. What I am advocating is not a return to the veneration of a host of deities but an exploration of the polytheistic spirit that promotes tolerance, generosity, and mutual coexistence.

What is manifestly noticeable is that there is no single book on the social history of the Bible in Asia. The continent has produced biblical interpreters with depth and insight, but most of their work, as I noted earlier, falls under the rubric of homiletics. They are largely apologetic, mission-oriented, and confessional. They seem to have been untroubled by the impact of the Bible outside the church compound. What is the social life of the Bible? And how individually and collectively is it received and appropriated by Hindus, Buddhists, Confucians, and Taoists? Asia is still to produce a cultural history of the Bible situating it firmly within the intersecting religious, literary, economic, and social contexts of the continent. The reception history of the Bible in Asia is not a uniform one. The economics of scripture publishing, the social cost of Bible distribution, the membership, recruitment, and pricing policy, and the image of various Bible societies remain unexplored. The impact of Bible translations, especially the

Sanskritization of Indian languages such as Tamil, the standardization of vernacular grammars, introduction of chapters and verses to Indian religious texts including the Bhagavad Gita, the obsession with the original meaning of texts, and the effect of the Bible on the sacred writings of India, have to be revisited again. Another side effect of Bible production was the introduction of the printing press in India, which led to a new type of religious and secular publishing that had to encounter the Christian Gospel and the European literary tradition. The effects printing had on the formation of national and religious identity and the orality of Indian tradition is worth examining. The Bible as an object of cultural transfer has yet to be investigated and documented. Its role in the articulation of caste affiliations, Protestant, Catholic, and Orthodox identities, and its contribution to the politics of language are yet to be articulated.

Linked to this is another task—that of raiding Asian archives. There are so many archives to be explored, narratives to be constructed and shared. We have no proper historians who can delve into the archives without carrying unnecessary ecclesiastical baggage or vested denominational interests. To name a few outstanding tasks, researchers have yet to explore the history of the Bible in Dutch-occupied Indonesia; the intriguing history of the role of the Bible in the Vietnam War; Korean readings of the Bible during the Japanese occupation; and, conversely, how Japanese Christians biblically justified or opposed the Korean conquest. There is so much material that has been scarcely studied and rarely explored, while materials on the same few topics are churned out routinely. Why should a Korean write the fortieth dissertation on Minjung theology, when he or she might be investigating the intertextual activities of Sir-hak Confucians, whose contrapuntal reading of Christian and Confucian texts were undertaken without the coaxing or the control of the missionaries in the eighteenth century? Why should a Japanese feminist write the thirtieth article on the eloquence of the Syrophoenican woman when she can bring out the first book on the hermeneutical implications of Matsumara Kaiseki's (1859–1939) Dokai Bible, which offered a countertext to the version of the New Testament introduced by the missionaries? Why should an Indian Dalit produce the eightieth dissertation on the wounded psyche of the Dalits when she or he could be writing the first history of Rajanaiken, supposedly the first Dalit biblical expositor in colonial India? Rajanaiken was a Roman Catholic convert who joined the Lutheran Church because he could not find a Tamil Catholic version of the Bible at that time. He was an army officer serving the Rajah of Tanjore—a small kingdom in South India. Rajanaiken was excited to find that the Tamil word used to describe the Roman soldier Cornelius in Acts—*servaikaran*—was similar to his rank, and he determined to model himself as a latter-day Cornelius. Yet very little has been written about Rajanaiken. We need to critically explore our archives and lift up the forgotten productive activity of an earlier generation.

Let me conclude with a few final observations. After being in the business for more than three decades, I get the sense that what Asian and, for that matter, African, Latin American, Caribbean, and Pacific biblical interpreters do is seen as relevant only to their immediate contexts rather than as having a universal appeal that spans continents and epochs. Their work is seen as little more than anticolonial and anti-Western protest and is not admired for its intellectual dynamism and creativity.

The often complacent claim of Asians and others that their interpretations are an "alternative discourse" may send a wrong signal. Such an assertion takes for granted a persisting and undisturbed preeminence of Western interpretation without making a serious and significant dent in it. It makes more sense to speak of a "coterminous" rather than merely an "alternative" or "derivative" discourse, with the same scope and range of meanings as the dominant Western scholarship. Such an altered perception, allowing for the coexistence of multiple interpretations with equal hermeneutical standing, would—to borrow a phrase from Mao—enable a hundred interpretative flowers to bloom and a hundred schools of thought to flourish.

Up to the present, an imaginary West has provided a valuable service for Asian biblical hermeneutics. This invented authority has functioned in a variety of ways for Asian biblical interpreters—as a benchmark to emulate, a body of knowledge to vie with, a standard system of reference, a contrasting entity, a pretext for dissension and discussion, an ideal to aspire after, and a cherished adversary. Asian biblical interpretation has been informed by this "West" and has evolved in dialogue with it. Asian biblical interpreters should break away from such a stranglehold now, however, and should initiate and broker new conversations that encourage people to look at scripture anew and transform their understanding. The new task that waits Asian biblical interpreters is to engage with multiple frames of reference so that our anxiety over the West is allayed, and productive work can flourish. I end this volume with the words of a mother to her daughter in Nozipo Maraire's novel *Zenzele: A Letter for My Daughter*. One may find her advice a bit bombastic, but its essence is a powerful encouragement for Asian interpreters. I beg her pardon for substituting "Asia" for "Africa": "You must absorb multiple frames of reality. Keep your eyes wide open. Take in the good and reject the bad insofar as you perceive them. Asia will be whatever you and others like you make of it. Without you it is nothing."[2]

Notes

Introduction

1. K. N. Chaudhuri, *Asia before Europe: Economy and Civilization of the Indian Ocean from the Rise of Islam to 1750* (Cambridge: Cambridge University Press, 1990), 22.

2. Korhonen, "Asia's Chinese Name," *Inter-Asia Cultural Studies* 3, no. 2 (2002): 266.

3. Ibid.

4. Ibid., 253.

5. Ibid., 267.

6. Donald F. Lach, *Asia in the Making of Europe,* vol. 1 (Chicago: University of Chicago Press, 1965), 4.

7. R. A. Palat, "India and Asia," *The Hindu,* April 12, 2000, http:/www.hindu /thehindu/2000/12/04/stories/05042534.htm.

8. Lach, *Asia in the Making of Europe,* 4.

9. Martin Palmer, *The Jesus Sutras: Rediscovering the Lost Scrolls of Taoist Christianity* (London: Judy Piatkus Publishers, 2001).

10. *After a Hundred Years: A Popular Illustrated Report of the British and Foreign Bible Society for the Centenary Year 1903–1904* (London: The Bible House, 1904), 99.

11. G. M. Soares-Prabhu, "Two Mission Commands: An Interpretation of Matthew 28:16–20 in the Light of a Buddhist Text," *Biblical Interpretation: A Journal of Contemporary Approaches* 2, no. 3 (1995): 270.

12. Ashis Nandy, *The Intimate Enemy: Loss and Recovery of Self under Colonialism* (Delhi: Oxford University Press, 1988), xi.

1. Merchandise, Moralities, and Poetics of Aryans, Dravidians, and Israelites

1. Randall C. Bailey, " 'Why He Is Wearing the King's Drapes?': Interse(ct)/(x)ionality of Race/Ethnicity, Gender and Sexuality in the Book of Esther" (unpublished paper).

2. D. T. Potts, *Mesopotamian Civilization: The Material Foundations* (London: Athlone Press, 1997), 261.

3. Ibid.

4. Ibid.

5. A. W. Streane, *The Book of Esther with Introduction and Notes* (Cambridge: Cambridge University Press, 1907), 7.

6. Lewis Bayles Paton, *A Critical and Exegetical Commentary on the Book of Esther* (Edinburgh: T. & T. Clark, 1908), 152.

7. P. T. Srinivasa Iyengar, *History of the Tamils: From the Earliest Times to 600 a.d.* (Madras: C. Coomarasawmy Naidu & Sons, 1929; reprint, New Delhi: Asian Educational Services 1982), 6.

8. Ibid., 202.

9. J. Kennedy, "The Indians in Armenia, 130 b.c.–300 a.d.," *Journal of the Royal Asiatic Society*, n.s., 36 (1904): 309–314. See also Srinivasa Iyengar, *History of the Tamils*, 205.

10. Stanley A. Cook, *The "Truth" of the Bible* (Cambridge: W. Heffer and Sons, 1938), 24.

11. M. F. Müller, *The Science of Language: Founded on Lectures Delivered at the Royal Institution in 1861 and 1863 in Two Volumes*, vol. 1 (London: Longmans, Green, and Co., 1899), 192.

12. M. F. Müller, *India: What Can It Teach Us?* (London: Longmans, Green, and Co., 1892), 10.

13. Müller, *The Science of Language*, 188.

14. Srinivasa Iyengar, *History of the Tamils*, 129.

15. J. Kennedy, "The Early Commerce of Babylon with India 700–300 B.C.," *Journal of the Royal Asiatic Society*, n.s. 30 (1898): 252. See also Zacharias P. Thundy, *Buddha and Christ: Nativity Stories and Indian Traditions* (Leiden: E. J. Brill, 1993), 213.

16. *The Periplus of the Erythraen Sea: Travels and Trade in the Indian Ocean by a Merchant of the First Century*, trans. Wilfred H. Schoff (London: Longman, Green, and Co., 1912), 153.

17. Srinivasa Iyengar, *History of the Tamils*, 101.

18. Robert Caldwell, *A Comparative Grammar of the Dravidian or South Indian Family of Languages* (London: Trubner and Co., 1875), 93–95. See also Müller, *The Science of Language*, 188–191.

19. Stuart Piggott, *Prehistoric India to 1000 B.C.* (Harmondsworth: Penguin Books, 1950), 208.

20. Potts, *Mesopotamian Civilization*, 261. See also Dominique Collon, "Ivory," *Iraq* 39, no. 2 (1977): 219–222; and A. L. Oppenheim, "The Seafaring Merchants of Ur," *Journal of the American Oriental Society* 74, no. 1 (1954): 6–17.

21. R. Champakalakshmi, *Trade, Ideology and Urbanization: South India from 300 BC to AD 1300* (Delhi: Oxford University Press, 1996), 117.

22. E. H. Warmington, *The Commerce between the Roman Empire and India* (Cambridge: Cambridge University Press, 1928), 38.

23. Srinivasa Iyengar, *History of the Tamils*, 196.

24. Müller, *India*, 11.

25. Max F. Müller, *Last Essays: Essays on Language, Folklore and Other Subjects. Collected Works of the Right Hon. F. Max Muller XVII* (London: Longmans, Green, and Co., 1901), 269–270.

26. "So the men turned from there, and went toward Sodom, while Abraham remained standing before the LORD" (18:22).

"The LORD said, 'Shall I hide from Abraham what I am about to do, seeing that Abraham shall become a great and mighty nation, and all the nations of the earth shall be blessed in him?'" (18:18–19).

27. Irwing F. Wood, "Folk-Tales in Old Testament Narrative," *Journal of Biblical Literature* 28, no. 1 (1909): 39.

28. M. James, "The Apocryphal Ezekiel," *Journal of Theological Studies* 15, no. 58 (1914): 236–243. See also *The Lost Apocrypha of the Old Testament: Their Titles and Fragments Collected, Translated and Discussed by Montague Rhodes James*, trans. M. R. James (London: Society for the Promoting Christian Knowledge, 1920), 64–68.

29. George Foot Moore, *Judaism in the First Centuries of the Christian Era: The Age of the Tannaim*, vol. 2 (Cambridge, MA: Harvard University Press, 1948), 148n206.

30. George Foot Moore, *Judaism in the First Centuries of the Christian Era: The Age of the Tannaim*, vol. 1 (New York: Schocken Books, 1971), 487.

31. Müller, *Last Essays*, 282.

32. E. J. Thomas, "Introduction," in *Jātaka Tales: Selected and Edited with Introduction and Notes*, ed. H. T. Francis and E. J. Thomas (Bombay: Jaico Publishing House, 1957), iv.

33. Thundy, *Buddha and Christ*, 217.

34. A. R. Venkatachalapathy, "Introduction: Tradition, Talent, Translation," in *Love Stands Alone: Selections from Sangam Poetry*, ed. A. Venkatachalapathy, trans. M. L. Thangappa (New Delhi: Viking, 2010), xx.

35. Chaim Rabin, "The Song of Songs and Tamil Poetry," *Studies in Religion* 3, no. 3 (1973–1974): 216.

36. Ibid., 211.

37. Peter C. Craigie, "Biblical and Tamil Poetry: Some Further Reflections," *Studies in Religion* 8, no. 2 (1979): 169.

38. Abraham Mariaselvam, *The Song of Songs and Ancient Tamil Love Poems: Poetry and Symbolism* (Rome: Editrice Pontificio Istituto Biblico, 1988), 285.

39. Ibid., 286.

40. E. S. Shaffer, *"Kubla Khan" and the Fall of Jerusalem: The Mythological School in Biblical Criticism and Secular Literature, 1770–1880* (Cambridge: Cambridge University Press, 1975), 83.

41. Henry Barclay Swete, *The Apocalypse of St. John: The Greek Text with Introduction Notes and Indices* (London: Macmillan, 1922), lxvi.

42. Nicol Macnicol, "India in the New Testament," *Expository Times* 55, no. 2 (1943): 51.

43. Richard Garbe, *India and Christendom: The Historical Connections between Their Religions* (La Salle, IL: Open Court Publishing Company, 1959), 59.

44. John W. McCrindle, *Ancient India as Described in Classical Literature* (Amsterdam: Philo Press, 1901), 78.

45. Roy C. Amore, *Two Masters, One Message: The Lives and Teachings of Gautama and Jesus* (Nashville: Abingdon, 1978).

46. Jean W. Sedlar, *India and the Greek World: A Study in the Transmission of Culture* (Totowa, NJ: Rowman & Littlefield, 1980), 238.

47. Charles Eliot, *Hinduism and Buddhism: An Historical Sketch in Three Volumes*, vol. 3 (London: Edward Arnold, 1921), 436.

48. Amore, *Two Masters, One Message*, 151.

49. R. Otto, *The Kingdom of God and the Son of Man: A Study in the History of Religion* (London: Lutterworth Press, 1938), 187.

50. Ibid., 189.

51. Ibid., 195.

52. Ibid., 205.

53. Ibid., 206.

54. Ibid., 205.

55. J. B. Lightfoot, *St. Paul's Epistles to the Colossians and to Philemon. A Revised Text with Introductions, Notes, and Dissertations* (London: Macmillan, 1879), 395.

56. Ibid., 386.

57. Ulrich Luz and Axel Michaels, *Encountering Jesus and Buddha: Their Lives and Teachings* (Minneapolis: Fortress Press, 2006), xiii.

58. *Buddhist Suttas: Vol. XI of The Sacred Books of the East,* trans. R. T. Davids (Oxford: Clarendon Press, 1881), 165.

59. S. Radakrishnan, *Eastern Religions and Western Thought* (Oxford: Clarendon Press, 1939), 186.

60. Albert J. Edmunds, "Buddhist Loans to Christianity with Special Reference to Richard Garbe," *The Monist* 22 (January 1912): 137.

61. Ibid.

62. Ibid., 136.

63. Albert J. Edmunds, "Buddhist Loans to Christianity with Special Reference to Richard Garbe: Second Article," *The Monist* 22, no. 4 (October 1912): 636.

64. Garbe, *India and Christendom,* 21.

65. Ibid., 60.

66. Ibid., 184.

67. Edgar J. Bruns, *The Christian Buddhism of St. John: New Insights into the Fourth Gospel* (New York: Paulist Press, 1971), vii.

68. Edmunds, "Buddhist Loans to Christianity" (January 1912), 138.

69. The Jesus Seminar is a group of critical scholars working on the questions of a historical Jesus and the origins of Christianity.

70. N. Cohn, *Cosmos, Chaos, and the World to Come: The Ancient Roots of Apocalyptic Faith,* 2nd ed. (New Haven, CT: Yale University Press, 1996).

71. J. C. Hindley, "A Prophet outside Israel? Thoughts on the Study of Zoroastrianism," *Indian Journal of Theology* 11, no. 3 (1962): 107.

72. Cook, *The "Truth" of the Bible,* 158.

73. Amore, *Two Masters, One Message,* 111.

74. Müller, *Last Essays,* 289.

75. Ibid., 272.

76. Ibid., 263.

77. Ibid., 275.

78. Ibid., 251–290.

79. Ibid., 279.

80. Edward W. Said, *Orientalism* (London: Penguin Books, 1978), 109–110.

81. Craigie, "Biblical and Tamil Poetry," 169.

82. Wilfred H. Schoff, "A Postscript to Indo-Roman Relations in the First Century," *The Monist* 22, no. 4 (October 1912): 638.

83. Ibid., 638.

84. Eliot, *Hinduism and Buddhism*, vol. 3, 429.

85. Ibid., 431.

86. A. Lillie, *India in Primitive Christianity* (London: Kegan Paul, Trench, Trübner & Co, 1909), 165.

87. McCrindle, *Ancient India as Described in Classical Literature*, 177.

88. S. Radakrishnan, *Eastern Religions and Western Thought* (Oxford: Clarendon Press, 1939), 188. See also Thundy, *Buddha and Christ*, 247–248.

89. H. G. Rawlinson, "India in European Literature and Thought," in *The Legacy of India*, ed. G. T. Garratt (Oxford: Clarendon Press, 1938), 8.

90. See Eusebius of Caesarea, *Praeparatio Evangelica (Preparation for the Gospel)*, trans. E. H. Gifford (1903), Web edition, http://www.tertullian.org.fathers /eusebuis_pc_11_book 11.htm. See also Rawlinson, "India in European Literature and Thought," 8.

91. Jorge L. Borges, *Fictions* (London: Penguin Books, 1998), 69.

92. Ibid., 71.

2. *Colonial Bureaucrats and the Search for Older Testaments*

1. John Muir, "St. Paul a Model for the Missionary," *Calcutta Christian Observer* 7, no. 69 (February 1838): 72.

2. A. M. Ramsay, *The Philosophical Principles of Natural and Revealed Religion. Part Second* (Glasgow: Robert and Andrew Foulis, 1749), 301.

3. Ibid., 183.

4. Ibid., 121.

5. For a succinct summary of the debate surrounding the authenticity of Holwell's text, see Urs App, *The Birth of Orientalism* (Philadelphia: University of Pennsylvania Press, 2010), 298–299.

6. J. Z. Holwell, *Interesting Historical Events Relative to the Provinces of Bengal and the Empire of Indostan, Part 3* (London: T. Becket and P. A. De Hondt, 1771), 52.

7. Ibid., 43; emphasis in original.

8. Ibid., 52.

9. Ibid.; emphasis in original.

10. J. Z. Holwell, *Interesting Historical Events Relative to the Provinces of Bengal and the Empire of Indostan, Part 2* (London: T. Becket and P. A. De Hondt, 1767), 23.

11. Holwell, *Interesting Historical Events, Part 3,* 50.

12. J. Z. Holwell, *Interesting Historical Events Relative to the Provinces of Bengal and the Empire of Indostan, Part 1* (London: T. Becket and P. A. De Hondt, 1765), 3–4.

13. Daniel Caracostea, "Louis-François Jacolliott (1837–1890): A Biographical Essay," *Theosophical History* 9, no. 1 (January 2003): 12–39.

14. Louis Jacolliot, *The Bible in India: Hindoo Origin of Hebrew Revelation of Science* (London: John Camden Hotten, 1870), 13; emphasis in original.

15. Ibid., viii.

16. Ibid., 17.

17. Ibid., 296.

18. Ibid., 127.

19. Ibid., 63.

20. Ibid., 13.

21. Ibid., 64.

22. Ibid., viii.

23. Holwell, *Interesting Historical Events, Part 3,* 36.

24. Ibid., 71.

25. Holwell, *Interesting Historical Events, Part 2,* 23.

26. Ibid., 12.

27. Holwell, *Interesting Historical Events, Part 3,* 37; emphasis in original.

28. Ibid., 38.

29. Ibid., 159.

30. Ibid., 50, 51.

31. Ibid., 71.

32. Ibid., 51.

33. Ibid., 89; emphasis in original.

34. Ibid., 36.

35. Ibid., 217.

36. Jacolliot, *The Bible in India,* 45.

37. Ibid., 181.

38. Ibid., 185.

39. Ibid., 98.

40. Ibid., 187.

41. Ibid., 113.

42. Ibid., 170.

43. Ibid., 169.

44. Ibid., 307.

45. Ibid., 298.

46. Jacolliot's contention that the Gospels are myths concurs with David Strauss's claim that the Gospels were mythological (*The Life of Jesus, Critically Examined*, 3 vols. [London, 1846]). Although it is not the main issue in this study, it would be worth probing whether these two interpreters understood myths in the same way.

47. Jacolliot, *The Bible in India*, 125.

48. Ibid., 175.

49. Ibid., 133.

50. Ibid., 317.

51. Ibid., 189.

52. Ibid., 264.

53. Holwell, *Interesting Historical Events, Part 3*, 154; emphasis in original.

54. Ibid., 161; emphasis in original.

55. Jacolliot, *The Bible in India*, 122.

56. Holwell, *Interesting Historical Events, Part 3*, 20.

57. Jacolliot, *The Bible in India*, 120.

58. Ibid., 210.

59. Ibid., 136.

60. Ibid., 161.

61. Ibid., 122.

62. Ibid., 122.

63. Ibid., 123.

64. Ibid., 168.

65. Ibid., 170.

66. Ibid., 168; emphasis in original.

67. Holwell, *Interesting Historical Events, Part 3*, 14.

68. Ibid., 19.

69. Ibid., 13.

70. Jacolliot, *The Bible in India*, 167.

71. Ibid., 167.

72. Ibid., 200.

73. Ibid., 54.

74. Holwell, *Interesting Historical Events, Part 3*, 65.

75. Ibid., 80; emphasis in original.

76. Holwell, *Interesting Historical Events, Part 2*, 7; emphasis in original.

77. Holwell, *Interesting Historical Events, Part 3*, 56; emphasis in original.

78. Ibid., 53.

79. Ibid., 146; emphasis in original.

80. Ibid., 145; emphasis in original.

81. Ibid., 63.

82. Jacolliot, *The Bible in India*, 300.

83. Ibid., 96.

84. Ibid., 319.

85. Holwell, *Interesting Historical Events, Part 3*, 222.

86. *The Travels of Several Learned Missioners of the Society of Jesus into Divers Parts of the Archipelago, India, China, and America* (London: Printed for R. Gosling, at the Mitre and Crown, over against St. Dunstan's Church, in Fleet Street, 1794), 3.

87. Ibid., 10.

88. Ibid., 25.

89. Ibid., 17.

90. Jacolliot, *The Bible in India*, 16.

91. Holwell, *Interesting Historical Events, Part 2*, 152.

92. Holwell, *Interesting Historical Events, Part 1*, 6.

93. Ibid., 5.

94. Holwell, *Interesting Historical Events, Part 3*, 221.

95. Ibid., 50.

96. Ibid., 8.

97. Jacolliot, *The Bible in India*, 56.

98. Holwell, *Interesting Historical Events, Part 1*, 7.

99. Ibid., 11.

100. Jacolliot, *The Bible in India*, 47.

101. Ibid., 47.

102. Ibid., 127.

103. Ibid., 130.

104. *The Life and Letters of the Right Honourable Friedrich Max Müller in Two Volumes*, vol. 2, ed. Georgina Adelaide Müller (London: Longmans, Green, and Co., 1902), 455.

105. Choan-Seng Song, "From Israel to Asia: A Theological Leap," *The Ecumenical Review* 28, no. 3 (1976): 258.

3. Enlisting Christian Texts for Protest in the Empire

1. *The English Works of Raja Rammohun Roy*, ed. Jogendra Chunder Ghose (New Delhi: Cosmo Print, 1906), 74.

2. Ibid., 943.

3. Lant Carpenter, *A Review of the Labours, Opinions, and Character, of Rajah Rammohun Roy* (London: Rowland Hunter, 1833), 57.

4. *The English Works of Raja Rammohun Roy*, 628.

5. Ibid., 876.

6. Ibid., 630.

7. Ibid., 605–606.

8. Ibid., 606.

9. Ibid., 608.

10. Joshua Marshman, *A Defence of the Deity and Atonement of Jesus Christ, in Reply to Ram-Mohun Roy of Calcutta* (London: Kingsbury, Parbury, and Allen, 1822), 10.

11. Ibid., 8.

12. Ibid., 2.

13. Ibid., 3.

14. For a detailed discussion of the debate, see R. S. Sugirtharajah, *Asian Biblical Hermeneutics and Postcolonialism: Contesting the Interpretations* (Sheffield, UK: Sheffield Academic Press, 1999), 29–53.

15. Marshman, *A Defence of the Deity and Atonement of Jesus Christ*, 18.

16. Ibid., 65.

17. Rajaiah D. Paul, *They Kept the Faith* (Lucknow: Lucknow Publishing House, 1968), 58.

18. *The English Works of Raja Rammohun Roy*, 875. See also Sophia Dobson Collet, *The Life and Letters of Raja Rammohun Roy, Edited by Dilip Kumar Biswas and Prabhat Chandra Ganguli* (Calcutta: Sadharan Brahmo Samaj, 1900), 151; emphasis in original.

19. Theodore Hamberg, *The Visions of Hung-Siu-Tshuen, and Origin of the Kwang-si Insurrection* (Hong Kong: China Mail, 1854), 10.

20. Ibid., 10–11.

21. J. C. Cheng, *Chinese Sources for the Taiping Rebellion, 1850–1864* (Hong Kong: Hong Kong University Press, 1963), 8.

22. *The Taiping Rebellion: History and Documents in Three Volumes:* vol. 2, *Documents and Comments*, ed. Franz Michael in collaboration with Chung Chung-li-Chang (Seattle: University of Washington Press, 1971), 156–157.

23. Ibid., 44.

24. Ibid., 114.

25. Ibid., 120.

26. Ibid., 74.

27. Ibid., 316.

28. Cheng, *Chinese Sources for the Taiping Rebellion,* 84.

29. Ibid.

30. Ibid., 83.

31. *The Taiping Rebellion,* 225.

32. Ibid., 113.

33. Thomas H. Reilly, *The Taiping Heavenly Kingdom: Rebellion and the Blasphemy of Empire* (Seattle: University of Washington Press, 2004), 99.

34. Jonathan Spence, *God's Chinese Son: The Taiping Heavenly Kingdom of Hong Xiuquan* (London: Flamingo, 1996).

35. *The Taiping Rebellion,* 313–314.

36. Ibid., 63.

37. Ibid., 62.

38. Joseph Edkins, "Narrative of a Visit to Nanking," in *Chinese Scenes and People,* ed. Jane R. Edkins (London: James Nisbet and Co., 1863), 295.

39. Thomas Taylor Meadows, *The Chinese and Their Rebellions* (London: Smith, Elder, and Co., 1856), 449.

40. *The Taiping Rebellion,* 222.

41. Silvester C. Horne, *The Story of the L.M.S 1795–1895* (London: London Missionary Society, 1895), 316.

42. Betram Wolferstan, *The Catholic Church in China from 1860–1907* (London: Sands and Company, 1909), 105.

43. Joseph Edkins, *The Religious Condition of the Chinese with Observations on the Prospects of Christian Conversion amongst That People* (London: Routledge, Warnes, & Routledge, 1859), 286.

44. Ibid., 273.

45. Griffith John, "The Chinese Rebellion" (1861), in *Western Reports on Taiping: A Selection of Documents,* ed. Prescott Clarke and J. S. Gregory (Honolulu: University of Hawai'i Press, 1982), 278.

46. Edkins, *The Religious Condition of the Chinese,* 286.

47. Ibid., 277.

48. J. C. Kumarappa, *Christianity, Its Economy and Way of Life* (Ahmedabad: Navajivan Publishing House, 1945), 23.

49. Ibid., 83.

50. Ibid., 87.

51. Ibid., 88.

52. Ibid., 91.

53. Ibid., 89.

54. Ibid., 91.

55. Ibid., 93.

56. Ibid.

57. Ibid., 98.

58. J. C. Kumarappa, *Practice and Precepts of Jesus* (Ahmedabad: Navajivan Publishing House, 1945), 1.

59. Kumarappa, *Christianity, Its Economy and Way of Life*, 22.

60. Edkins, "Narrative of a Visit to Nanking," 274.

61. William James Hail, *Tsêng Kuo-Fan and the Taiping Rebellion, with a Short Sketch of His Later Career* (New Haven, CT: Yale University Press, 1927), 102.

62. *The Taiping Rebellion*, 159.

63. Ibid., 305.

64. *The English Works of Raja Rammohun Roy*, 567.

65. Kumarappa, *Christianity, Its Economy and Way of Life*, 63.

66. Kumarappa, *Practice and Precepts of Jesus*, 37.

67. *The Taiping Rebellion*, 234.

68. Edkins, "Narrative of a Visit to Nanking," 292.

69. *The English Works of Raja Rammohun Roy*, 484.

70. Kumarappa, *Practice and Precepts of Jesus*, 107–108.

71. Kumarappa, *Christianity, Its Economy and Way of Life*, 77.

72. *The Taiping Rebellion*, 159.

73. *The English Works of Raja Rammohun Roy*, 552.

74. Kumarappa, *Christianity, Its Economy and Way of Life*, 10.

75. Spence, *God's Chinese Son*, 233.

4. A Buddhist Ascetic and His Maverick Misreadings of the Bible

1. Anagarika Dharmapala, *Return to Righteousness: A Collection of Speeches, Essays and Letters of Anagarika Dharmapala*, ed. Ananda Guruge (Colombo, Sri Lanka: The Government Press, 1965), 701.

2. Ibid., 699.

3. Ibid., 684.

4. Ibid., 685.

5. For the life, work, and contemporary assessment of Dharmapala, see Ananda Guruge, "Introduction," in *Return to Righteousness*, xvii–lxxxv.

6. Spence R. Hardy, *The Sacred Books of the Buddhists Compared with History and Modern Science* (Colombo, Sri Lanka: Wesleyan Mission Press, 1863), 157.

7. Spence R. Hardy, *Christianity and Buddhism Compared* (Colombo, Sri Lanka: The Wesleyan Methodist Book Room, 1908), 82.

8. Hardy, *The Sacred Books of the Buddhists*, 162–163.

9. John Henry Barrows, *The Christian Conquest of Asia: Studies and Personal Observations of Oriental Religions* (New York: Charles Scribner's Sons, 1899), 178.

10. Ibid., 211.

11. Ibid., 181.

12. J. M. Peebles, ed., *Buddhism and Christianity: Being an Oral Debate Held at Panadura between the Rev. Migettuwatte Gunananda, a Buddhist Priest, and the Rev. David de Silva, a Wesleyan Clergyman* (Colombo, Sri Lanka: P. K. W. Siriwardhana, 1955), i.

13. Dharmapala, *Return to Righteousness*, 26.

14. Ibid., 441.

15. Ibid., 157.

16. Ibid.

17. Ibid., 408.

18. Ibid., 405.

19. Anagarika Dharmapala, *The Arya Dharma of Sakya Muni, Gautama the Buddha or the Ethics of Self Discipline* (Calcutta: Maha Bodhi Book Agency, 1917), 157.

20. Dharmapala, *Return to Righteousness*, 160.

21. Ibid., 409.

22. Ibid., 441.

23. Ibid., 439.

24. Ibid.

25. Ibid., 3.

26. Ibid., 64.

27. Ibid., 391.

28. Ibid., 418.

29. Ibid., 148.

30. Ibid., 419.

31. Ibid., 342.

32. Ibid., 500.

33. Ibid., 412.

34. Ibid., 410.

35. Ibid., 468.

36. Ibid., 441.

37. Ibid.

38. Ibid., 445.

39. Ibid., 29.

40. Ibid., 465.

41. Ibid., 286.

42. Ibid., 499.

43. Ibid., 500.

44. Ibid., 448.

45. Ibid.

46. Ibid., 449.

47. Ibid., 19–20.

48. Ibid., 189.

49. Ibid., 352.

50. Ibid., 27.

51. Ibid., 462.

52. Ibid., 24.

53. Ibid., 106.

54. Edward W. Said, *Orientalism* (London: Penguin Books. 1978), 154.

55. Dharmapala, *Return to Righteousness*, 578.

56. Ibid., 667.

57. Ibid.

58. Ibid., 481.

59. Ibid., 410.

60. Ibid., 123.

61. Ibid., 438.

62. Ibid., 515.

63. Ibid., 482.

64. Ibid., 479.

65. Ibid., 541.

66. Ibid., 494.

67. Ibid., 718.

68. Ibid., 667.

69. Ibid., 25.

70. Ibid., 286.

71. Ibid., 409.

72. Ibid., 442.

73. Ibid., 700.

74. Ibid., 215.

75. Ibid., 157.

76. Ibid., 468.

77. Ibid., 26.

78. Ibid., 57.

79. Ibid., 400.

80. Ibid., 798.

81. Ibid., 410.

82. Ibid., 406.

83. Ibid., 530.

84. Ibid., 666.

85. Ibid., 42.

86. Ibid., 35.

87. Ibid., 491.

88. Ibid., 158.

89. Ibid., 158.

90. Anagarika Dharmapala, "Colonel Olcott and the Buddhist Revival Movement," *Journal of the Maha Bodhi Society* 28 (January–March 1907): 26–28.

91. Dharmapala, *Return to Righteousness*, 24–25.

92. Spence R. Hardy, *Jubilee Memorials of the Wesleyan Mission, South Ceylon 1814–1864* (Colombo, Sri Lanka: Wesleyan Mission Press. 1864).

93. Dharmapala, *Return to Righteousness*, 25.

94. Ibid., 684.

95. Ibid., 464.

5. Paul the Roman in Asia

1. W. M. Ramsay, *The Teaching of Paul in Terms of the Present Day* (London: Hodder and Stoughton, 1913), 17.

2. John Robertson, *Pastoral Counsels Being Chapters on Practical and Devotional Subjects* (London: Macmillan, 1867), 222.

3. Ramsay, *The Teaching of Paul in Terms of the Present Day*, 50.

4. Matthew Arnold, *St. Paul and Protestantism with Other Essays* (London: Smith, Elder and Co., 1896).

5. Ibid., 21.

6. W. M. Ramsay, *St. Paul the Traveller and the Roman Citizen* (London: Hodder and Stoughton, 1902), 34.

7. Adolf Deissmann, *The Religion of Jesus and the Faith of Paul*, trans. William E. Wilson (London: Hodder and Stoughton, 1923), 271.

8. W. Wrede, *Paul*, trans. Edward Lummis (London: Philip Green, 1907), 2.

9. Ibid., 78.

10. Ibid., 77.

11. Deissmann, *The Religion of Jesus and the Faith of Paul*, 202.

12. Ibid., 155.

13. Adolf Deissmann, *Paul: A Study in Social and Religious History* (London: Hodder and Stoughton, 1926), 6.

14. Deissmann, *The Religion of Jesus and the Faith of Paul*, 222.

15. Ibid., 257.

16. Deissmann, *Paul: A Study in Social and Religious History*, 6.

17. Adolf Deissmann, *Light from the Ancient East: The New Testament Illustrated by Recently Discovered Texts of the Graeco-Roman World* (London: Hodder and Stoughton, 1910), 392.

18. Ibid., 302.

19. Wrede, *Paul*, 169.

20. Deissmann, *Light from the Ancient East*, 240.

21. Suzanne L. Marchand, *German Orientalism in the Age of Empire: Religion, Race, and Scholarship* (New York: Cambridge University Press, 2009), 285.

22. Ibid., 287.

23. Ramsay, *St. Paul the Traveller and the Roman Citizen*, 130.

24. W. M. Ramsay, *A Historical Commentary on St. Paul's Epistle to the Galatians* (London, 1899), 320–321.

25. Ibid., 322.

26. Brigitte Kahl, "Galatians and the 'Orientalism' of Justification by Faith: Paul among Jews and Muslims," in *The Colonized Apostle: Paul through Postcolonial Eyes*, ed. Christopher D. Stanley (Minneapolis: Fortress Press, 2011), 212.

27. Roland Allen, *Missionary Methods: St. Paul's or Ours?* (Grand Rapids, MI: Wm. B. Eerdmans, 1962), vii.

28. Ibid., 147.

29. Bernard Lucas, *The Empire of Christ Being a Study of the Missionary Enterprise in the Light of Modern Religious Thought* (London: Macmillan, 1907), 150.

30. Joachim Jeremias, *Unknown Sayings of Jesus*, trans. Reginald H. Fuller (London: SPCK, 1957), 91.

31. E. F. Brown, *The First Epistle of Paul the Apostle to the Corinthians with Introduction and Notes* (London: Society for Promoting Christian Knowledge, 1923), xlvii.

32. Arthur Crosthwaite, *The Second Epistle to the Corinthians* (Madras: SPCK Depository, 1916), 17.

33. Brown, *The First Epistle of Paul the Apostle to the Corinthians*, xlvi.

34. Ibid., xlv–xlvi.

35. W. B. Harris, *A Commentary on the Epistle of St. Paul to the Romans*, The Christian Students' Library, vol. 33 (Madras: Christian Literature Society, 1964), 46–47.

36. Ibid., 47.

37. Ibid.

38. Ibid., 52.

39. T. Walker, *The Epistle to the Philippians* (London: Society for Promoting Christian Knowledge, 1909), 69.

40. Ibid., xxxvii.

41. Ibid., 70.

42. Ibid., 62.

43. Lucas, *The Empire of Christ*, 149.

44. Ibid., 150.

45. Ibid., 151.

46. Walter Kelly Firminger, *The Epistles of St. Paul the Apostle to the Colossians and to Philemon with Introduction and Notes* (Madras: SPCK Depository, 1921), 15.

47. J. C. Kumarappa, *Practice and Precepts of Jesus* (Ahmedabad: Navajivan Publishing House, 1945), 105.

48. Ibid., 107.

49. Ibid., 104.

50. Ibid., 96.

51. J. C. Kumarappa, *Christianity, Its Economy and Way of Life* (Ahmedabad: Navajivan Publishing House, 1945), 63.

52. Ibid.

53. *The Complete Works of Kanzo Uchimura with Notes and Comments by Taijiro Yamamoto and Yoichi Muto*, vol. 30 (Tokyo: Iwanami Shoten, 1982), 192.

54. Shinsui Kawai, *My Spiritual Experiences* (Tokyo: Christ Hear Church, 1970), 12.

55. *The Theology of Chenchiah with Selections from His Writings*, ed. D. A. Thangasamy, Confessing the Faith in India Series no. 1 (Bangalore: Christian Institute for the Study of Religion and Society, 1966), 73.

56. Ibid., 72.

57. Ibid.

58. Ibid., 76.

59. Ibid., 80.

60. Ibid., 159.

61. *The Complete Works of Kanzo Uchimura with Notes and Comments by Taijiro Yamamoto and Yoichi Muto*, vol. 3 (Tokyo: Kyobunkwan, 1972), 123–124.

62. Ibid., 56.

63. Khiok-Khng Yeo, "The Rhetorical Hermeneutic of 1 Corinthians 8 and Chinese Ancestor Worship," *Biblical Interpretation: A Journal of Contemporary Approaches* 2, no. 3 (1994): 311.

64. Gordon Zerbe, "Constructions of Paul in Filipino Theology of Struggle," in *The Colonized Apostle: Paul through Postcolonial Eyes*, ed. Christopher D. Stanley (Minneapolis: Fortress Press, 2011), 237.

65. Satoko Yamaguchi, *Mary and Martha: Women in the World of Jesus* (Maryknoll, NY: Orbis Books, 2002); Hisako Kinukawa, *Women and Jesus in Mark: A Japanese Feminist Perspective* (Maryknoll, NY: Orbis Books, 1994); Hisako Kinukawa, "Alternative Leadership Shown by Mary of Magdala," *In God's Image* 29, no. 2 (June 2010): 6–14; and Seong See Kim, *Mark, Women and Empire: A Korean Postcolonial Perspective* (Sheffield, UK: Sheffield Phoenix Press, 2010).

66. Hyunju Bae, "The Typology of Women's Leadership in Early Christianity," *In God's Image* 26, no. 2 (June 2007): 6–25; Hyunju Bae, "Women's Leadership and Authority in Pauline Christianity II: Deconstructing Paul's Ambivalence to Women in Later Pauline Christianity," *In God's Image* 26, no. 2 (June 2007): 26–32.

67. Hyunju Bae, "Paul, Roman Empire and Ekklesia," *CTC Bulletin* 22, no. 2 (2006): 12.

68. Ibid., 14.

69. Kumarappa, *Practice and Precepts of Jesus*, 97.

70. Lucas, *The Empire of Christ*, 150.

71. Deissmann, *Light from the Ancient East*, 391.

72. *The Life and Letters of the Right Honourable Friedrich Max Müller in Two Volumes*, vol. 2, ed. Georgina Adelaide Müller (London: Longmans, Green, and Co., 1902), 81.

73. Firminger, *The Epistles of St. Paul the Apostle to the Colossians and to Philemon*, 287.

74. K. M. Banerjea, "A Lecture on the Claims of Christianity in British India," in *Krishna Mohan Banerjea: Christian Apologist*, ed. T. V. Philip (Madras: Christian Literature Society, 1982), 175.

75. Firminger, *The Epistles of St. Paul the Apostle to the Colossians and to Philemon*, 317.

76. Raymond Panikkar, *The Unknown Christ of Hinduism* (London: Darton Longman and Todd, 1964), 137.

77. Ibid., 17.

78. Ibid., 131; emphasis in original.

79. R. H. S. Boyd, *Khristadvaita: A Theology for India* (Madras: Christian Literature Society, 1977), 317; emphasis in original.

80. Deissmann, *Light from the Ancient East*, 260.

81. John Muir, "St. Paul a Model for the Missionary," *Calcutta Christian Observer* 7, no. 69 (February 1838): 65.

82. Daniel Boyarin, *A Radical Jew: Paul and the Politics of Identity* (Berkeley: University of California Press, 1994), 236.

83. Ibid., 7.

84. Ibid., 156.

85. Ibid., 9.

86. Richard J. Cassidy, *Paul in Chains: Roman Imprisonment and the Letters of Paul* (New York: Crossroad Publishing Company, 2001), 16.

87. Richard J. Cassidy, *Society and Politics in the Acts of the Apostle* (Maryknoll, NY: Orbis Books, 1987), 118.

88. Ibid., 124.

89. Richard A. Horsley, ed., *Paul and Empire: Religion and power in Roman Imperial Society* (Harrisburg, PA: Trinity Press International, 1997).

90. Richard A. Horsley, "General Introduction," in Horsley, *Paul and Empire*, 8.

91. Richard A. Horsley, "Introduction," in Horsley, *Paul and Empire*,, 209.

92. *The Colonized Apostle: Paul through Postcolonial Eyes*, ed. Christopher D. Stanley (Minneapolis: Fortress Press, 2011).

93. Gordon Zerbe, "The Politics of Paul: His Supposed Social Conservatism and the Impact of Postcolonial Readings," in *The Colonized Apostle*, 73.

94. Ramsay, *St. Paul the Traveller and the Roman Citizen*, 132.

95. Ramsay, *A Historical Commentary on St. Paul's Epistle to the Galatians*, 322.

96. Ramsay, *St. Paul the Traveller and the Roman Citizen*, 132.

97. For a postcolonial critique of these volumes, see R. S. Sugirtharajah, *Asian Biblical Hermeneutics and Postcolonialism: Contesting the Interpretations* (Sheffield, UK: Sheffield Academic Press, 1999), 54–85.

98. Walker, *The Epistle to the Philippians*, xxxvii.

99. Deissmann, *Light from the Ancient East*, 392.

100. Boyarin, *A Radical Jew*, 8.

101. Shlomo Pines, *The Jewish Christians of the Early Centuries of Christianity According to a New Source* (Jerusalem: Israel Academy of Sciences and Humanities, 1966), 26.

102. Ibid., 28.

103. C. S. Lewis, "Introduction," in *Letters to Young Churches: A Translation of the New Testament Epistles*, ed. J. B. Phillips (London: Geoffrey Bles, 1947), x.

104. See Matthew Arnold, *St. Paul and Protestantism with Other Essays* (London: Smith, Elder and Co., 1896), 1.

105. Helen Barrett Montgomery, *The Bible and Missions* (West Medford, MA: Central Committee on the United Study of Foreign Missions, 1920), 176–177.

106. Zha Changping, "Studying the New Testament in the Chinese Academic World: A Survey 1976–2006," in *Reading Christian Scriptures in China*, ed. Chloë Starr (Lodon: T. & T. Clark, 2008), 81–94.

107. Gordon Zerbe, "Constructions of Paul in Filipino Theology of Struggle," in *The Colonized Apostle*, 253.

108. Robertson, *Pastoral Counsels*, 223.

109. Deissmann, *Paul: A Study in Social and Religious History*, 4.

6. Exegesis in Eastern Climes

1. Aloysius Pieris, "Cross-Scripture Reading in Buddhist-Christian Dialogue: A Search for the Right Method," in *Scripture, Community and Mission: Essays in Honor of D. Preman Niles*, ed. Philip L. Wickeri (Hong Kong: Christian Conference of Asia, 2003), 244.

2. Ibid.

3. Ibid., 253.

4. Ibid.

5. Archie Chi Chung Lee, "Transformative Readings: Convergence of Scriptural Traditions in Negotiating for Asian Christian Identities" (unpublished paper), 12.

6. George M. Soares-Prabhu, "Two Mission Commands: An Interpretation of Matthew 28: 16–20 in the Light of a Buddhist Text," *Biblical Interpretation: A Journal of Contemporary Approaches* 2, no. 3 1995: 264–282.

7. Byung-Mu Ahn, "Jesus and the Minjung in the Gospel of Mark," in *Voices from the Margin: Interpreting the Bible in the Third World*, ed. R. S. Sugirtharajah (Maryknoll, NY: Orbis Books, 1995), 85–104.

8. Cyrus Hee-Suk Moon, "An Old Testament Understanding of Minjung," in *Minjung Theology: People as the Subjects of History*, ed. Commission on Theological Concerns of the Christian Conference of Asia (London: Zed Press, 1983), 132.

9. Teruo Kuribayashi, "Recovering Jesus for Outcasts in Japan," in *Frontiers in Asian Christian Theology*, ed. R. S. Sugirtharajah (Maryknoll, NY: Orbis Books, 1994), 16.

10. Ibid.

11. Hisao Kayama, "The Cornelius Story in the Japanese Cultural Context," in *Text & Experience: Towards a Cultural Exegesis of the Bible*, ed. Daniel Smith-Christopher (Sheffield, UK: Sheffield Academic Press, 1995), 194.

12. Wati A. Longchar, "Reading the Bible from the Perspective of Indigenous People's Experience: A Methodological Consideration," *MIT Journal of Theology* 4 (2003): 51.

13. Ibid., 52.

14. Ibid., 54.

15. Nirmal Minz, "A Theological Interpretation of the Tribal Reality in India," in Sugirtharajah, *Frontiers in Asian Christian Theology*, 46.

16. James Massey, "Introduction to Our Liberative Traditions and Their Contribution to Our Doing Theology," in *The 7th Minjung-Dalit Theological Dialogue: Our Liberation Tradition, Church and Theology*, October 2007, South Korea, 2007, 45.

17. A. Maria Arul Raja, "Breaking Hegemonic Boundaries: An Intertextual Reading of the Madurai Veeran Legend and Mark's Story of Jesus," in *Voices from the Margin: Interpreting the Bible in the Third World; Revised and Expanded Third Edition*, ed. R. S. Sugirtharajah (Maryknoll, NY: Orbis Books, 2006), 108.

18. Surekha Nelavala, "Smart Syrophoenician Woman: A Dalit Feminist Reading of Mark 7.24–31," *Expository Times* 118, no. 2 (2006): 64.

19. Ibid., 66.

20. M. Gnanavaram, "'Dalit Theology' and the Parable of the Good Samaritan," *Journal for the Study of the New Testament* 50 (1993): 59–83.

21. Satoko Yamaguchi, *Mary and Martha: Women in the World of Jesus* (Maryknoll, NY: Orbis Books, 2002), 141.

22. Hisako Kinukawa, *Women and Jesus in Mark: A Japanese Feminist Perspective* (Maryknoll, NY: Orbis Books, 1994).

23. Mai-Anh-Le Tran, "Lot's Wife, Ruth, and To Thi: Gender and Racial Representation in a Theological Feast of Stories," in *Ways of Being, Ways of Reading: Asian American Biblical Interpretation*, ed. Mary Foskett and Jeffery Kah-Jin Kuan (St. Louis: Chalice Press, 2006), 132.

24. Edward Said, *Power, Politics, and Culture: Interviews with Edward W. Said*, ed. with introduction by Gauri Viswanathan (New York: Pantheon Books, 2001), 222.

25. See Mary O'Hara, "Western Plague," *Society Guardian* 6, no. 4 (2011): 5.

26. For history, theory, practice, and recent developments, see R. S. Sugirtharajah, *Exploring Postcolonial Biblical Criticism: History, Method, Practice* (Oxford: Wiley-Blackwell, 2012).

27. Philip Chia, "On Naming the Subject: Postcolonial Reading of Daniel 1," in *The Postcolonial Biblical Reader*, ed. R. S. Sugirtharajah (Oxford: Blackwell Publishers, 2005), 171.

28. Ibid., 181.

29. Ibid., 179.

30. Ibid., 181. See also Archie Lee's reading of the return of the postexilic community in Isaiah (55–66) in light of the handover of Hong Kong to China in 1997: "Returning to China: Biblical Interpretation in Postcolonial Hong Kong," *Biblical Interpretation* 8, no. 2 (1999): 156–173.

31. Seong See Kim, *Mark, Women and Empire: A Korean Postcolonial Perspective* (Sheffield, UK: Sheffield Phoenix Press, 2010), 5.

32. Uriah Y. Kim, *Decolonizing Josiah: Toward a Postcolonial Reading of the Deuteronomistic History* (Sheffield, UK: Sheffield Phoenix Press, 2005).

33. For Kim's comparative reading of the fate of Uriah the Hittite, a career soldier in David's army, and Asian Americans' struggle for identity, see "Uriah the Hittite: A (con)Text of Struggle for Identity," *Semeia* 90/91 (2002): 69–85. For further examples of Asian American postcolonial readings, see Hyun Chul Paul Kim, "Interpretative Modes of Yin-Yang Dynamics as an Asian Hermeneutics," *Biblical Interpretation* 9, no. 3 (2001): 287–308; Tat-Siong Benny Liew, "Tyranny, Boundary and Might: Colonial Mimicry in Mark's Gospel," in *Journal of the Study of the New Testament* 73 (1999): 7–31; Tat-Siong Benny Liew, "Margins and (Cutting-)Edges: On the (Il)Legitimacy and Intersections of Race,Ethnicity, and (Post)Colonialism," in *Postcolonial and Biblical Criticism: Interdisciplinary Intersections*, ed. Stephen D. Moore and Fernando F. Segovia (London: T. & T. Clark International, 2005), 114–165.

34. Leng Leroy Lim, "'The Bible Tells Me to Hate Myself': The Crisis in Asian American Spiritual Leadership," *Semeia* 90/91 (2002): 315–322.

35. Roy I. Sano, "Shifts in Reading the Bible: Hermeneutical Moves among Asian Americans," *Semeia* 90/91 (2002): 108.

36. Gale A. Yee, "Yin/Yang Is Not Me: An Exploration into an Asian American Biblical Hermeneutics," in Foskett and Kuan, *Ways of Being, Ways of Reading*, 152–163.

37. Russell G. Moy, "Resident Aliens of the Diaspora: 1 Peter and Chinese Protestants in San Francisco," *Semeia* 90/91 (2002): 51–67.

38. Mary F. Foskett, "The Accidents of Being and the Politics of Identity: Biblical Images of Adoption and Asian Adoptees in America," *Semeia* 90/91 (2002): 141.

39. Ibid., 142.

40. Sze-Kar Wan, "Betwixt and Between: Toward a Hermeneutics of Hyphenation," in Foskett and Kuan, *Ways of Being, Ways of Reading*, 144.

41. J. N. M. Wijngaards, "The Co-Existence of the Bible and the Non-Christian Sacred Scriptures," in *Research Seminar on Non-Biblical Scriptures*, ed. D. S. Amalorpavadass (Bangalore: National Biblical, Catechetical and Liturgical Centre, 1974), 96.

7. Between the Lines of Asian Fiction

1. David Norton, *The King James Bible: A Short History from Tyndale to Today* (Cambridge: Cambridge University Press, 2011), 189.

2. Sarah Joseph, *Othappu: The Scent of the Other Side*, trans. Valson Thampu (New Delhi: Oxford University Press, 2009), 129.

3. Ibid., 161.

4. Ibid., 92.

5. Ibid.

6. Ibid., 159.

7. Ibid., 219.

8. Ibid., 55.

9. Ibid., 153.

10. Ibid.

11. Ibid., 137.

12. Ibid., 14.

13. Gish Jen, *World and Town* (New York: Alfred A. Knopf, 2010), 308.

14. Ibid., 150.

15. Ibid., 156.

16. Ibid., 157.

17. Ibid., 210.

18. Ibid., 173.

19. José Rizal, *Noli Me Tangere (Touch Me Not)*, trans. Harold Augenbraum (1887; reprint, London: Penguin Books, 2006), 83.

20. Ibid., 85.

21. Esther David, *Book of Rachel* (New Delhi: Viking, 2006), 49.

22. Ibid., 145.

23. Esther David, *Book of Esther* (New Delhi: Viking, 2002), 43.

24. David, *Book of Rachel*, 182.

25. Ibid., 6.

26. Ibid., 143.

27. Ibid., 48.

28. Esther David, *Shalom India Housing Society* (New York: Feminist Press at the City University of New York, 2009), 22.

29. David, *Book of Rachel*, 9.

30. Ibid., 36.

31. David, *Book of Esther*, 39.

32. David, *Book of Rachel*, 169.

33. Paul Zacharia, *Praise the Lord, What News, Pilate? Two Novellas* (New Delhi: Katha, 2001), 93.

34. Ibid., 70–71.

35. Ibid., 72.

36. Ibid., 71.

37. Ibid., 72.

38. Ibid., 81.

39. Ibid., 80.

40. Ibid., 66.

41. Ibid., 69.

42. Shusaku Endo, *White Man, Yellow Man: Two Novellas,* trans. Teruyo Shimizu (Norwalk, CT: EastBridge, 2006).

43. Ibid., 78.

44. Yiyun Li, *A Thousand Years of Good Prayers* (London: Fourth Estate, 2006), 117.

45. Ibid., 119.

46. Ibid.

47. Ibid., 118.

48. Ibid., 126.

49. Ibid.

50. Ibid., 118.

51. Rishi Reddi, *Karma and Other Stories* (New Delhi: HarperCollins, 2007), 193.

52. Ibid., 194.

53. David, *Book of Esther*, 364.

54. Endo, *White Man, Yellow Man*, 67.

55. David, *Book of Rachel*, 36.

56. Amy Tan, *The Joy Luck Club* (London: Minerva, 1990), 116.

57. Chan Koonchung, *The Fat Years* (London: Doubleday, 2011), 190.

58. Shusaku Endo, *Stained Glass Elegies*, trans. Van C. Gessel (Harmondsworth, UK: Penguin Books, 1986), 120.

59. Jen, *World and Town*, 160.

Conclusion

1. Karen Armstrong, *The Bible: The Biography* (London: Atlantic Books, 2007), 16.

2. Nozipo Maraire, *Zenzele: A Letter for My Daughter* (London: Weidenfeld & Nicolson, 1996), 70.

Acknowledgments

The publication of this volume would not have been possible but for the immense interest shown by Sharmila Sen of Harvard University Press; the relentless support and encouragement of Dan O'Connor for all my research projects, which has persisted over nearly thirty years; and finally, the love, care, and intellectual sustenance provided by my wife, Sharada, without whom nothing is possible.

Index of Scriptural References

Buddhist Scriptures

General Index